ASSOCIATIVE
LEARNING

a cognitive analysis

THE CENTURY PSYCHOLOGY SERIES

James J. Jenkins
Walter Mischel
Willard W. Hartup
Editors

ASSOCIATIVE LEARNING

a cognitive analysis

James G. Greeno

University of Pittsburgh

Carlton T. James

Rutgers University

Frank J. DaPolito

University of Dayton

Peter G. Polson

University of Colorado

PRENTICE-HALL, INC. *Englewood Cliffs, New Jersey 07632*

Library of Congress Cataloging in Publication Data

MAIN ENTRY UNDER TITLE:

Associative learning.

    Bibliography: p.
Includes index.
    1. Learning, Psychology of. 2. Cognition.
3. Association of ideas. I. Greeno, James G.
BF318.A84   153.1'526   77–17096
ISBN 0–13–049650–2

© 1978 by Prentice-Hall, Inc., Englewood Cliffs, New Jersey 07632

Printed in the United States of America

10 9 8 7 6 5 4 3 2 1

Acknowledgments

Figure 2-1: Adapted from Quillian, M. R., Semantic memory. In M. Minsky (Ed.), *Semantic information processing.* Cambridge, Mass.: MIT Press, 1968. Reprinted by permission of The MIT Press, Cambridge, Massachusetts.

Figure 2-3: From *Explorations in Cognition,* by Donald A. Norman, David E. Rumelhart, and the LNR Research Group. W. H. Freeman and Company. Copyright © 1975.

(Acknowledgments continued on p. 241)

PRENTICE-HALL INTERNATIONAL, INC., *London*
PRENTICE-HALL OF AUSTRALIA PTY. LIMITED, *Sydney*
PRENTICE-HALL OF CANADA, LTD., *Toronto*
PRENTICE-HALL OF INDIA PRIVATE LIMITED, *New Delhi*
PRENTICE-HALL OF JAPAN, INC., *Tokyo*
PRENTICE-HALL OF SOUTHEAST ASIA PTE. LTD., *Singapore*
WHITEHALL BOOKS LIMITED, *Wellington, New Zealand*

Contents

Chapter 3
PROCESSES OF STORING INFORMATION IN MEMORY   29

Chapter 4
PROCESSES IN THE LEARNING OF ASSOCIATIONS   53

Chapter 5
ABSTRACTION AND POSITIVE TRANSFER
OF ASSOCIATION   95

Chapter 6
NEGATIVE TRANSFER   124

Chapter 7
FORGETTING: PROACTIVE INTERFERENCE   165

Chapter 8
FORGETTING: RETROACTIVE INTERFERENCE   186

Chapter 9
CONCLUSIONS   213

REFERENCES   222

AUTHOR INDEX   233

SUBJECT INDEX   237

Preface

The origin of this book probably occurred when I became a research assistant in the group working with James Jenkins at Minnesota in 1960. Our task was to demonstrate the associationist principles that we thought were required to explain some of the syntactic knowledge people use when they speak grammatically. These experiments were massively unsuccessful, and this fact discouraged the effort prevailing at the time of developing an associationist explanation for language behavior. But a kind of desperate attempt to show that mediated transfer could be demonstrated in our experimental design led to the kind of study in which Joseph Scandura and I later applied statistical methods based on Markov models to analyze transfer of training.

From 1964 to 1966, DaPolito was conducting experiments for his dissertation at Indiana University with the intention of showing that the elegant experimental design and statistical methods developed by Estes could be applied to the analysis of forgetting of individual items. They could indeed, but the results were quite surprising. DaPolito expected to measure the degree of interference between items from statistical dependencies between the responses to a single stimuli. When the responses were found to be independent, we had an unexpected and important result to consider.

In 1966 and 1967, Polson conducted experiments and analyses of the acquisition of verbally mediated concepts. He succeeded in providing a quantitative analysis of the process of acquiring a categorical concept, and his results were consistent with the hypothesis that such acquisition is an

all-or-none process. Polson also was able to derive the mathematical properties of a system in which the subject acquires general knowledge about the
nature of the concepts to be acquired, at which time the probability of
acquiring new concepts increases.

James and I worked on the process of stimulus selection at Indiana in
1964 and 1965. James' experiments showed that the subjects stored partial
representations of stimuli as long as they were still acquiring further items
in the list, but acquired more complete representations during overtraining
after all the items in the list had been learned. This seemed to implicate a
deliberate attentional strategy in the process of stimulus selection. Allen
Harrington's dissertation conducted in 1967 and 1968 included further evidence that stimulus encoding is a process governed by systematic attentional
strategies involving the complete task, rather than selection of aspects of
individual stimuli on an item-by-item basis.

While I was visiting at Stanford University in 1966, Michael Humphreys
and I began working on the analysis of some data he had collected earlier,
expecting to find support for the two stages of response learning and connection learning that most theorists assumed for the acquisition of paired
associates. The pattern of results that was obtained involved effects on the
first stage of both stimulus and response difficulty, and only an effect of
stimulus difficulty on the second stage. This led to the idea that the first
stage of learning a paired associate should be considered as a process of
storing a representation of the stimulus-response pair, and the second stage
as learning a reliable way of retrieving the pair on tests.

James and I collaborated on several experiments on negative transfer in
the A-B, A-B$_r$ paradigm from 1965 to 1967. Much of this experimental work
was done by James at Indiana during the 1965–1966 year that I spent at
Stanford University. The two-stage Markov analysis indicated that nearly
all the interfering effect was in the second stage of learning, which contradicted our expectation based on the hypothesis of associative interference
that most of the difference between negative transfer and control conditions
would occur early in learning, when the interfering associations would be
the strongest.

By the time James conducted his dissertation experiment on retroactive
forgetting at Indiana in 1967 and 1968, we finally expected to obtain results
inconsistent with associationist hypotheses. In order to obtain a coherent
account of James' rather complex findings, it seems necessary to postulate
a set of retrieval processes considerably more complex than simple retention
of associative connections.

James and I worked together at Michigan in the summer of 1969, where
we reviewed the evidence we had obtained regarding negative transfer and
forgetting. We prepared a draft manuscript for what we thought might be

a long chapter on the topic, and I used the ideas we developed there in a paper that I read at the American Psychological Association meetings.

During those APA meetings in 1969, Jenkins and I happened to meet and had dinner together. I described the work that I was reviewing in my presentation there, and I believe I said that except for a single remaining experiment, I was intending to set aside the study of paired-associate learning in favor of studying problem solving and mathematics learning. Jenkins wondered whether I might collect the various published and unpublished studies of paired-associate memorizing in a book. It seemed a reasonable suggestion, since virtually all the writing was already done. The dissertations written by James, DaPolito, and Polson had not been published (though Polson's subsequently was), and it seemed that a book would provide both an opportunity to present those results in a general context, and to reinterpret earlier findings in the light of conclusions that we had reached in the meantime.

Of course, the job of cutting and pasting that I had imagined for compiling the book turned out to be insufficient. The material now in Chapters 5 through 8, being largely taken from earlier writing—especially Polson's, DaPolito's, and James' dissertations and the draft chapter that James and I had written—did fit together in a simple way. But before returning to that part of the job, I wrote and rewrote a number of introductory sections, incorporating the results in Chapter 4 in various ways, and trying to fit together a coherent argument concerning the general issues. This was a task that seldom had my primary attention. I did move my main research focus to problem solving and mathematics learning, and maintaining that ongoing research program took priority over the completion of this book. It was not until the summer of 1974, during a sabbatical leave, that I found a period of time sufficient to complete a first draft. I am grateful to the John Simon Guggenheim Foundation for support during that period. A subsequent draft was submitted to Jenkins and Prentice-Hall, and Jenkins was helpful in identifying some remaining incoherencies in the presentation that I hope have now been improved.

I am grateful to my co-authors for their patience during the inexcusably long time I took to get my writing for this book done. I am also grateful to many other colleagues with whom I had the pleasure and good furtune to interact during the time this work was carried out. I am especially indebted for interactions concerning various aspects of the substance of this book with Frank Restle, Edwin Martin, and Arthur Melton, whom I count as most supportive and stimulating colleagues, as well as valued friends. Many other teachers, colleagues, and students have enriched my cognitions as well, of course, and I thank you all.

J.G.G.

But association is far from being synonymous with experience. It is one way of coping with experience, one conception to treat experience scientifically. Therefore a criticism of associationism, however negative it may be, is not a rejection of a genetic theory. There are other, and I believe better, ways of treating experience than the concept of association.

—Kurt Koffka (1935, p. 589)

chapter 1

Association and the Nature of Knowledge

In this book we present results of experimental and theoretical research on paired-associate memorizing, transfer, and forgetting that we carried out during a 15-year period beginning in the 1960s. Some of the results have not been published previously, or have been published only in brief summary form. Our interpretations of some of our previously published results have changed because of more recent empirical findings and theory.

In the 1970s, the study of human memory changed dramatically. Investigators began concentrating mainly on studying ways in which knowledge is organized in memory and mechanisms used to retrieve organized knowledge in answering questions and solving problems; they had set aside questions about the process of storing new components of knowledge. We, however, will discuss just those questions: those that explore the way in which new components of knowledge are stored in memory.

It is clear now that a theory of human memory must represent knowledge as a complex relational structure, with concepts and procedures linked through specific relations. Such a theory seems incompatible with the basic premises of associationism, which provided the conceptual basis for nearly all the research on human verbal learning carried out in this century. It might be thought that a massive gap exists between current conceptualizations of memory and the considerable accumulation of research developed prior to 1970.

We believe that the gap is real and compelling at the level of theory—that is, we believe that the associationist theory of memory is fundamentally in error. However, the empirical phenomena of rote learning should not just be set aside as irrelevant to current theoretical issues. When a new theory is advanced, it is important to show that it can explain the phenomena that were formerly explained by the theory it replaces. This book takes up that part of the task concerning the main phenomena of paired-associate memorizing.

The conclusion that associationist theory is mistaken was not apparent when we began our research in the early 1960s. In all but our latest experiments, the initial goal was to provide quantitative analysis of such processes as response acquisition, formation and loss of associative bonds, and facilitation of and interference with associative learning. We thought our research would contribute to the use of modern methods of analysis to further clarify and specify the nature of processes that have been generally believed to operate in paired-associate learning, transfer, and forgetting.

Our experimental results have led to quite a different conclusion. Instead of allowing us to fill in details of generally accepted theories, our results have led us to question the validity of those theories. In case after case, the conclusion has been that something was going on other than what we—and most others working on the problem—initially thought was going on. Our results were much more compatible with the Gestalt theory of association as that theory has been presented by such writers as Koffka (1935), Köhler (1947), and Selz (1913).

Gestalt theorists and associationists have differed in their views of the relationship between association and other cognitive processes. For associationists, association is a basic process in nearly all cognitive activity, such as conceptual behavior (Underwood, 1952), problem solving (Maltzman, 1955), and perceptual learning (Postman, 1955). In Gestalt theory, association is but one rather peculiar special instance of more general processes of cognitive organization, such as grouping and differentiation.

A conclusion that Gestalt theory is closer to the truth about paired-associate memorizing than associationist theory seems to us to have important implications. Paired-associate memorizing is the best task we have for studying the formation of associations in a pure and simple form. Once one becomes persuaded, as we have, that the cognitive processes involved in paired-associate memorizing are different from the processes of connection between elements that are central in associationist theory, then it becomes difficult to foresee any important use of that theory in explaining other kinds of cognitive activity.

ASSOCIATIONIST THEORY AND EMPIRICISM

The views stated suggest that this book will have a negative tone, primarily aimed at showing associationist theory to be false. This is only partly true. We believe that our empirical results permit some significant extensions and elaborations of Gestalt theory, including incorporation of some modern concepts of information processing. But to a considerable extent, we feel the importance of this book is in the evidence against formation of undifferentiated connections as a basic process in memorizing and learning. We present this evidence with a strong sense of the importance of associationism not only as a substantive hypothesis but also as part of the attitude of empiricism that has provided a revolutionary concept of human nature in the last three centuries.

Associationism became a fully developed theory of learning in the eighteenth and nineteenth centuries, when Hartley, James Mill, John Stuart Mill, and Bain worked out the implications of epistemological ideas introduced in the seventeenth century, primarily by Locke (Boring, 1950). It was natural and important that the associationist theory of learning be developed at that time, since it fit naturally with the general view of empiricism, that human knowledge is derived from experience.

Empiricism was an idea of great philosophical importance in itself, but a considerable part of its significance lies in its relationship with a whole Zeitgeist of liberalizing ideas that were developed in Europe starting with the Renaissance. Of course, to characterize social change in the last 600 years as a consistent enfranchising of ordinary persons would oversimplify history in the extreme. But it is not unreasonable, even for us amateurs, to note that a greater proportion of human beings in Western society now have significantly more responsibility and freedom in their political, social, moral, and intellectual affairs than they did in medieval Europe.

We maintain that just as the development of democratic government provided a framework for political liberalization, and as the Reformation provided a framework for religious liberalization, so the development of empiricism and science provided a framework for intellectual liberalization. As long as people believed that knowledge was derived from divine revelation or from innate reason, the possession of knowledge was controlled as rigidly as the possession of material wealth. Not everyone was in a position to discover truth. Only persons skilled in the interpretation of scripture or disciplined in receptive meditation or trained in the rigors of correct argument could achieve new truths in systems of theological or rationalist epistemology. These skills and disciplines and training were not universally available; in fact, only a very small number of individuals were admitted to seminaries and academies where they could learn how to judge whether an idea was true or false. Furthermore, the knowledge that untrained persons achieved could only be received from persons who had become expert and who deigned to transmit their wisdom. In theological or rationalist systems that were dominant, basic principles could only be accepted on authority. As Locke remarked in 1690 concerning innate ideas,

> it was of no small advantage to those who affected to be masters and teachers, to make this the principle of principles,—*that principles must not be questioned*. For,

having once established this tenet,—that there are innate principles, it put their followers upon a necessity of receiving *some* doctrines as such; which was to take them off from the use of their own reason and judgment, and put them on believing and taking them upon trust without further examination: in which posture of blind credulity, they might be more easily governed by, and made useful to some sort of men, who had the skill and office to principle and guide them. (Locke, 1690/1894)

In contrast, when it is believed that knowledge derives from experience rather than divine revelation or innate reason, a liberalized view of knowledge results. The source of knowledge—experience—now becomes something that everyone has and can use; therefore, the possibility of discovering truth is no longer a restricted privilege. To be sure, a certain amount of training helps a person to observe carefully and to draw correct conclusions; moreover, an individual with greater experience can provide useful training for a person of limited experience. But the differences that greater experience produces are quantitative. In an empiricist epistemology, no person is completely dependent on training from others for acquiring knowledge. And a corollary is that every person has at least some basis for evaluating the truth of pronouncements made by alleged authorities.

Associationist theory played a critical role in the development of empiricist epistemology. According to early empiricism, all people start life with very simple sensory experiences. The problem with this view is that it is difficult to explain how complex concepts and ideas are developed. The solution given by early empiricists was to attribute it to the process of association. Thus, the formation of association was a hypothesis that contributed critically to the plausibility of empiricism, in that associationism provided the learning mechanism needed for an empiricist epistemology to work.

The hypothesis that learning is a process of forming associations among impressions and ideas has enjoyed nearly doctrinal status in European and American psychology for three centuries. When the problem of learning was dealt with directly, as it was by Hartley, James Mill, John Stuart Mill, and Bain, the question asked was how associations are formed; not whether formation of associations is the basis of learning. In this century, functionalists have elaborated on the theory of association, incorporating concepts such as response competition (McGeoch, 1942), unlearning (Melton & Irwin, 1940), response acquisition (Mandler & Heinemann, 1956; Underwood & Schulz, 1960), and response-set selection (Postman, 1963). When a theory of learning was needed in the analysis of another psychological process, as with Wundt's analysis of illusions of similarity and contrast, Titchener's theory of meaning, and Freud's analyses of neurotic symptoms, the concept used to explain changes in cognitive structure was association between impressions or ideas. Behaviorists have analyzed changes in stimulus-response functions using a somewhat operationalized version of William James' and Pavlov's idea of associations between brain processes.

ALTERNATIVE GESTALT HYPOTHESES

Gestalt psychologists objected and offered an alternative hypothesis to the idea of undifferentiated associative connections. The Gestalt hypothesis may have been foreseen by John Stuart Mill, who postulated a kind of mental chemistry in which the compound formed by association between ideas has properties that are not inherent in either of the ideas when they are not associated. An explicit alternative view was formulated by Selz in 1913. The Gestalt theory of association was developed in fairly extensive discussions by Köhler in 1929, Koffka in 1935, and Katona (1940), who carried out an extensive series of empirical studies.

Selz identified the critical hypothesis of associationist theory, which he called the hypothesis of diffuse reproductions—the idea that information is stored in the form of undifferentiated connections and that retrieval of a response is determined solely by the combined strength of connections leading to the response. In place of this idea, Selz proposed what he called a hypothesis of specific responses. The substance of this hypothesis is illustrated in the following example, which deals with performance in a task of giving generic concepts as associations to a set of stimulus words. Suppose that when the stimulus is "farmer," a subject gives the response, "occupation." Selz said,

> . . . the task "generic concept" and the relevant stimulus word "farmer" cannot be treated as factors acting in isolation, but rather that they act like the coherent question "What is the generic concept for farmer?" This question of the experimenter already anticipates schematically the knowledge-unit (or structure) "Farmer is an occupation" which the subject has previously acquired. The question contains one member (A) of the known facts of the case and the relation (γ) to the other, sought-for member; in this case the relation is of species to genus. The question can, therefore, act as an eliciting condition for the intellectual operating of knowledge-production [*Wissensaktualisierung*], whereby the uncompleted knowledge-unit (A γ) which the question represents is completed by restoring the reproductive unit (AγB). Instead of a diffuse play of competing reproductive tendencies, this theory offers a comprehensive process wherein the question acts as a unitary total task along with a uniquely relevant operation of knowledge-production. This operation can be shown to be a special case of structure-completion, since the fragmentary structure of the question is made complete by the operation of knowledge-production. (Selz, 1964, pp. 227–228)

For our purposes, the main point of Selz' hypothesis of specific responses is that knowledge units are relational structures, not undifferentiated connections. Köhler (1947) similarly argued that the cognitive structure produced by learning an association is a single memory trace, representing the associated elements as "relatively segregated subunits," rather than as two individual traces connected by a bond.

Köhler also presented an objection to the associationist view that ideas become connected merely by occurring together. In no other branch of science, Köhler pointed out, do we assume that objects or events become functionally related regardless of their individual properties. For example, "in chemistry, atoms react or remain indifferent to each other depending upon their given characteristics" (Köhler, 1947, p. 153).

The view taken by Köhler was that an association is learned when the elements to be associated are organized into a unit, so as to form a unitary trace of the experience that incorporates both elements. He said,

> . . . contiguity in space and time favors association only because, under the name of proximity, it is a favorable factor in organization. Now, this condition is just one among many others which all have a favorable influence on organization, and since it now appears that organization is the really decisive condition of what is commonly called association, the rule of association may have to be reformulated accordingly. (Köhler, 1947, p. 158)

Köhler discussed recall primarily in terms of attitudinal factors. He also remarked that recall depends on a compromise. On the one hand, recall of an association presupposes a stable organization of the associated elements, that is, a unitary trace. On the other hand, if one associated element is presented, it will not produce recall if it is too thoroughly absorbed in the organization of the trace that constitutes the association in memory. Recall—or as we will say, retrieval—thus requires that "the process which is now given resembles some region within the organized trace of the whole experience" (Köhler, 1947, p. 17).

Koffka (1935) also took the view that learning is a process of organization, with an association being the formation of a unitary trace representing both of the associated items. Koffka strengthened the Gestalt analysis of learning by focusing attention on the concept of a trace's stability. He postulated "that a trace will influence a process in such a way that the reactive influence exerted by the process on the trace will not diminish, but if possible increase, the latter's stability" (Koffka, 1935, p. 563).

In addition to the implications of this idea for processes of acquisition, the postulate provides the basis of a theory of retrieval. An implication of the postulate is that "if a process communicates with part of a trace system, the *whole* trace system will exert a force on the process in the direction of making it as complete as it was when it created the trace system" (Koffka, 1935, p. 567). This implication follows because if part of a trace system were activated without the whole system becoming active, the stability of the system would decrease. This implication explains the retrieval of associations. When a part of the trace system that constitutes an association (presumably a "relatively segregated subunit") becomes active, the whole trace system becomes active, because trace systems tend to maintain their stability. Retrieval of associations is therefore a process of redintegration.

GESTALT THEORY AND EMPIRICISM

If an empiricist epistemology like Locke's is taken as a starting point, the Gestalt theory of association is simply unacceptable. Locke's empiricism requires a theory of learning that can start from a blank tablet; association-ism asserts that concepts and other complex ideas are formed out of elementary impressions. But Gestalt theory claims that associations are produced by cognitive organization. The concepts and relationships that are the basis of grouping and differentiation among objects are also the basis of association. If the views of Selz, Köhler, and Koffka are accepted, we must reject the important epistemological idea that knowledge derives entirely from experience.

If Locke's empiricism were the only kind possible, the acceptance of a Gestalt theory of association would be paradoxical. Our preference for an extension of Selz', Köhler's and Koffka's hypotheses over those of McGeoch, Melton, Underwood, and Postman is based on evidence. We have been led to a view that opposes our initial hypotheses by the evidence of our observations—that is, by our experience. It would be paradoxical if this event forced us to give up the view that knowledge is based on experience.

On the other hand, the way that experience leads to knowledge may be different from that given in Locke's kind of empiricism. An alternate formulation has been given by Popper (1935, 1959) in which evidence is used not to support hypotheses but rather to correct theories by showing that hypotheses are false. In an epistemology like Popper's, concepts and relationships are not induced from experience. Rather, a person's present beliefs form the basis of expectation about what the person will experience. When experience is incompatible with expectations, the person can then change beliefs, moving, one would hope, closer to the truth. Popper's philosophical arguments seem consistent with Piaget's general hypotheses about cognitive development, in that experience that does not fit with present schemata can lead to an accommodation of cognitive structure that gives a more adequate basis for interacting with the environment.

Popper's idea of falsification and Piaget's concept of accommodation give a theory of knowledge that emphasizes observation and experience as much as the older empiricist view. Concepts and ideas are not derived initially from experience—the mind is not originally a blank tablet. But concepts and ideas must be checked against experience. And most important, when people disagree about the way things are, their disagreement can be settled, if it can be settled at all, by testing their respective views against empirical observation. Experience is the court of last resort in resolving differences of opinion, and arcane texts or authoritarian pronouncements about what is "reasonable" do not provide valid resolutions of disputes.

EMPIRICISM AND LIBERALISM

If the empiricist philosophy of knowledge is modified to permit innate concepts and ideas of relations, one must ask whether empiricism loses its effectiveness as a libertarian viewpoint. In at least one respect, its liberalizing effect is strengthened. Persons with governmental power, academic seniority, and other positions of institutional authority tend to have an advantage of experience and access to evidence. If knowledge-claims are valid to the extent that they are supported by evidence, then a person with institutional authority is in a strong position, because opposition almost always rests on a smaller quantity of data than that which can be collected in support of an official view.

But if experience is mainly a corrective factor, the advantage of institutional authority is greatly reduced. The empirical status of a theory depends less on the quantity of evidence supporting the theory than on the quality of that evidence, especially as it relates to competing alternative theories. An established theory can be disproven by documenting a single falsifying fact. This implies a considerable advantage to the dissenter. A person does not need a lifetime of experience nor access to all the accumulated data to develop effective opposition to the prevailing view. If a weakness of assumption in the established theory is understood, then it is reasonable to expect that an item of falsifying evidence can be discovered and documented. When this is done, the established view is shown to be false, regardless of the quantity of evidence consistent with that view. Thus, while classical empiricism was a liberalizing idea regarding knowledge, the view that evidence serves mainly as a corrective of false opinions leads to a further liberalization by showing the extent to which all persons have access to the basis of knowledge and dissent.

SUMMARY

We will present evidence that we think argues convincingly against commonly held views about the process of learning associations. Rather than the view that associations are etched by experience on a blank tablet, we are led to a hypothesis that association is a form of cognitive organization, depending on relational ideas that the learner already has in cognitive structure.

Because of the central role of associationism in classical empiricism, we recognize that our evidence and the conclusions we draw from it tend to undercut a widely held version of the empiricist theory. However, the views we develop about learning are consistent with a reconstructed empiricism in which experience is used mainly to correct false opinions. This revised empiricism is reasonable and strengthens the libertarian implications of empiricism regarding accessibility of the basis of knowledge. Our main interest in this book is scientific; the central issue is the truth of alternative hypotheses about how simple associations are acquired in experiments. We believe that our evidence leads to a more nearly correct hypothesis about the nature of simple associative learning than the view that ideas simply become connected. But we are pleased that it also encourages an epistemology that seems to us more nearly correct and more strongly libertarian than the philosophical views in which associationism was originally embedded.

chapter 2

Organization and Association

The central claim in Gestalt theory about association is that it is merely one form of cognitive organization. Organization is fundamental, although it occurs in various ways. One outcome of organization can be association between two elements into a new cognitive unit.

In this chapter, we first briefly review two groups of theories that consider general principles of organization. The first group deals with organization of knowledge about concepts and events. The second specifies ways in which knowledge is organized to permit recognition of patterns. We then present an overview of the theory of association developed from our studies of paired-associate memorizing.

THEORY OF SEMANTIC AND FACTUAL MEMORY

A strong achievement in the theory of memory since the late 1960s has been the development of representations of organized knowledge. A review of the early developments was given by Frijda (1972). One important early theory was given by Quillian (1968), who analyzed some of the knowledge structures needed to support comprehension of language. Quillian's model gives a representation of the kind of information found in a dictionary about the meanings of words. Quillian recognized that our knowledge about word meanings is like a network, consisting of relations among concepts. To represent this knowledge, Quillian used five types of connections:

1. category membership; for example, "tree" is in the category "plant," and "plant" is in the category "structure."

2. modification; for example, a plant is a structure of a particular kind, namely, a living structure.
3. disjunction; the relation between members of a set of alternatives.
4. conjunction; the relation between members of a set of requirements.
5. connections between relations and their arguments; for example, the information that people use machines has the relation "use" connected to "people" and "machine" through this relation. The system must distinguish different forms of this kind of connection, since many relations are not symmetric.

In addition to the connections, Quillian's system uses quantitative modifiers to represent information such as plants frequently have leaves, or plants are not animals.

An example of a knowledge structure that can be constructed in Quillian's model is given in Figure 2-1. The diagram represents the information for the first dictionary definition for "plant": Living structure that is not an animal, frequently with leaves, getting its food from air, water, or earth. The diagram shows plants as members of the category "structure," modified by a conjunction of four concepts: they are living; they are not animal; they frequently

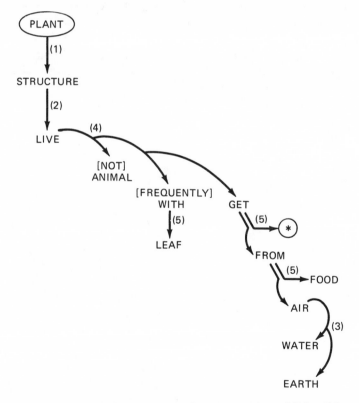

Figure 2-1   Knowledge structure for one meaning of "plant," in Quillian's (1968) model.

have the relation "with" to leaf; and they have the relation "get" to a structure consisting of the relation "from" between food and a disjunction of air, water, or earth.

Anderson and Bower's (1973) model, Human Associative Memory (HAM) uses a somewhat different set of relational connections. The information encoded in HAM represents propositions. To represent a proposition, HAM constructs a tree in which nodes designate components of the proposition, and labeled connections indicate what relation each node has with other nodes and with the proposition as a whole. One node represents the proposition. A second optional node, representing a context, can be included. A third node represents the fact—something that occurred. Related to the node for context can be nodes representing location and time. Related to the node for a fact are nodes representing subject and predicate, and related to a predicate can be nodes representing relation and object. HAM also provides quantitative relations, specifically, set membership, set inclusion, and the universal quantifier.

Figure 2-2 gives an example of a knowledge structure that HAM can construct. The proposition represented here would be expressed by the sentence, "A hippie touched a debutante in the park at night." The topmost node represents the proposition. There is context (C), consisting of a location (L), some park, and a time (T), an unspecified night. The fact (F) includes a subject (S), a hippie, and a predicate (P), which designates a relation (R), touching, and an object (O), a debutante.

Still another model, by Norman and Rumelhart (1975), develops the rep-

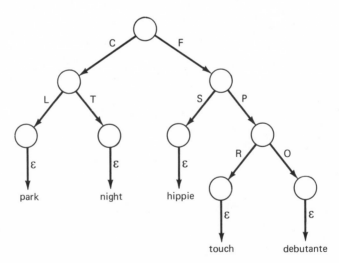

Figure 2-2 Representation of "A hippie touched a debutante in the park at night," in HAM (Anderson & Bower, 1973).

resentation of propositions in somewhat greater detail, using many semantic relations of the kind analyzed by Fillmore (1968). The central nodes represent actions or other kinds of relations specified by verbs. These relational terms are connected to other relations in ways that are specified in the structure.

The example shown in Figure 2-3 corresponds to the sentence, "Peter put the package on the table." The upper part of the diagram indicates that someone named Peter put something that is a package onto a location that is the top of something that is a table. The lower part of the diagram represents general knowledge about the meaning of "put." Norman and Rumelhart's model uses this kind of general knowledge in processing the information presented in sentence form. "Put" refers to an event in which some action, performed by an agent, causes a change in location of some object from one place to another. Thus, hearing the sentence, "Peter put the package on the

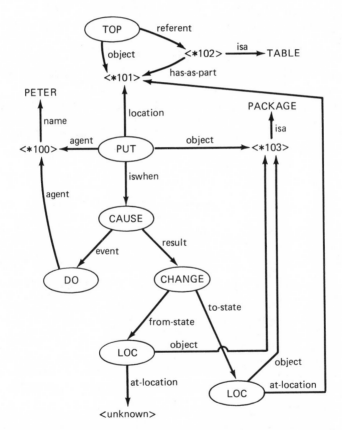

Figure 2-3 Representation of "Peter put the package on the table," in Norman and Rumelhart's (1975) model.

table," the system fills in specific components in various slots that are specified in the schema that corresponds to knowing what "put" means.

The propositional structure corresponding to various sentences and paragraphs has been studied extensively by Kintsch (1974). Two analyses that were used in an experiment by Kintsch and Keenan (1973) are shown in Figure 2-4. The information in each sentence appears as a set of propositions—four propositions in the sentence about Romulus, and eight propositions in the sentence about Cleopatra. Each proposition specifies a relation, named by the first word in parentheses, and one or more ideas that are connected to the relation in the proposition. For example, the proposition indicated by "TOOK, ROMULUS, WOMEN, BY FORCE" has "TOOK" as the relation (in HAM we would find a relation "TAKE," with "PAST" as part of the context). "ROMULUS" could be identified as the agent of the relation, "WOMEN" as its object, and "FORCE" as its instrument. In the case of propositions such as "LEGENDARY, ROMULUS" and "SABINE, WOMEN", the first terms are properties, rather than relations, and modify the respective second terms.

In all the theories reviewed here, information is stored in memory in the form of relational structures and the information is relational at two levels. The first level includes such relations as category membership and subset relations, as well as grammatical relations such as subject and predicate, and case relations such as agent and object. At another level, much of the stored information involves relations that are named by the system and treated as

---

Romulus, the legendary founder of Rome, took the women of the Sabine by force.
1. (TOOK, ROMULUS, WOMEN, BY FORCE)
2. (FOUND, ROMULUS, ROME)
3. (LEGENDARY, ROMULUS)
4. (SABINE, WOMEN)

Cleopatra's downfall lay in her foolish trust in the fickle political figures of the Roman world.
1. (BECAUSE, α, β)
2. (FELL DOWN, CLEOPATRA) = α
3. (TRUST, CLEOPATRA, FIGURES) = β
4. (FOOLISH, TRUST)
5. (FICKLE, FIGURES)
7. (PART OF, FIGURES, WORLD)
8. (ROMAN, WORLD)

Figure 2-4 Propositional representations of two sentences (Kintsch & Keenan, 1973).

concepts, connected to other concepts in the network. In Kintsch's analyses, in fact, the structural details are suppressed in order to focus attention on the properties and relations specified in propositions.

For our purpose, the major conclusion to be drawn is that storing of relatively complex relational structures occurs naturally and frequently in ordinary human cognitive activity. This does not imply that the theories reviewed here give a complete and accurate explanation of such processes as language comprehension. On the contrary, the task of explaining such processes is far from complete and much is still not understood. However, it seems very likely that persons store most of their knowledge in a form similar to that specified in these theories.

THEORY OF PATTERN RECOGNITION

Another group of theories deals with the organization of information used in identifying patterns. For several years it has been generally agreed that the process of recognizing a familiar pattern such as a letter or word, or a friend's face, involves analyzing the features of the stimulus pattern, rather than comparing the stimulus with a stored template of the pattern (see Neisser, 1967).

One system that recognizes patterns by analyzing features is a program called Pandemonium (Selfridge, 1959). Pandemonium begins with a set of feature detectors, each of which is set to respond if a specific feature is present in the stimulus. Some, for example, detect oblique lines, others detect horizontal lines, and still others, curved lines. When the stimulus is the letter A, the detectors for oblique lines and a horizontal line respond, and the detectors for curved lines are silent. At the next level are cognitive demons, that listen to the responses of the feature detectors. Each pattern that the system can recognize has a cognitive demon that corresponds to a set of features. For example, the demon for A could have these features: two oblique lines, a horizontal line, three acute angles, and two obtuse angles. Each cognitive demon listens and responds to the feature demons corresponding to those included in its set of features. If all the feature detectors corresponding to the cognitive demon's features are responding, and no other feature detectors are responding, then that cognitive demon responds at full strength. If one or more features in a cognitive demon's set are absent, or if features are present that are not in the demon's set, that demon's response will be reduced. The system makes a final decision about the pattern by comparing the strengths of response of the various cognitive demons, choosing the pattern that corresponds to the demon who is shouting the loudest.

Pandemonium, true to its name, has its knowledge of patterns organized very weakly. Each pattern that can be recognized is represented by a unit of the system, constituting a "bundle" of features.

Systems with more structure have also been developed, which recognize patterns by an analysis that uses a decision network. Two systems that develop network structures for pattern recognition are Concept Learning System (CLS), developed for learning categorical concepts (Hunt, Marin & Stone, 1966), and Elementary Perceiver and Memorizer (EPAM), developed as a theory of verbal learning (Feigenbaum, 1963).

Hunt's CLS includes features in its decision net for a concept based on a sample of stimuli that are designated as positive and negative instances of the concept. As an example, suppose a category is defined by the following combination of properties: triangle, *and* either red in color or having a striped border. Several stimuli are shown, and for each stimulus it is indicated whether the stimulus is or is not an instance of the concept. All positive instances of the concept will be triangles with striped borders or red in color or both. Negative instances will be triangles with neither striped borders nor red color and any figure that is not a triangle. Note that any nontriangular figure with either a striped border or red color or both is also a negative instance. By comparing sets of negative and positive instances, CLS can arrive at a correct way of classifying the stimuli, showing the result in the form of a decision tree. Figure 2-5 illustrates the example discussed here. Note that the information is a structure of features, connected by links that are labeled either "yes" or "no," which are the two possible outcomes of tests that can be applied to a stimulus.

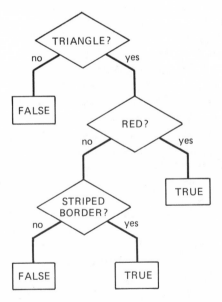

Figure 2-5 Representation of a categorical concept, "Triangle, and either red in color or having a striped border," in CLS (Hunt, Marin & Stone, 1966).

When CLS has learned a concept, it has a structure that uses feature detectors, just as Pandemonium does. However, the feature tests are carried out in a serial order, and the outcome of each test determines what other tests will be carried out. This interdependence among tests means that some stimuli can be classified more quickly than others. For example, in Figure 2-5, a negative instance that is not a triangle would be rejected more quickly than a triangle that has neither red color nor a striped border. In experimental tests of differences predicted between time to classify various stimuli the results have been in agreement with predictions of the kind illustrated here (Trabasso, Rollins & Schaughnessy, 1971).

Another model, designed to simulate rote verbal learning, is EPAM (Feigenbaum, 1963). EPAM constructs a recognition network that identifies the items in a list of nonsense syllables that might be presented in a paired-associate or serial learning experiment. The main process carried out in the system is discrimination learning. The network that EPAM constructs includes a set of features that allows the system to differentiate each item from other items in the list.

When a list of associations has been learned by EPAM, the system has stored a structure of tests and branches. Each test examines a stimulus attribute, such as the identity of a letter or a phonemic or graphemic feature. The outcome of each test determines which feature will be tested next. The discrimination net that is acquired is detailed enough so that each stimulus and each response gives a unique pattern of outcomes of the tests included in the net. Then, when a stimulus is presented, a series of tests occurs leading to a unique terminal node. At that node is stored a (usually partial) image of the stimulus.

Each stimulus image has stored with it information about the response paired with that stimulus. This information, called a cue, comprises a partial list of the properties of the appropriate response. When a stimulus has been presented and the terminal node for that stimulus has been reached, the response cue stored is used as another entry in the discrimination net, and the features specified in the cue are examined in another pass through the network. This process should end at a terminal node containing a response image, which must be detailed enough to permit production of the response.

Acquisition of the discrimination net involves adding new test nodes whenever the present net is inadequate for correct performance in the paired-associate task. This occurs when the series of tests on a stimulus fails to lead to a response cue, or when the response cue that is obtained leads to a terminal node without a response image or with an incorrect image. When this happens, one or more new nodes are added to the net, so that the stimulus and response will be represented appropriately at terminal nodes and will be distinguished from other terms already included in the net.

Figure 2-6 illustrates the kind of net EPAM builds (Feigenbaum, 1963). At

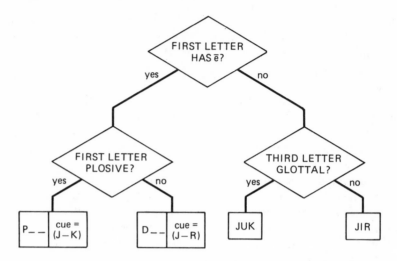

Figure 2-6 Discrimination network for two paired associates (Feigenbaum, 1963).

the point shown, the experiment has included two pairs of nonsense trigrams: *DAX—JIR* and *PIB—JUK*. In the example, EPAM created a test to discriminate the two terms of the first pair. This first test examines a feature of the first letter; it could be a visual feature such as "curved line at right," or a phonemic feature such as ē present in the sound of the letter's name. The first test gives a positive result when the stimulus *DAX* is presented; however, this test does not discriminate *PIB* from *DAX*. A positive result is also obtained on the first test for *PIB*. Therefore, a second test is needed. The second test uses an additional feature of the first letter—if the features being tested are phonemic, the second test might be the feature "plosive." Then *PIB* gives positive results for both tests while *DAX* gives a positive result for the first test but a negative one on the second.

Both response terms in this example sort down the negative side from the first test; neither response passes a test such as the one for ē in the name of the letter. To discriminate the two responses, a letter different from the first letter must be tested. A third test could use a feature of the last letter that would separate *K* from *R*. The terminal nodes for stimuli contain cue information used to identify responses. When the terminal marked *P* is reached, the system must find information that results in a second pass that will terminate at *JUK*, and similarly the system needs to store information with *D* that will result in a sort to *JIR*.

An important theoretical study was conducted by Hintzman (1968), using the idea of a discrimination net similar to that used by Feigenbaum. Hintzman's program, called Stimulus and Association Learner (SAL), is simpler than EPAM in some ways. Instead of storing a series of tests to identify each response, SAL stores only the response item at the terminal node of the tree used to sort stimuli. This means that SAL cannot be used to investigate ideas about response acquisition, and serial learning cannot be accomplished by SAL, as it can be by EPAM. On the other hand, this simplification provides a theoretical advantage. Hintzman wished to investigate the extent to which a process of stimulus discrimination can be used to explain a variety of phenomena in associative learning. If the system used to simulate learning involves a complicated set of processes, it is more difficult to determine which of the several processes or their interactions are important in producing the performance of the system, and theoretical inference is therefore more difficult.

As with EPAM, learning in SAL is a process of adding test nodes to a discrimination net. However, SAL includes stochastic parameters. Whereas EPAM always adds a test node whenever an error occurs, SAL does this with probability a. This means that there are trials when SAL's response is different from the one called correct by the experimenter, but SAL does not change its way of sorting the stimulus. In these cases, the response called correct by the experimenter on that trial replaces SAL's previous response with probability b. The basic mechanism used by SAL explains a considerable variety of experimental facts, such as the effect of similarity between stimuli in the list being learned, and effect of the number of different responses used. The use of stochastic processes enabled Hintzman to run simulated experiments, obtaining several different sequences of data for each condition used and getting information about the amount of intersubject variability that SAL produces.

To deal with some additional phenomena, two other processes were studied. In SAL II, when a correct response is given there is a probability c that an additional test node will be formed for the item. This process causes SAL II to produce overlearning and explains some effects due to amount of practice and similarity between stimuli in different lists in retroactive interference. Finally, in SAL III there is a push-down stack for storage of responses. Recall that when an error occurs there is probability $(1 - a)\,b$ that the discrimination net will not be changed but that the correct response will be stored at the terminal node reached in the series of tests. In SAL III the new response is placed in the first slot of a stack; responses already stored there are moved to lower positions in the stack. A process of change over time was postulated, during which responses from lower positions in the stack move up and displace responses that arrived in the stack more recently; this process explains proactive interference effects. An explanation of some effects caused by the type of test given, such as the difference between recognition and recall, was obtained by assuming that SAL III scans the complete response stack at a terminal node when it is appropriate to do so.

In addition to finding that the idea of stimulus discrimination as realized in a discrimination net has explanatory power for a very large set of experimental phenomena, Hintzman also discovered that a number of phenomena probably depend on additional processes. Effects of list length cannot be explained with the discrimination process of SAL and may be related to limitations of short-term memory. Also, SAL provides no explanation of negative transfer, and it may be necessary to postulate storage of list-identifying information to explain transfer effects, although EPAM can explain negative transfer in A–B, A–C by postulating that storage of new response images requires a large amount of time.

An application of EPAM has been developed by Simon and Gilmartin (1973) for a task involving retrieval of information from a very large structure of stored knowledge. Simon and Gilmartin gave an analysis of pattern recognition in chess. It is known (Chase & Simon, 1973; deGroot, 1966) that chess masters have exceptional ability in a task requiring fast encoding of complex information about a chess position. If a board is arranged with pieces from a position that could be reached during a game, then shown to a master player for a few seconds, the player often can accurately replace nearly all the pieces and generally can accurately replace as many as 15–18 pieces—well beyond the number of discrete elements that a person can hold in short-term memory. Simon and Gilmartin explained this ability on the basis that the master player perceives patterns rather than individual pieces, and recognizes the patterns by using information stored in the form of an EPAM net. Simon and Gilmartin's system, called MAPP (for Memory-Aided Pattern Perceiver) learned somewhat fewer than 600 patterns, each with an average of two to three pieces, with the information stored in a network containing somewhat fewer than 2000 nodes. This memory store was then used to simulate the performance of a subject whose task was to reproduce a sample of board positions after brief viewing. MAPP succeeded in reproducing about 50% of the pieces in the positions used. This was not as good as the performance of a chess master, who replaced an average of 74%, but was somewhat better than performance of a Class A player, who replaced an average of 43%. It was estimated that a system organized like MAPP could perform at the level of the chess master if it had a network permitting recognition of some thousands, or perhaps tens of thousands of patterns.

ASSOCIATION AND STRUCTURE

Any theory that describes an organized system specifies components of the system and relations among the components. Thus, all theories about organization must be about association, at least in a general sense. However, the theory we are calling the associationist theory has made a specific claim regarding the organization of memory—that is, that organization of knowledge consists of a network of simple connections between ideas, or between stimuli and responses. Connections have been assumed to vary in strength, but only in strength. In other words, associationist theory states that memory can be represented as a graph in which ideas, or stimuli and responses, are denoted by nodes, and the connections between nodes vary only in strength.

Theories about memory structure of the kind that we have reviewed here differ from the traditional associationist theory in one fundamental way: they assume that associations in memory are of different kinds. Theories of semantic and factual memory specify different kinds of relations among components of knowledge, and concepts are associated because they enter into those relations. In theories of pattern recognition, the various component features of concepts are linked by branches that depend on the features found in the stimulus.[1]

It seems to us that there are two views that an associationist might reasonably take regarding current theories about the organization of memory. One is simple skepticism. It might be argued that the structures and mechanisms assumed in recent theories are wrong—or at least unnecessarily complex. Such an argument would be tantamount to belief that a theory based on simpler principles would be closer to the truth. We disagree with this view; in our judgment the weight of evidence strongly favors theories whose basic principles are relatively more complex. But we will not try to support that general position here. The task of developing and evaluating a general theory of human memory is not in the domain of this book.

The second response available to an associationist is to maintain that the basic mechanism of learning is the formation of simple connections, and that the more complex structures found in semantic and factual knowledge, in complex pattern recognition, and in other complex cognitive domains involve complex combinations of these basic connections. According to this view, it could be accepted that analysis of knowledge structures seems to lead to the idea of different kinds of associations corresponding to various relations among components, but this diversity is only apparent. It would be expected

---

[1]Pattern-recognition systems like Pandemonium, CLS, and EPAM can actually be realized as simple stimulus-response machines, if the systems are assumed to receive input from their own feature detectors. The contingent branching in EPAM and CLS can be accomplished by assuming that the stimulus situation is modified at each test node by the feature that is found. Then only a simple association is needed to link to the next test or terminal node. However, more complex forms of pattern recognition require more detailed structure, including recognition of relations among components of patterns. There has been some analysis of processes of recognizing complex relational concepts (e.g., Huesmann & Cheng, 1973), and there is considerable literature concerning psychological processes involved with serial patterns (e.g., Egan & Greeno, 1974; Greeno & Simon, 1974; Jones, 1974; Restle & Brown, 1970; Simon & Kotovsky, 1963).

that an appropriate analysis would show how these complex relations are composed of simple connections that vary only in strength.

It is the second associationist response that this book attempts to discourage. According to an associationist view, formation of connections is simple; understanding relations is complex. We take the opposite view: relating cognitive elements is basic and simple, but learning associations between apparently unrelated elements involves a relatively more complex process that can best be understood as a composition of processes. Various aspects of building a relational structure are the component processes in associative learning—not the other way around.

NATURE OF ASSOCIATIONS

The central assertion in the theory we are presenting is: Formation of an association consists of storing in memory a new structure in which the associated elements are in some way related. As Bower (1972a) and Köhler (1947) indicated, the relation may be only that the two elements occurred together in the same context. However, mere proximity in place and time provides relatively weak relational connection; stronger learning should occur if there is some more substantial basis for relating the elements.

Some experiments have compared associations with terms that could be related easily to others that seem less easy to relate. According to the hypothesis that associative formation is basically a process of finding relations, associations should be easier to memorize when there is a stronger basis for relating the items.

In an early contribution to the Gestalt theory of association, Köhler (1941) showed that, in a list of items with some numeric terms and some alphabetic terms, learning was faster on pairs with both stimulus and response terms from the same class than on pairs with the stimulus from one class and the response from the other. Köhler presented this result as an illustration of the importance of organization in learning, citing the Gestalt principle of grouping by similarity as the probable basis of the effect.

However, further analysis shows that effects of this kind are open to another interpretation. Postman and Riley (1957) responded to Köhler's argument, noting that before learning an item, subjects could be selecting responses in a biased way, preferring responses that are in the same class as the stimulus, and they presented evidence that such biases exist. On Postman and Riley's hypothesis, Köhler's finding was due not to differential ease of learning the similar and dissimilar items, but to differences in guessing biases prior to learning that produced more correct responses to unlearned similar items than to unlearned dissimilar items.

Data that seem to avoid Postman and Riley's objection were presented by Asch (1969), who manipulated the conditions of presentation of items rather than the properties of items themselves. Asch studied the association between properties, such as a form having the shape of a triangle, a line being composed of small circles, and other features of geometric stimuli. In one condition, Asch presented the properties to be associated as features of single objects. An example would be a triangular shape formed by three lines of small circles. In the other condition, the properties were presented but not integrated in that way. A triangle made of ordinary lines was presented beside a line composed of small circles. Asch's idea is that when two properties are features of the same object, they will be easily organized into an integrated unit, but that when the properties are presented side by side, it would be more difficult to do so. In tests of retention Asch obtained large differences favoring the condition with integrated presentation of properties.

An associationist analysis of this kind of effect probably is possible, but at least the argument of response bias prior to learning does not seem to apply. Asch's demonstration is especially interesting in that it relates directly to one of the original uses of the concept of association—explanation of the development of complex concepts (such as "table") based on association between properties that are experienced together. The simplest interpretation of Asch's result is that when we learn that an object has several properties, we learn it partly because the properties are all parts of the same object, and are therefore experienced in an integrated and unified way. But on this interpretation, principles of cognitive organization (in this case, perceptual principles) are used to explain an aspect of associative learning, whereas the associationists were attempting to explain cognitive organization using principles of associative learning.

In many ways, the most compelling demonstrations of the potency of organizational factors in associative learning come from experiments dealing with elaborative coding strategies. An especially strong demonstration was given by Jensen and Rohwer (1963), studying associative learning by adult retardates. The task involved associating pictures of objects like a hat and a table. When one of the pictures was presented (say, the hat) the subject was to select a lever under the picture of the associated picture (the table) from a set of pictures. Jensen and Rohwer reported that many of their subjects had great difficulty in learning the pairings, sometimes working for many daily sessions without making noticeable progress. But a dramatic change in learning occurred when subjects were instructed to form sentences involving the objects. (For example, "The hat is on the table.") When subjects were taught to use this strategy, learning occurred at a reasonable rate.

Many experimental demonstrations have shown that subjects can be greatly aided in memorizing associations by use of appropriate kinds of cognitive additions to the material being memorized. The material added by the subject may be verbal, such as the sentences used by Jensen and Rohwer's subjects (also see Adams, 1967), or it may be pictorial (see Bower, 1972b; Paivio,

1971). Evidence from experiments indicates that the main use of a pictorial image comes in integrating the elements to be associated as parts of an interacting scene, thus performing an organizational function similar to that discussed by Asch (see Bower, 1970; Wollen & Lowry, 1971).

Evidence of strong facilitation based on elaborative encoding supports the importance of organization in associative learning. In many situations where elaborative encoding helps, it would seem that simple associative learning should be easier without it. Suppose that a subject is to learn to associate the words "wheel" and "pencil." Learning is made easier by using an image of a wheel with spokes made of pencils. But in terms of associative connections, the subject who learns by using imagery has associated the pictorial representation with the stimulus (for example, imagining a wheel pictorially in response to reading the word "wheel") *and* the response with the image (say "pencil" in response to the pictorial image). Why should this be easier than simply connecting the word "pencil" with the word "wheel?" The reason seems to come naturally from the Gestalt idea that association is a form of cognitive organization. The image provides a way of forming an integrated unit of the two elements to be associated.[2]

RETRIEVAL OF ASSOCIATIONS

We argue that in storing an association, a subject has formed a new mental pattern. Under this assumption, retrieval of an association is a form of pattern recognition. We believe that recently developed theories of pattern recognition, reviewed earlier in this chapter, provide an appropriate set of concepts for understanding the process of retrieving associations.

The idea we propose is a modified version of Feigenbaum's (1963) EPAM system. We will adopt Feigenbaum's idea that pattern recognition is based on an organized set of feature tests carried out on a stimulus that is presented. However, our analysis differs from Feigenbaum's in that we assume that the pattern stored at each terminal node represents the cognitive unit formed when the stimulus-response pair is stored. The features tested in retrieving the association must be features of the stimulus, since that is what is presented on the test. However, the engram that is retrieved is the stimulus-response association, represented as a pattern.

---

[2]Anderson and Bower (1973) also have recognized that associations are easier to memorize if their elements can be made to fit easily into a cognitive relation that is already known. This fact is consistent with their view that information is stored in memory in propositional structures, such as that illustrated by Figure 2-2. Anderson and Bower note that their representation contradicts a strong Gestalt hypothesis that a proposition must be encoded in its entirety or not at all. On the other hand, like other representations in which elements enter into relations rather than simply being connected, Anderson and Bower's representation also contradicts a strong associationist hypothesis that knowledge is organized as a set of undifferentiated connections among elements. We believe that the second of these facts has the greater theoretical significance.

An example is shown in Figure 2-7. The list to be learned is shown, along with a set of feature tests that would identify the associations as a result of testing features of the stimuli. The questions contained in the diamonds are tests carried out by the pattern recognizer, and identification occurs when the sequence of tests and results arrives at a terminal node. Since the system can be represented as a set of nodes denoting feature tests and patterns, connected by a set of links denoting the sequence of carrying out tests, the system has the form of a network. We will refer to systems like Figure 2-7 as retrieval networks (or retrieval systems).

We think that the selection and arrangement of features in a retrieval network are determined mainly by two factors. First, if the items all have different responses, the features included in the network must provide for discrimination among all the associations. The subject cannot give correct responses to all the items if two different stimuli are sorted to the same terminal node. (Of course, if different stimuli are paired with the same response, the subject can benefit from grouping the items. We will discuss the positive transfer that can occur from such grouping in Chapter 5.) Since discrimina-

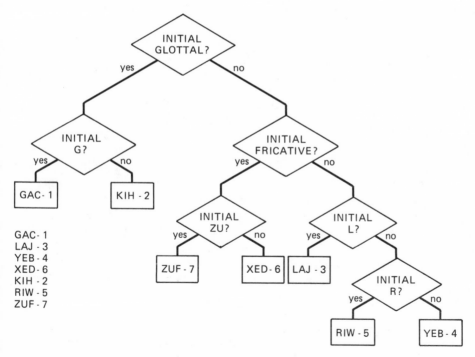

Figure 2-7 Hypothetical retrieval network for a list of paired associates.

tion among patterns is a minimal requirement for successful performance, Feigenbaum (1963) referred to the structures built by EPAM as discrimination nets, and Hintzman's (1968) simplified version of EPAM, described earlier, was based solely on its capability for discriminating among stimuli. (The general problem of discriminating among patterns is a major issue in the formal theory of pattern recognition; see, for example, Minsky & Papert, 1969.)

However, the requirement of discriminability does not determine all the characteristics of a recognition network; many different arrangements of feature tests would provide complete discrimination among the items shown in Figure 2-7, or any list of associations. We propose, therefore, as a second factor, that the arrangement of the network must also be influenced by a need for efficiency of retrieval. Different arrangements of feature tests can produce simpler or more complex networks. A simpler network has two advantages: first, it involves less information that has to be held in memory, so it should be easier to retain; second, use of a simpler network requires fewer steps, and therefore retrieval can take place more quickly and easily.

One way to arrange a network for efficient retrieval is to take advantage of features that are shared among subsets of stimuli. Suppose one stimulus feature is shared by half the items in a list. Testing for that feature then enables the system to eliminate half the items. More generally, a simpler network will result if stimulus features shared by subsets of items are tested early in the recognition process. This corresponds to having these shared features located in relatively high-level positions in a graph such as Figure 2-7.

Although the features needed to retrieve associations must be properties of stimuli, we expect that properties of responses will also influence the selection of features in the network and their arrangement. A major reason for this opinion is our view that individual associations are generally represented in a way that involves a relation between the stimulus and response terms. Concurring with Selz (1913) and later Gestalt theorists, we have concluded that in learning associations, a representation of the stimulus-response pair is generally stored in memory, after which features of the stimulus are incorporated into a retrieval system. But this means that the features most likely to be selected are those that are incorporated in the relational representation of the stimulus-response pair. It is also likely that relations among responses can be utilized in developing an efficiently organized system of retrieval. An illustration is included in Figure 2-7, where the items sorted under "initial glottal" have the responses 1 and 2. Relationships among responses as such cannot make the retrieval network more efficient. However, it seems likely that if items have responses that are interrelated, subjects will more probably notice relationships among their stimuli, and therefore will more probably incorporate those interstimulus relationships into the retrieval networks they develop for the list.

The hypotheses we have given here about retrieval systems imply that organizational factors are important in associative learning, as they have been shown to be in free-recall learning (Mandler, 1967; Tulving, 1962; Wood, 1972). With a few exceptions, theories of learning associations have neglected organizational processes, although Battig (1968) recognized that subjects do acquire groupings of items as they learn the list. Our view that an organized retrieval system is developed by subjects plays an important role in our understanding of phenomena of negative transfer and forgetting, which we discuss in Chapters 6, 7, and 8. However, if we consider only the process of acquisition, there seem to be fairly strong theoretical reasons for expecting organizational factors to play a significant role in associative learning.

SUMMARY

This chapter has presented an overview of the theory of association developed from studies reported in later chapters. The theory consists of two major claims: First, storing an association in memory consists of forming a new cognitive unit that includes the stimulus and response terms as components, and will generally occur through the finding of a relational connection that links the terms. Second, retrieval of associations occurs through a process of pattern recognition based on an organized system of tests on stimulus features.

The first claim, that associations correspond to relational structures rather than connections between otherwise independent entities, violates the fundamental claim of associationist theory—that associations form through the coincidence of ideas. To form a relational structure, the learner must be able to recognize the relation used to form the structure. In assuming that learning of associations is mainly a process of identifying relations rather than forming connections, we think our theory agrees closely with the claims made by Gestalt theorists and with recent theories about the organization of knowledge in memory, in which concepts are stored in complex relational structures.

The second claim, that retrieval is based on a system of tests of features, departs from both classical associationist theory and Gestalt theory. The idea that subjects acquire representations involving a rich set of interitem relationships seems consistent with the spirit of Gestalt theory; we can hardly imagine Köhler or Koffka arguing against the idea of a relational representation of an entire list. However, the concepts in this theory of retrieval have not come from analyses given by Gestalt theorists, but rather from the modern theory of pattern recognition.

Because of the strong continuity between our theory and the Gestalt tradition, we would consider it quite appropriate if our theory were to be called a Gestalt theory of association. On the other hand, Gestalt concepts are combined with concepts developed within a theoretical framework of information processing, with roots in computer science. A more accurate label, historically then, would be a cognitive theory of association.

chapter 3

Processes of Storing Information in Memory

In traditional associationist theory, especially in its behaviorist forms, the outcome of learning has been conceptualized as a change in a person's tendency to do something. Association has been considered a conditional relation between stimulus and response (Martin, 1972; Postman, 1972). In this way of thinking, when a person is learning an association between A and B, the strength of connection between A and B is increased, and this corresponds to an increasing tendency to perform B whenever the person perceives the stimulus A.

Contemporary theories of memorizing take a different point of view. In recent analyses, memorizing has been conceptualized as a process of storing information; remembering, as a process of retrieving stored information. A rich set of concepts and hypotheses was developed during the 1960s by experimental psychologists who analyzed performance in a variety of memorizing tasks and who formulated their conclusions in terms of hypothetical models about processes of storing information in memory.

In Chapter 2, we sketched our main hypotheses about the process of memorizing associations. In our view, the main questions to be considered about associative learning concern the nature of information that is stored in memory when a person has acquired new associations between ideas. Thus, our theory of associative learning belongs in the recent information-processing tradition rather than in the behaviorist tradition of analyzing stimulus-response contingencies.

In this chapter, we will review some major contributions to the theory of memory storage based on concepts of information processing. Many of the empirical studies that have been used have involved memorizing individual items and lists of items, rather than memorizing associations. In this respect, the present chapter is a digression from the development of our main analysis, which focuses on the learning of associations. But theories of recognition memory and recall are important to the conceptual framework in which we have developed our hypotheses about associative learning, and thus the present chapter does provide relevant substantive background for the remainder of the book.

Another reason for presenting the material in this chapter is technical. We give special emphasis to models formulated as Markov chains, and we describe statistical methods for Markov models in some detail. Analyses presented throughout the book depend on measurements of the difficulty of various aspects of learning, and these measurements will consist of estimates obtained from Markov models of the kind we present here. This chapter presents the basic statistical methodology that is later used in testing substantive hypotheses about the process of learning associations, and about transfer between different associative learning tasks.

ALL-OR-NONE LEARNING

We begin with the simplest case, in which learning of each item involves a single transition between states. Then learning is an all-or-none event, and a subject's state of knowledge about an item is that either it is unknown or it has been learned. The graph in Figure 3-1 shows the two states.

Empirical results agreeing with the all-or-none model have been obtained in two kinds of memorizing experiments: recognition memory and simple associative learning with a small number of response alternatives. In an experiment on recognition memory, a list of several items is presented, one item at a time. Then a test is given, in which each item in the original list is presented again, but this time intermixed with new items. The subject's task is to indicate whether or not each item was in the original set. Again the original list is presented alone, then recognition is tested a second time by intermixing a new set of items with those being learned. By continuing this way, the items to be learned are shown repeatedly until the subject correctly recognizes all of them.

In simple paired-associate memorizing, a similar procedure is used. A set

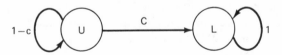

Figure 3-1 Graphical representation of all-or-none learning.

of pairs is constructed—for example, stimuli of simple drawings paired with numerical responses. The pairs are studied, then in a test each stimulus is shown and the subject is asked to give the paired response. The pairs are then shown again, followed by tests on the stimuli. This procedure is repeated until the subject can give the correct responses for all items.

In experiments of these kinds, the items are usually unknown at the beginning. At this point each item is in State U. The all-or-none hypothesis is that each time an item is presented, there is a fixed probability c that the item will become learned—that is, with probability c the item transits to State L. If learning does not occur, the item remains in State U, and will have the same probability of becoming learned on the next trial. As long as the item is unlearned, the probability of a correct response on a test is a constant g, presumably the probability of guessing correctly. It is assumed that the probability of correct response in the learned state is 1.0, but since subjects are likely to occasionally fail to give responses they know, a criterion of about five successive correct responses on an item is used in analyzing the data to indicate the learned state; errors that occur after the criterion has been reached are ignored.

When the model is correct, we can use it to measure the difficulty of learning. In the simple all-or-none model, the difficulty of learning is indicated by the value of c; when c is large, learning is easy, and when c is small, learning is more difficult. For example, Kintsch and Morris (1965) found that the all-or-none model agreed with data of recognition memorizing in two conditions: one in which a list of 10 nonsense syllables was learned, and one in which a list of 15 nonsense syllables was learned. For the 10-item list, the estimate of c was .37; the interpretation is that each time an item was studied there was probability .37 that information about the item would be stored in memory in a way that would permit the item to be recognized throughout the experiment. With the longer 15-item list, the memorizing task was somewhat harder; the estimate of c in that condition was .28. In later chapters, we will be considering more complex models and using the values of parameters like c to estimate the difficulty of different stages of the learning process.

If the assumptions of a model are not at least approximately correct, the parameter values that could be estimated would have no meaning. Therefore, there are two important practical questions about the statistical methods for Markov models. First, how do we obtain the estimates of parameters such as c? Second, how do we decide whether a model is applicable for the analysis of a set of data?

Both questions are answered by the same general approach. From a model such as the all-or-none model, we can derive formulas that show probabilities of various aspects of data. These probabilities are functions of the parameters of the model. Then using empirical observations, we can use some of these formulas to estimate the parameters of the model; if the model is correct, these estimates provide measurements of the difficulty of learning. Having obtained the numerical estimates, we then test whether the data agree with predictions that are calculated from other formulas. Usually, estimates are obtained from some general summary properties of data, such as the mean number of errors and the mean number of trials before criterion.

Predictions to test the model usually involve more detailed properties of data. For example, a formula can be derived for the probability distribution of the number of errors. The numerical estimates obtained from summary statistics give a predicted frequency distribution of the number of errors per item. This predicted frequency distribution is compared with the frequencies in the data, and if the two agree to an acceptable extent, the model is judged applicable for those data.

The analytic power gained by representing a learning process as a Markov chain results from the possibility of calculating the probability of any sequence of events that can occur in an experiment. This can be illustrated easily in relation to the all-or-none model. When an item is tested, there are three possibilities: an item may be learned, denoted by L; it may be unlearned but guessed correctly, denoted by G; or it may be unlearned and an error given, denoted by E. One possible sequence in such an experiment is

$$G\ E\ E\ G\ E\ G\ L\ L\ L. \ldots$$

This sequence has probability

$$g \cdot (1 - c)(1 - g) \cdot (1 - c)(1 - g) \cdot (1 - c)g \cdot (1 - c)(1 - g) \cdot (1 - c)g \cdot c$$
$$= (1 - c)^5(1 - g)^3 g^3 c.$$

The events that can be observed in data are correct and incorrect responses. Let 1 denote an error and let 0 denote a correct response. One possible sequence of data is

$$0\ 1\ 1\ 0\ 1\ 0\ 0\ 0\ 0\ 0\ldots$$

Since correct responses due to guessing cannot be distinguished from correct responses that occur because learning has occurred, the probability of a response sequence corresponds to probabilities of several theoretical sequences. The response sequence listed above has probability

$$g \cdot (1 - c)(1 - g) \cdot (1 - c)(1 - g) \cdot (1 - c)g \cdot (1 - c)(1 - g)$$
$$\cdot [c + (1 - c)gc + (1 - c)^2 g^2 c + \ldots],$$

where the sum of terms inside the brackets involves probabilities of learning immediately after the last error (c), or failing to learn but guessing correctly, then learning ($(1 - c)gc$), or failing to learn twice and guessing both times, then learning $((1 - c)^2 g^2 c)$, and so on. The infinite series inside the brackets can be simplified, giving the result

$$P(0\ 1\ 1\ 0\ 1\ 0\ 0\ 0\ldots) = (1 - c)^4 g^2 (1 - g)^3 \left(\frac{c}{1 - g + gc}\right)$$

The probability of any kind of response sequence can be computed as a function of the parameters. In principle, then, the assumptions of the model could be tested by computing the theoretical probability of each possible kind of response sequence and comparing the results with the proportions obtained in the experiment. In practice, experiments are far too small to permit meaningful comparisons at this level of detail. Therefore, certain summary statistics are used in evaluating the model. Two that are often used are the trial of last error on an item, denoted L, and the total number of errors per item, T. These have distributions

$$P(L = k) = \begin{cases} \dfrac{gc}{1 - g + gc} & k = 0, \\[2ex] \dfrac{(1 - g)c}{1 - g + gc}(1 - c)^{k-1} & k \geq 1. \end{cases} \tag{3-1}$$

$$P(T = j) = \begin{cases} \dfrac{gc}{1 - g + gc} & j = 0, \\[2ex] \dfrac{(1 - g)c}{(1 - g + gc)^2}\left(\dfrac{(1 - g)(1 - c)}{1 - g + gc}\right)^{j-1} & j \geq 1. \end{cases} \tag{3-2}$$

Derivations of these and several other summary statistics were given by Bower (1961). Similar derivations with some attention to general methods of calculation can be found in Atkinson, Bower, and Crothers (1965), in Laming (1973), and in Restle and Greeno (1970).

As we have mentioned earlier, a mathematical model has two uses. It provides a structural description of the process being studied, and as such it is a hypothesis that must be evaluated. It also is a basis of measurement; in a learning model, the model has parameters whose values indicate difficulty of learning. Both uses require estimation of the values of parameters of the model. Various procedures for estimation are possible; some discussion will be given in Chapter 4. For the present discussion, it is sufficient to note that numerical values are required and can be obtained. Numerical values are required if equations like those given above are to be compared with data. Empirical proportions of sequences with zero, one, two, . . . , errors can be observed. These can be compared with theoretical proportions calculated from Equation 3-2, but numerical values must be substituted for the parameters g and c. One reasonably good method of estimation uses the observed mean of one or more statistics in the data, such as the number of errors per item. From Equation 3-2 it can be shown that

$$E(T) = \frac{1-g}{c},\tag{3-3}$$

and if the value of g is known, an easy estimate of c is obtained:

$$\hat{c} = \frac{1-g}{E(T)}.\tag{3-4}$$

If g is not known, then additional data must be used in estimation. The mean trial of last error, derived from Equation 3-1, is

$$E(L) = \frac{1-g}{c(1-g+gc)}.\tag{3-5}$$

Equations 3-3 and 3-5 can be solved simultaneously to obtain estimates of g and c.

To illustrate these methods, consider an experiment in paired-associate memorizing by Polson, Restle, and Polson (1965). The stimuli used are shown in Figure 3-2. Note that eight of the stimuli are distinctive; the other eight form four pairs of highly similar drawings that Polson, et al., called twinned stimuli. The responses were five short words, *cost, hope, part, rush,* and *only,* that the subjects memorized before working on the pairs. Responses were

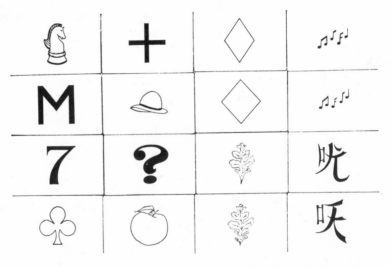

Figure 3-2   Stimuli used in paired associates by Polson, Restle, and Polson (1965).

assigned randomly to the 16 stimuli, with the restriction that the two stimuli of each pair had different responses.

The experiment of Polson, et al., was based on Restle's (1964) idea that paired-associate memorizing would become a more complicated process when similarity between stimuli substantially increases the difficulty in discriminative learning. The items with distinctive stimuli might be learned in an all-or-none fashion. But then it would be expected that the learning of items with twinned stimuli should involve another stage, in which the finer stimulus discriminations would be acquired. In other words, learning a distinctive pair would be a relatively simple process of storing a memorable representation, and it would not be surprising if this were an all-or-none process. But in learning an item with a twinned stimulus, subjects might often store a representation that did not include the features needed to distinguish between the two twinned items. In that case, the first representation in memory would have to be changed by adding additional features to avoid confusions between the twinned items.

For the distinctive items, the mean number of errors was 2.80, and the mean trial of the last error before criterion was 3.61. Using Equations 3-3 and 3-5, the estimated parameter values are $\hat{c} = .25$, $\hat{g} = .30$. When these values are substituted in Equation 3-2, the function drawn in Figure 3-3 is obtained. The empirical distribution of the number of errors per item is shown in Figure 3-3 by solid dots. The empirical and theoretical distributions of the

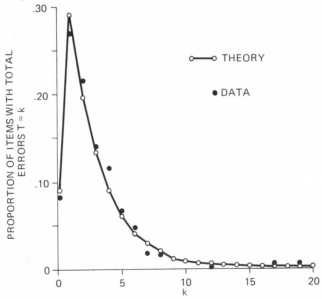

Figure 3-3 Theoretical and empirical distributions of number of errors for individual paired-associate items, from Polson *et al.* (1965).

trial of last error are shown in Figure 3-4. Both comparisons show that the data and the theoretical predictions were in good agreement for these items. (In the present discussion evaluation of goodness of fit, like estimation of parameters, is informal. More rigorous methods will be used in later discussions and will be defined as they are introduced.)

It was not expected that the data from the twinned items would agree with the all-or-none model. However, it is important to understand that testing a model involves a kind of sorting procedure—some sets of data agree with a model, others do not. The twinned items had an average of 5.96 errors. If we assume that g was .30, as estimated for the distinctive items, then Equation 3-4 gives the estimate $\hat{c} = .117$ for the twinned items. This gives the function shown in Figure 3-5. The data from the twinned items shown in Figure 3-5 clearly disagree with the predicted frequencies, confirming the expectation that learning the twinned items would be a more complicated process—not just a slower one. Since the data show the all-or-none model is not a correct description of the learning of these items, it would be a mistake to attribute any meaning to the value of the learning parameter estimated from these data.

The purpose of comparing data and theoretical predictions like those in Figures 3-3, 3-4, and 3-5 is to provide a test of assumptions in the model being considered. Note that this test uses considerably more information from the data than is often the case. In most psychological experiments the mean score of some statistic like total errors is used to measure performance,

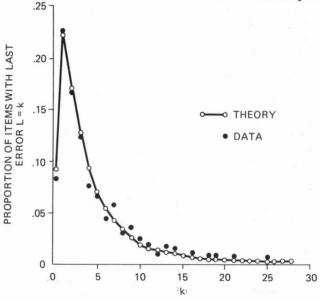

Figure 3-4 Theoretical and empirical distributions of trial of last error for individual paired-associate items, from Polson *et al.* (1965).

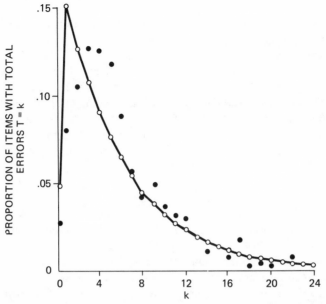

Figure 3-5 Theoretical and empirical distributions of number of errors for paired-associate items with confusable stimuli, from Polson *et al.* (1965).

and analysis of variance is carried out to judge the importance of effects produced by experimental variables. In the analysis of variance, variation among individuals in a single condition, or among measurements taken on the same individual, is considered noise, often called error variance. In that framework the amount of such variation is not informative about theoretical questions and is generally taken as a quantity that should be made as small as possible. In contrast to the analysis of variance, analysis based on a specific quantitative model uses the entire distribution of a variable, such as number of errors or trial of last error, as empirical information to be used in making theoretical inference.

The statistical methodology described here represents only one way of testing hypotheses of the kind represented in the all-or-none model. Regarding the hypothesis of all-or-none learning of simple associations, Estes (1960) gave evidence that if an item was missed on one test, the probability of a correct response on a second test was equal to chance guessing. This supports the idea that items have two states of performance that we have called unlearned and learned. Rock (1957) compared a condition where a list was learned in the normal way with a condition where any item that was missed on a test was replaced by a new item. Subjects in the replacement condition achieved a criterion of no errors as quickly as subjects in the control condition, supporting the idea that as long as an item was not learned, its probability of being learned remained a constant even though it had several previous study trials. There is considerable literature on whether simple associative learning is all-or-none (e.g., Postman, 1963b; Restle, 1965; Underwood, Rehula, & Keppel, 1962). Clearly, it often is not. But we conclude that the weight of evidence favors the idea that learning proceeds through a series of discrete changes, rather than gradual strengthening of traces or connections (cf. Crowder, 1976, chap. 9), and that the all-or-none model provides a good approximation of the course of learning in the simplest cases, in which only one discrete transition is required for a learning criterion to be achieved.

ANALYSIS OF SHORT-TERM RETENTION

The all-or-none model gives a useful statistical description of simple learning, based on transitions occurring between successive trials. However, the model says virtually nothing about the mechanisms of information processing that result in storage of information. A great deal is now known about processing that occurs when items are studied. A composite of most theories is summarized in Figure 3-6.

Information enters the system through the various perceptual systems, which have brief holding capacities in the form of short-term sensory storage (STSS). Attentional mechanisms select information for further processing in short-term memory (STM), which has a capacity of approximately five to seven chunks of information, and when information is arriving at fairly high rates, an individual item typically is maintained in short-term memory for a few seconds. When a subject memorizes a list of items, a representation of the list is stored in intermediate-term memory (ITM), where relatively large amounts of information are held for periods of minutes or hours. Information can become integrated with the person's general structure of semantic and factual knowledge and thus become part of the person's permanent store of organized knowledge.

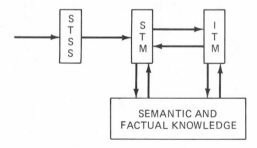

Figure 3-6   A model of information-processing systems.

Markov Chain with Short-Term Memory

During study of a list of items, subjects sometimes know the correct answer on a test before the item has been learned because the tested item was studied recently and is still in short-term memory. A simple change in the all-or-none model provides a system that can be used to analyze some aspects of short-term memory.

A fairly general version of the appropriate Markov model is shown in Figure 3-7. Two changes from the all-or-none model are important. First, there are three states rather than two; an item that is in short-term memory is in State S. Note that State S in the Markov model is not the same as the short-term memory *system* indicated in Figure 3-6. The Markov model describes what happens to a single item during an experiment. The item may be in State S—this occurs on a trial when the item is part of the contents of short-term memory (STM). State L in Figure 3-7 applies after the item has been learned. In most experiments, an item is counted as learned if the subject gives its response correctly for a few tests. It probably is not necessary for an item to be integrated into the subject's permanent store of semantic and factual knowledge to be counted as learned in most experiments. Thus, entry into State L probably corresponds to storage in intermediate-term memory (ITM) in a way that permits reliable retrieval. State U is the state of an item that is not stored in the subject's memory when it is presented.

Second, the transitions assumed when an item is presented correspond to assuming that all items are processed through short-term sensory storage at

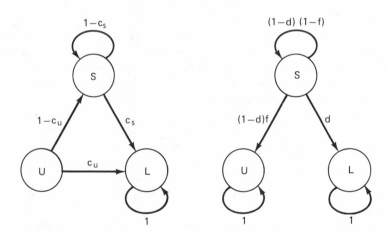

Figure 3-7 All-or-none learning with short-term retention. Transitions shown on the left can occur when an item is presented. Transitions on the right can occur when other items are presented.

least to the level of short-term memory. If an item is in State U when it is presented, there is probability c_u that it will be learned; otherwise, the item goes into short-term memory. If the item is already in State S when it is presented, it is learned with probability c_s; otherwise, it remains in short-term memory. Between an item's presentations, it can make a transition from State S to State L; this has probability d, and a probable mechanism is rehearsal of the item during presentations of other items. If the item does not go into State L, it will remain in State S with probability $1-f$; otherwise it is forgotten, which corresponds to going into State U.

The model shown in Figure 3-7 has been used in analyses of interactions between short-term retention and transfer of information to long-term memory. Bjork (1966), Greeno (1967), and Kintsch (1966) used the model to study effects of spacing between presentation of an item. When two presentations of an item are given with few or no other items between them, performance on a later test is less good than if presentations of an item are separated by presentation or test of several other items.

This effect of spacing can be explained in two general ways. One way notes that with successive or nearly successive repetitions, the item will probably be in State S when the second presentation occurs, and that c_s might be smaller than c_u in the model. This could occur for either of two reasons. The first possible assumption is that if an item is in State S when it is presented, the subject does not try as hard to process that item for long-term retention. This could be due to a simple strategy of conserving information-processing capacity; that is, the subject relaxes a bit when the item that is presented is one that the subject already knows. Another possible assumption implied by the EPAM-type theory given in Chapter 2 is that subjects add a minimum number of features to the discrimination net. An item that had just been studied would be discriminated correctly even if its encoding was not sufficient to prevent later confusions; however, if other items were studied between the item's presentations, inadequacies in the encoding of the item would be more likely to lead to a failure to retrieve the item, and a change in encoding would then occur.

The second general idea that can be used to explain the effect of spacing is that transition from S to L can occur between the item's presentations, because of rehearsal that the subject carries out for items still in short-term memory. In the model the parameter d would be larger for longer interpresentation intervals. This idea explains ineffectiveness of massed presentations by saying the first presentation is less effective than the second because there is less time in which rehearsals are carried out before the second presentation occurs.

Both of these ideas seem plausible, and experimental evidence has been obtained supporting each of them. A reasonable conclusion based on present data is that both kinds of factors are operating to some extent in most experiments: that is, some interpresentation rehearsal occurs, but it is reduced when interpresentation intervals are short; at the same time, when an item is shown that is already in short-term memory, subjects tend to reduce their processing or maintain the encoding they already have achieved. (A thorough review of this issue has been given recently by Hintzman, 1974.)

Additional features of the interaction between short-term retention and longer-term memorizing have been inferred when temporal variables have been analyzed in greater detail. Rumelhart (1967) showed that an interaction between the interval separating two presentations and the interval separating presentations and test can be explained by assuming that the subject does not always attend to a presented item. In the model this would be represented as a nonzero probability of remaining in State U during a presentation. Young (1971) showed that further facts about spacing, including an eventual reversal of the spacing effect (very long interpresentation intervals are worse than moderately long ones) and some time-dependent effects of test trials, can be explained by assuming that two levels of short-term memory exist. Young's theory includes an immediate short-term memory state from which items can always be retrieved, and a more remote short-term memory state from which failures of retrieval can occur, but from which learning occurs with nonzero probability on presentations and tests. Izawa (1971) has given an alternative explanation to Young's hypothesis of two levels of short-term memory. Izawa's idea is that a test can have a potentiating effect on later study trials, thereby causing improvement in performance by indirect means, rather than by learning that occurs during the test.

An important application of the model shown in Figure 3-7 was developed by Atkinson (1972). When students work on a memorizing task such as foreign-language vocabulary, they should benefit from selecting items for study in some optimal way. For example, if c_u is substantially larger than c_s, then putting long intervals between successive presentations of a single item will be more effective.

Atkinson used the model to select items for study in a vocabulary-learning task. Students worked on a set of 84 German vocabulary items in daily sessions. The items were divided into seven sets of 12 items each, and each trial of the experiment involved one set, with a single item selected from the set for study. In different conditions different methods were used to select the item to be studied. As a baseline, there was a condition involving random selection. In a second condition, the subject selected the item to be studied on each trial.

In the remaining two conditions, the model shown in Figure 3-7 was used to select items. On each trial, a calculation was made for each item in the set for that trial to determine the probability that if the item was presented, it would cause a transition into State L. The calculation used all the responses the subject had made on that item on previous trials. The item with the highest probability according to the model was selected and presented. In one condition these calculations were based on a single set of parameter values estimated for all 84 of the vocabulary items. In the final condition, separate parameter values were estimated for the different items in the experiment.

The results showed that the method used to select items had a substantial effect on subjects' learning. In a test given a week after the sequence of study sessions, subjects in the random condition remembered .38 of the items. Subjects who selected their own items and subjects whose selection was based on the model with a single set of parameters did considerably better, with .58 and .54 retention, respectively. But the best performance was achieved by subjects for whom items were selected according to calculations based on the model with separate parameter estimates for individual items. These subjects recalled .79 of the vocabulary items they had studied.

Non-Markovian Stochastic Models

The Markov chain shown in Figure 3-7 gives a rough approximation to the transitions that occur in processing an item that is being studied. A more detailed analysis can be given, and several more specific models have been developed.

One major contribution to the theory of short-term memory was made by Atkinson and Shiffrin (1968). The main ideas of Atkinson and Shiffrin's analysis are: items being studied are transferred into short-term memory from the sensory store; short-term memory has a small capacity although items held there can be easily retrieved; items in short-term memory are kept active through a process of rehearsal; information about an item is transferred to long-term memory throughout the time that the item is held in short-term memory; and information transferred to long-term memory is assumed to decay at a constant rate.

When subjects have to study many items, as they almost always do in experiments, processing of any one item probably is cut short by the entry of later items into the buffer. The amount of time that an item remains in the buffer depends on the condition of the buffer when it enters and the events that occur while it is there. If an item is presented at the beginning of a series, it will take some time before the buffer becomes crowded, and there will thus be some time for processing that item before it becomes likely that the item will be dropped out. During the time shortly after an item is put into the buffer, if many different and unfamiliar items are presented, the item will probably not remain in the buffer very long; however, if the time shortly after its entry is used to present fewer different items or items that the subject has already memorized, an item will remain in the buffer longer and therefore receive more processing.

If an item being tested is still in the short-term buffer, the subject can retrieve it with probability 1.0. If the item is not in the buffer, a search of long-term memory is conducted, and the probability of retrieval depends on the amount of information stored in long-term memory while the item was in the buffer. Thus, the probability of correct response depends on the time an item resided in the buffer; hence, on variables like those described above. The quantitative effects of these variables can be calculated in the form of theoretical predictions when parameters of the model are estimated. Parameters include the size of the buffer, rate of transfer of information to long-term memory, the rate at which information is lost from long-term memory, and the number of times information is taken from long-term memory in the search for the item. The model has given good explanations of an impressive variety of experimental findings, and interesting variations and elaborations of the model have been developed for special experimental conditions.

A theory dealing with many of the same empirical phenomena as Atkinson and Shiffrin's, but based on a different idea, was given by Bernbach (1969). Rather than assuming that short-term and long-term memory constitute discontinuously different systems, Bernbach postulated a single memory system. The main assumptions of Bernbach's analysis involve a process of rehearsal that has the effect of creating replicas of studied items in memory. When a subject studies an item there is specific rehearsal that results in storage of some replicas of the presented item. Following specific rehearsal of the presented item, a general rehearsal process is carried out, involving all items having one or more replicas in memory. The number of replicas created in each process is a random variable. During specific rehearsal k_p replicas of the presented item are made, and k_p has the Poisson distribution with parameter λ_p; a total of k_g replicas are made during general rehearsal, and k_g has the Poisson distribution with parameter λ_g. Each time a replica is created in general rehearsal, every item having one or more replicas in memory is equally likely to be the item getting the added replica. Replicas are lost when a new item is studied. Each time specific rehearsal occurs, every item with replicas in memory loses a single replica with probability δ.

It is harder to calculate theoretical predictions for many experiments using Bernbach's model than it is using Atkinson and Shiffrin's. Computations have been carried out for a number of experiments, and results show that a single-system theory of the kind Bernbach developed has many of the same implications for experimental results as the theory with separate short-term and long-term memory systems developed by Atkinson and Shiffrin. The important theoretical point established in Bernbach's work is that transient phenomena of the kind studied intensively in memorizing experiments do not necessarily require a theory having a discontinuous distinction between long-term and short-term memory systems. On the other hand, the theory with separate systems seems to be more tractable, and because the two theories have similar empirical content, it is reasonable to use the theory with separate systems in analyzing effects of empirical variables that affect the ease of memorizing, and thereby develop rigorous analyses of the process of storing information in memory. Conclusions reached using either model probably can be translated into the other's concepts and assumptions, in the event that future work should provide convincing evidence that one is more accurate than the other.

The analyses given by Atkinson and Shiffrin (1968) and Bernbach (1969) consider the process of storing information about items in some detail. A process of loss or decay of information from memory is included in each of these models, but no specific assumptions about the process of information loss are made. An important theoretical analysis given by Bower (1967b) treats the memory trace of an item as a vector of components, and investigates implications of the idea that the loss of information from memory involves loss of components of the stored vector.

The main concept in Bower's analysis is that when information about an item is stored in memory, that information can be represented as a vector whose elements represent features of the item. Sometime later the individual will be tested in some way to determine whether he remembers the item. The subject's success on the test will depend on the number of the item's features retained in memory. Assuming that enough features are stored initially to allow the subject to reconstruct the item, analysis of retention performance involves two main problems. One is the problem of information loss—what the process is by which the memory trace is degraded. Bower considered a number of alternatives, including a hierarchical system in which important elements are retained longer than components of less importance. But an assumption of independent loss of individual components from the memory trace turns out to be sufficiently rich to allow explanation of many known facts about retention.

The other problem in understanding retention performance involves understanding the requirements imposed by the nature of the test. Bower analyzed relationships between many kinds of recognition tests, showing that the idea of a degraded memory trace provides a basis for understanding a considerable variety of phenomena, including the effect of similarity between studied items and distractors used in tests of recognition. Assumptions were also proposed about the process of recall—primarily that the subject attempts a recall only if some threshold number of component features are retained in memory. This gives a way of analyzing important phenomena such as "tip-of-the-tongue," in which subjects can be shown to perform above the level of chance on items they could not recall but believed they could recognize if shown the items.

Bower's theory provides the beginning of analysis of the structure of information stored and retained in memory. An important contribution by Norman and Rumelhart (1970) used Bower's idea of a multicomponent memory trace, incorporating the concept in an analysis of relationships between perception, short-term memory, and long-term memory.

Norman and Rumelhart's theory incorporates hypotheses about perception given by Rumelhart (1970), where it is assumed that features of a stimulus are registered, and recognition of a stimulus occurs if a sufficient number of features is extracted. Norman and Rumelhart postulated a naming mechanism that includes a dictionary, containing names and vectors of features for the set of items that the subject is expecting. A name is assigned to the stimulus if all the features extracted in perception match elements in only one of the feature-vectors in the dictionary. (An alternative assumption is also described, in which a subject guesses between alternative items if more than one dictionary entry matches the perceived features. However, it is assumed that the more conservative strategy of assigning a name only if all the perceived features match is probably used in most situations.) When a name is assigned, the named item's vector of features is registered in short-term memory.

The attributes in short-term memory are assumed to decay as they are held, and Norman and Rumelhart obtained evidence that loss of attributes' clarity in short-term memory depends mainly on the amount of time since the item was registered rather than on the number of items presented during its residence. While the item's features remain in short-term memory, information is in the form of an association between an attribute and the context in which the attribute was perceived. At any specific time, the attention given to each item in short-term memory is proportional to the clarity of that item's attributes relative to all the items then in short-term memory. And the probability of transferring an attribute-context association to long-term memory depends on the amount of attention the subject is giving to the item. The theory thus describes a system in which a recognized item is represented in short-term memory as a vector of its attributes, and association between some of the attributes and the context in which they were perceived is transferred to long-term memory. A more complete representation, involving more of the item's attributes, will result if fewer other items are in short-term memory, and a more complete representation will be favorable to performance on retention tests.

If a subject is shown an item and asked whether it was in the list studied, the features of the test item are compared with attributes stored in long-term memory to see whether an item matching the present one was included in the list. If a criterion number of the test item's features are found associated with a context from the list, the subject responds that the item is recognized. The theory provides a way of explaining performance with different criteria of recognition (a stricter criterion corresponds to requiring a larger number of found features) and the effect of presenting test items that are more or less similar to the studied items (more similar items share more features with the studied items, and there is a high probability of finding a match for an item not in the set studied). In a recall test, the information given tells the subject what context to use, and features of items retrieved are those associated with the context. Then the subject responds by giving those items that can be generated on the basis of the features retrieved from memory.

Computer Simulations of Memory Processing

Ideas that are similar to those used in the stochastic models just described have been used as the basis of a number of models developed as computer programs.

One model of short-term effects was given by Reitman (1970). Following a suggestion by Bower (1967a), Reitman assumed that items entering short-term memory are processed in a way analogous to customers waiting to be served by a clerk. In Reitman's analysis, when an item is recognized it is placed in a queue. The rate at which items enter the queue depends on the rate at which they are presented in the experiment, although there is a limiting rate of recognizing items, and if items are presented more rapidly some items will not be processed at the initial stage. Items in the queue are waiting to be processed for storage in working memory, which holds items long enough for correct performance during an experiment. At any given time the coder that transfers items to working memory will be processing a single item, and it is assumed that each time an item is selected for this processing it will be the item that has been in the queue longest. If items were presented slowly, then every item could be processed by the coder and transferred to working memory. However, in most experiments items are presented at a rate exceeding that of the coder, so they queue up. Also, the queue has limited capacity, so after several items have been placed in the queue, addition of new items causes older items to be bumped out and thus lost from short-term memory before being processed for working memory. An additional factor producing loss from short-term memory is a decay process that is assumed to remove any item that has been in the queue more than a certain amount of time.

A simulation model given by Laughery (1969) incorporates hypotheses about both the structural properties of short-term memory and the form in which information is stored in short-term memory. Laughery's model includes a long-term memory containing a vocabulary of letters and digits. The information in long-term memory is in the form of a discrimination net, with the sorting based on phonemic or visual features of the vocabulary items. For example, the phonemic features defining S are ϵ (as in *pen*) and s (as in *sue*), and the visual features for S are half curve, open left, bottom and half curve, open right, top.

Structural properties of the system for memory storage and retention are like those of Bernbach's (1969) theory, rather than Atkinson and Shiffrin's

(1968). Laughery postulated a single short-term memory system in which input items are stored and held, if possible, until needed for output on a test. A rehearsal mechanism was postulated, and a process of updating the contents of short-term memory by rehearsal preserved information in the system. In Laughery's theory, long-term memory holds the dictionary of items known by the subject. Long-term memory is not a separate storage system used to hold the items presented during a specific memorizing task.

Laughery's program simulates performance in memorizing tasks where items are presented either visually or auditorily. With visual presentation, the items' visual features are given as input; with auditory presentation, the inputs are vectors of phonemic features. Inputs are placed in a "window"— actually, a set of computer memory locations that the simulation program interrogates from time to time to receive new items. Laughery assumed that items are represented in short-term memory by vectors of phonemic features. When inputs are received by auditory presentation, phonemic features are transferred directly from the "window" to short-term memory in the form of a memory structure containing the name of the structure and phonemic features as substructures. Each component substructure includes a time tag and a decay parameter. The decay parameter used at initial storage of a component is a characteristic of that component. If visual presentation is used, input visual features are sorted through long-term memory. This should result in finding the input item, a process of recognition. When the item is recognized a short-term memory structure based on its phonemic features is created.

Each time a new memory structure is created, the structure created just previously is given a substructure that links it to the new item. This linking information consists of the address in memory where the newly created item can be found. Links are themselves components of memory structures, and as such they have time tags and decay parameters. They provide the mechanism for determining the order in which information is stored and retained.

Laughery's theory is like Bower's (1967b) multicomponent theory of the memory trace in assuming that individual components of the memory structure are lost over time. Each component has a characteristic decay parameter B, and is assumed to decay in such a way that the probability of retrieval at time t is $p = e^{-Bt}$, t being the time since the component was stored or updated by rehearsal, and e being a standard constant. Rehearsal occurs whenever there is time for it. When rehearsal is carried out, items in short-term memory are retrieved in order, the order being determined by the linking components of the memory structure. Rehearsal of an item consists of retrieving the components of the item, and then updating the time tag and reducing the decay parameter for the components of the item found in long-term memory. Rehearsal thus resets the time clock associated with the components of an item and also produces a reduced rate of decay for the components.

Since the retrieval of components is probabilistic, the rehearsal process may fail, and in fact may result in insertion of erroneous items in short-term memory. Since phonemic features provide the basis of storage in short-term memory, the intrusions that occur are likely to be phonemically similar to the correct items.

Laughery also discussed a process of coding individual inputs into groups or chunks. Chunking was assumed to have lower priority than rehearsal, but when it occurs, memory storage is condensed. In Laughery's discussion, chunking is based on information stored in long-term memory about combinations of elementary vocabulary items that can be formed. A common basis for chunking is probably the pronounceable unit that can be formed by a consonant-vowel-consonant sequence. Laughery proposed that when such a sequence is encountered, if there is time for recoding processes to occur, the system could find consonant-vowel-consonant (CVC) sequences by scanning short-term memory and could create new memory structures for the chunks thus formed. The components of the new structure would be the phonemic features of the pronounceable syllable. This process would include creating a new entry in long-term memory corresponding to the newly formed chunk, thus permitting later rehearsal of the memory structure. And a linking substructure would be established, connecting the chunk's memory structure to the element following the chunk's last letter in the sequence. The facilitating effect of chunking would come from reduced rehearsal time; the time needed to rehearse a three-letter chunk would be about the same as the time needed to rehearse a single letter, so the formation of chunks in short-term memory would permit more frequent rehearsals of the memory's contents.

TWO-STAGE LEARNING

We began this chapter by discussing learning of the simplest kind, in which memorizing a single item involves a single transition. The analysis of short-term retention discussed in the preceding section is mainly about transitory effects that occur during study. An item may be remembered for a short time, even if it has not been learned. Such transitory effects do not violate the hypothesis of all-or-none learning; the learning of an item still can be an all-or-none process in the sense that there is a constant probability of the transition to the learned state independent of previous practice on the item.

On the other hand, learning is not generally or even usually an all-or-none process. The conditions needed to produce all-or-none learning are quite special. To apply the analytic methods provided by Markov models to most experiments a more general system is needed. For the experiments we present in this book, a two-stage system is sufficiently complex to handle the data satisfactorily. Figure 3-8 is a graph of a two-stage learning system. An item is initially in the unlearned State U and remains in State U until the first stage of learning is accomplished. State U is a Markov state, so there is a constant

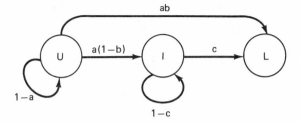

Figure 3-8 Graphical representation of two-stage learning.

probability a of leaving State U on each trial. The value of a therefore gives a measure of the difficulty of the first stage of learning. If a is large, the first stage is easy, but if a is small then many trials may be needed before the first stage of learning is accomplished.

The second stage of learning is accomplished when the item goes into State L. This may occur on the same trial as the transition from State U; with probability b the second stage takes no trials beyond those needed for Stage 1. But with probability $1 - b$ an item that has left State U goes into an intermediate State I, and some trials are needed before the second stage of learning is accomplished. The values of b and c give measures of the difficulty of the second stage of learning. Large values of b and c correspond to short residence in State I and therefore indicate that the second stage of learning is easy. Small values of b and c indicate that the second stage is difficult since the system will be in State I for many trials.

In the first section of this chapter we described statistical methods that can be used to test whether learning in some situation is all-or-none. Those same methods can be used to test a two-stage model, although the formulas involved are somewhat more complicated. We will discuss the statistical properties of two-stage learning in somewhat more detail in Chapter 4, where we will begin to make substantive inferences based on measurements of difficulty of the two stages of learning. But to illustrate the general ideas involved, we will give a brief introduction here.

According to the Markov model, the two stages of learning are independent all-or-none events. Let Z_1 be the number of trials that are spent in State U, and let Z_2 be the number of trials spent in State I. In other words, Z_1 is the number of trials needed to complete the first stage of learning, and Z_2 is the number of trials needed to complete the second stage. The distributions of Z_1 and Z_2 are

$$P(Z_1 = i) = (1 - a)^i a$$

$$P(Z_2 = j) = \begin{cases} b & \text{for } j = 0, \\ (1 - b)(1 - c)^{j-1}c & \text{for } j \geq 1. \end{cases} \tag{3-6}$$

The total number of trials needed for learning to be completed is the sum of Z_1 and Z_2. When a and c differ, its distribution is

$$P(Z_1 + Z_2 = k) = (1 - a)^k a\left[\frac{ab - c}{a - c}\right] + (1 - c)^k \frac{a(1 - b)c}{a - c}. \qquad (3\text{-}7)$$

The function differs from those derived from the all-or-none assumption mainly in having two terms $(1 - a)$ and $(1 - c)$ that are raised to the power k. This gives a different appearance to the distribution of statistics such as the total number of errors made on individual items. With all-or-none learning, the theoretical distributions of most statistics decrease monotonically after the first term. If learning has two stages, many statistics have modes displaced somewhat to the right, although distributions will still typically be strongly skewed. An example in Figure 3-9 shows the data of Polson, Restle, and Polson (1965) again, but with the theoretical function derived from assuming that there were two stages in learning. Note that the character of the data is represented much more satisfactorily here than by the all-or-none predictions for these data shown in Figure 3-5.

It should be recognized that the use of the two-stage model is not confined to any specific psychological ideas about the process of learning in the two stages, or about what information is stored in the two stages of learning.

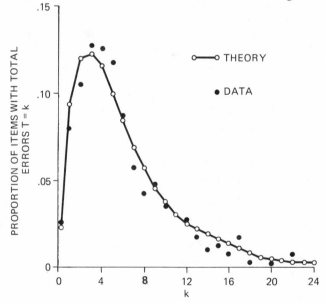

Figure 3-9 Theoretical and empirical distributions of number of errors for paired-associate items with confusable stimuli, from Polson *et al.* (1965). This theoretical function assumes two stages of learning.

Polson et al. proposed that the first stage involves storing a representation of the association, and the second stage involves refining that representation if necessary to avoid confusions between similar stimuli. But there are other interpretations that have been given to the two stages of memorizing, depending on the nature of the task studied and the kind of process inferred to be occurring in the learning situation.

One alternative that has been used by Atkinson and Crothers (1964), Bjork (1966), Rumelhart (1967), and Young (1971) assumes that State U refers to a state in which an item has not yet been coded to permit short-term retention, while in State I an item will be held in short-term memory for a while after each presentation. In this interpretation, the elevation of performance that occurs when an item leaves State U is due to occasional retention of items in short-term memory and the coding that permits this is a partial step in learning.

Another idea that leads to a two-stage process is that an item can begin with a wrong response associated with the stimulus. Then the first stage of learning consists of unlearning the wrong association; an item in State I has no stimulus-response connection and the subject will be able to guess the correct response. Once the wrong association has been unlearned, the correct response will be learned in an all-or-none fashion. This idea was used by Bower and Theios (1964) in an application of the model to an experiment in which responses were changed after subjects had learned them. State U was thus interpreted as a state in which the response learned first was still connected to its stimulus, after the experimenter had begun reinforcing a different response for that stimulus. Bernbach (1965) used a similar idea, but assumed that learning of wrong responses could occur during an ordinary paired-associate experiment if the subject had to guess a response and retained the wrong guess rather than the response declared correct by the experimenter. Along similar lines, Millward (1964) and Nahinsky (1967) considered a system in which partial learning consists of learning to avoid giving certain errors. The probability of correct response for an item increases before the correct association is learned because the subject learns that some subset of response alternatives is incorrect.

A hypothesis we will discuss thoroughly in Chapter 4 is that Stage 1 of paired-associate learning is acquisition of the response while Stage 2 is learning the correct stimulus-response connection. This idea was developed by Mandler and Heinemann (1956) and by Underwood and Schulz (1960). Kintsch (1963) used it in a quantitative analysis.

Another hypothesis has been used by Estes and DaPolito (1967) and by Kintsch and Morris (1965). The first stage of learning is assumed to involve an accomplishment that allows the subject to recognize the item, but not necessarily to recall it. The transition to State L occurs when the subject becomes able to recall the item. Estes and DaPolito used the idea in connection with recognition and recall tests of paired associates, while Kintsch and Morris used it in analyzing recognition and free recall memorizing of nonsense trigrams. Heine (1970) analyzed serial position effects in free recall memorizing. Heine showed that the two-stage model gave a good approximation for a process involving storage of information about an item in the first stage by a process like that postulated by Atkinson and Shiffrin (1968). The inference was that during the first stage, information was transferred to long-term memory and once sufficient information was stored, it became possible for the subject to develop a reliable way of retrieving the item. This analysis of free recall by Heine relates closely to analyses of paired-associate memorizing carried out by Humphreys and Greeno (1970), which will be discussed in Chapter 4.

CONCLUSION

In this chapter, we have reviewed a variety of theories about the processing of information that results in storage of items in memory. Part of the reason for presenting this material is technical; later chapters depend strongly on results obtained from statistical methods based on Markov models, introduced in this chapter in an elementary way. The conceptual developments presented are less directly relevant to our main topic of learning associations; however, the strong development of theory about information processing in memory provides a general framework within which issues about associative learning can be formulated, and much of our discussion in subsequent chapters is formulated in these terms.

chapter 4

Processes in the Learning of Associations

The question considered in this chapter is how new associations between ideas are acquired. We begin by considering the formation of complex ideas, an important general problem that was solved using the concept of association between ideas. We suggest that the classical associationist account of this process presents difficulties, but that analyses of cognitive structure such as those discussed in Chapter 2 provide a promising basis for developing new approaches to the problem.

The main task of this chapter involves analysis of the process of learning new associations between ideas as this is observed in laboratory experiments. It is generally agreed that the process of memorizing paired associates is not a simple, unitary process except under quite special circumstances. We review two hypothetical subprocesses—response learning and stimulus encoding—that have been incorporated into standard associationist analyses of paired-associate memorizing. We will argue that the cognitive theory sketched in Chapter 2 provides an alternative interpretation for the kinds of phenomena that led associationists to postulate these auxiliary processes. Finally, we include quantitative analyses of the process of paired-associate memorizing, using the two-stage Markov model discussed at the end of Chapter 3.

COMPLEX IDEAS

The concept of association is important because it offers solutions for fundamental intellectual problems. One of the major questions this concept has been used to answer is, How do people come to have complex ideas?

To a person who believed in innate ideas or in revelation, acquisition of complex ideas would not be problematic. If the mental structures corresponding to concepts such as a table or a human face or a nation or justice were inherited or were received from God, then there would be no reason why a person should not be endowed with complex and abstract ideas as well as with simple and concrete ideas.

But consider what happens if we adopt the brash assumption that knowledge is derived from experience. Then, complex and abstract ideas present a problem, although the exact nature of the problem depends on what is meant by "experience." Many psychologists and philosophers use a meaning based on so-called sense-data—elementary impressions such as the impression of a blue patch of color in the visual field. It was natural to think that the mental capacity to experience blue-ness, brightness, loudness, middle-C-ness, roughness, sharpness, and other sensory qualities would be given directly in our physical makeup.

If we take the view that knowledge comes from experience and assume further that experience is made up of elementary sense-data, understanding how people can know about complicated things like tables or can recognize their friends becomes a problem; furthermore, people's understanding of abstract concepts such as chemical valence or justice seems even more mysterious. The solution offered in associationist theory is that complex concepts are combinations of elementary ideas that are built up because the component ideas frequently occur together in experience. The process by which the needed combinations occur was postulated to be a process of association, and the ability to form associations among ideas was assumed to be a fundamental property of the mind.

Toward the end of the nineteenth century, psychological laboratories were established and experimental studies were conducted to analyze and better understand the processes of mental life. The main focus of this early work was the analysis of the properties of sensory experience, with the goal of obtaining a systematic description of the fundamental entities of experience. A table of the psychological elements was to be obtained. This enterprise was indeed appropriate in that it was based on the assumption that the complex concepts and ideas of our thought and experience are the product of association among elementary sensory experiences. In this framework, then, the experimental study of association was begun.

Because a principal use of the concept of association was to explain how simple psychological entities combine to form more complex ideas, the main goal of experimental study of association was to investigate the way in which that takes place. Given the framework of concepts and theory in which he worked, Ebbinghaus (1913) chose exactly the right situation for investigation. By combining letters that did not form words in German, he formed nonsense syllables and memorized lists of these syllables. His observation led to a conclusion that an intricate pattern of forward, backward, and remote associations is involved when mental elements are combined in a complex structure. It is revealing that nonsense syllables were chosen as the elements. In our present understanding, a word like "dog" is considered to be relatively simple and unitary, and a nonsense syllable such as "dwg" is assumed to be more complex. But a century ago, words were assumed to have meaning by virtue of association with other words and ideas. Thus, a familiar word was believed complex because of its many associations with other ideas in cognitive structure, while an unfamiliar syllable was believed more simple because of its lack of associative connection with ideas already in the mind.

General Critique

For complex concepts, the basic idea of the associationist analysis seems indisputable. Certainly persons develop ideas that are composites of other ideas, and surely an understanding of the rules of combination by which component ideas are composed into complex ideas is a central theoretical goal.

However, the associationist analysis assumes that connections among the component ideas of a complex concept occur in an unrestricted way. For Ebbinghaus' analysis to be relevant to the problem of forming complex ideas, it must be assumed that a complex idea can be composed of arbitrary components, arranged in an arbitrary sequence. Contrast this with the kind of complex idea illustrated in Figure 2-3. That idea represents an event in which Peter put a package on a table, and is analyzed in Norman and Rumelhart's theory as a combination of component ideas. However, the form of the combination is strongly restricted. Component ideas are related in specific ways, rather than by undifferentiated connections. And the whole idea is organized by the constraints of a schema: the general idea of "putting" is known, and the specific event involving Peter uses a pattern of relations that is known.

The question arises, then, of whether the associationist solution to the problem of complex ideas has any generality beyond the artificial compositions of unrelated words and nonsense syllables that were contrived by investigators to minimize the meaningfulness of the complex idea to be acquired. We emphasize that we are not questioning the scientific practice of studying artificial tasks in order to test ideas about acquisition of complex ideas in experiments on rote memorizing; the failure is not due to the artificiality of the situation studied. On the contrary, the failure, if it has been a failure, was brought about by use of a mistaken theory that wrongly characterized the nature of complex ideas. If complex ideas are really complex relational structures, not simply connected networks, information about their formation will come from studies of comprehension and learning of relations.

It must be recognized that our objection to the associationist analysis of complex ideas is informal. We have not described the domain of complex ideas or formulated the limits of simple associative connections with sufficient rigor to prove a theorem of impossibility. However, we are skeptical about the capability of a system limited to formation of undifferentiated connections to generate complex ideas that correspond to relational structures. Although the issue is still open, and other investigators (notably Estes, 1976) have taken a more hopeful view, our current conclusion makes us doubt whether the hypothesis of associationism does, in fact, solve the problem of complex ideas in a satisfactory way.

Complex Ideas in Cognitive Theory

Present knowledge does not permit anything like an adequate explanation of the acquisition of new complex concepts. However, some promising beginnings have been made and it seems appropriate to comment briefly on the relationship of some recent work to the classical problem.

The theory of natural language understanding has been developed to a considerable degree (Norman & Rumelhart, 1975; Schank, 1972; Winograd, 1972) and provides a set of very promising ideas about possible mechanisms for generating complex concepts. When a sentence or paragraph is presented to a system, interpretive mechanisms use knowledge about the meanings of words and interrelationships among concepts to develop relational structures. When a sentence or a paragraph is understood, the result is a structure that represents the meaning of the message. Figures 2-2 and 2-3 are examples of the kinds of structures built by these systems. These structures are complex concepts that are stored in memory and represent information about events and facts.

Like the associationist theories of concept formation, the theory of language understanding assumes strong prior knowledge about specific ideas that are combined into the complex concepts that the system acquires. It is recognized that more powerful mechanisms must be involved in the acquisition of the schemata than are used in the comprehension of specific information. For example, the structure in Figure 2-3 is constructed by a system that already knows what it means for something to be put somewhere. The next problem is to understand how general schemata develop for concepts such as "putting."

Some promising beginnings have been made. Winston (1973) has studied characteristics of a system that can learn certain spatial concepts, such as "arch" and "pedestal," by combining component ideas that refer to surfaces and edges of solid objects. Klahr and Wallace (1973) have studied relationships between concepts of quantity and number, which children understand at differing ages, and have begun to analyze possible processes of development as the addition of new procedures of comparison and the assignment of quantitative symbols to sets. Gentner (1975) has studied relationships between different concepts relating to possession, such as "give," "trade," and "sell."

These involve schemata of varying complexity, and the more complex concepts have components that are present in the less complex concepts. The process of developing these schemata can probably be understood as an elaboration in which new components are added to previous structure.

ASSOCIATION AS STIMULUS-RESPONSE CONNECTION

During the first half of the twentieth century, American psychologists who studied learning became increasingly influenced by behaviorism, a methodological program developed in biology and imported to psychology by Watson (1919), among others. They turned their attention away from questions about association between ideas in the mind and toward questions about association between stimuli and responses. A sharp distinction between stimulus and response does not arise naturally when the concept of association is used to explain the emergence of complex ideas, but it does arise in the experimental situations that have been used to investigate processes of association. This is particularly true of paired-associate memorizing, and in recent years most of the experiments used to develop and test concepts of association theory have used the method of paired associates.

If one considers an association to be a connection between a stimulus and a response, then paired-associate memorizing represents a paradigm case for association theory, in that the process of forming an association can be observed in a relatively simple and pure form. The investigator can specify what the stimulus is on each trial, to a greater degree than in other memorizing tasks such as serial or free recall memorizing (see Underwood, 1964). Further, a single correct response for each stimulus is specified. It is not surprising, then, that the process of learning to give the correct response for a single paired associate has been considered to be a kind of two-body problem, in which relationships among pairs in the list are assumed to be of minor importance, although they undoubtedly exist and can be shown to have effects, as Battig (1968) pointed out.

Paired-associate memorizing has been studied intensively in recent years, and two fundamental changes have been made in the associationist theory. The process of memorizing a paired associate is no longer assumed to involve only formation of a connection between stimulus and response. Instead, it is assumed to include two additional processes: response learning and stimulus learning, or stimulus encoding.

RESPONSE LEARNING

The concept of response learning recognizes two discrepancies between what happens in real paired-associate memorizing and in the ideal process of forming a connection between two elementary mental entities. First, materials used in paired-associate experiments often do not form unitary mental elements. If a subject has to connect a response like "gwk" with a stimulus, the task is more complicated than connecting a single element with another single element, because "gwk" is really a three-element list. In fact, the subject's task has features in common with the task of list learning, studied by Ebbinghaus. The theoretical response to this fact was developed by Mandler and Heinemann (1956), McGuire (1961), and Underwood and Schulz (1960). It was hypothesized that when the response to be associated with a stimulus is not unitary, a process of response integration occurs. This preserves the idea that association is basically a process of connecting a response to a stimulus. But it asserts that in some situations, an additional process, that of forming a unitary response to be connected, occurs also.

Second, an aspect of response learning occurs whether or not the items used as responses are familiar and integrated at the start of the experiment. It is implicit in the nature of the paired-associate experiment that to perform correctly, the subject must perform the assigned response—not the stimulus. This means that readiness to perform the response for an item will be a factor in the subject's retention. This factor of readiness, or availability, appears in many situations and is related to groups or sets of responses that are formed by subjects. For example, when subjects solve a series of anagrams, creating words that are names of animals, and then see the anagram, EOSRH, they are likely to find the solution "horse"; if they have been solving anagrams into words naming bodies of water, they are more likely to find "shore" (see Rees and Israel, 1935). Associationist theory was elaborated to include a process called formation of a response pool. Thus, recent versions of associationist theory assume that, even when responses are familiar and meaningful to the subject, a process of response learning constitutes part of the subject's task in a paired-associate experiment (Postman 1963a; Underwood & Schulz, 1960).

A considerable amount of experimental evidence has been gathered in support of the idea that response learning has significant effects in paired-associate memorizing. One important fact involves the kind of items used as the response terms in a list of pairs. Large differences in ease of learning paired associates can be produced by varying the meaningfulness and ease of pronounciation of response terms. An item's meaningfulness is measured by determining how easily subjects can think of words as associations to the item. Thus, the trigram CAL is highly meaningful, because several words come to mind ("call," "calorie," "California"), while QWL is much less meaningful.

When pairs have highly meaningful responses, associations are much easier to learn than when they have nonmeaningful responses. Associationist theory offers the explanation that response learning is a component process of memorizing an association, and meaningful responses are easier to learn than nonmeaningful ones. The idea that meaningfulness primarily affects the response learning component is supported by the fact that varying the meaningfulness of stimuli leads to far smaller effects on difficulty of learning than does varying the meaningfulness of responses (e.g., Cieutat, Stockwell & Noble, 1958). Apparently, meaningfulness has a more important influence than pronounceability on the difficulty of remembering items: a list of such items as AFL and TWA has been found easier for subjects to remember than a list of the same items with their letters rearranged to make them pronounceable (FAL, TAW); however, the pronounceable list was easier than items that were neither pronounceable nor meaningful, for example, LFA and WTA (Gibson, Bishop, Schiff & Smith, 1964).

Another finding that has been interpreted as support for the hypothesis of response learning involves transfer to paired-associate memorizing after free recall pretraining. If subjects are first trained to recall a list of items, and these items are subsequently used as responses for paired associates, then the associations are easier to memorize. This effect is especially strong with response terms low in meaningfulness, but it has also been shown to occur for highly meaningful (word) responses (Underwood, Runquist, & Schulz, 1959). An explanation in associationist theory is that during pretraining the subjects accomplish the response-learning phase of association learning; therefore, only the connections between responses and stimuli remain to be learned during the paired-associate training.

Another finding by Underwood, Runquist and Schulz (1959) suggests an interesting interaction between the hypothetical processes of response learning and learning of stimulus-response connections. In the experiment, responses were meaningful words, but in one condition the responses were similar in meaning, while in another the responses were more distinctive. Subjects were given paired-associate training for varying numbers of trials, then were stopped and asked to recall only the response terms. The result was that when response terms were similar to each other, paired-associate learning was harder, although more responses could be recalled. The associationist interpretation is that similarity among responses facilitates response learning but, because of a difficulty in discrimination, retards learning of stimulus-response connections.

Critique of Associationist Interpretation

An important question is whether response learning, as conceived in the modification of associationist theory, undermines the basic premise of associationism that all knowledge is built by forming connections between subunits. The importance of response learning might be taken as evidence that even in memorizing associations there is a critical nonassociative process.

Associationist theory can comfortably assimilate a process of response learning if an analysis of response learning shows that it is itself a process of forming associations. Such an analysis is theoretically possible. Response integration could be a process consisting of forming associations between the elements of the response. Integrating the components of a response probably involves processes like those involved in learning a list, and a theoretical analysis like that given by Ebbinghaus could be carried out. An associative explanation of the process of forming a response pool also has been given; the theoretical mechanism is forming associations between the responses and the background or context stimuli in the situation, thus increasing the availability of the responses.

Although an associationist analysis of response learning is possible, the problem is whether response integration and availability are in fact produced by formation of associative connections. There are substantial reasons to doubt the associationist analysis of response integration. One source of doubt is Underwood and Schulz' (1960) finding that the ease of learning a list of trigrams was more strongly dependent on the pronounceability of the trigrams than on the frequency with which the trigrams appear in written English. One might have thought that frequent experience with the letter combinations would be optimal for producing an advantage in a process of forming connections among the components. Instead, the result that pronounceability matters more suggests that integration is better aided by having components that can easily be fit together into a pattern of phonetic relationships.

The plausible analogy between response integration and list learning gives an additional reason to doubt that response integration is a process of forming connections between components. Recent analyses have increasingly emphasized that subjects learn lists by finding relationships among the items, thereby organizing a structure of a few groups of items, rather than a simple list of all the items. Subjects make strong use of relationships that are deliberately put into serial lists (Restle & Brown, 1970) and lists presented for free recall (e.g., Bower, Clark, Lesgold & Winzenz, 1969; Bousfield, 1953; Jenkins & Russell, 1952). Strong correlations are found between measures of categorical organization and success in recall (Mandler, 1967). Furthermore, measures of consistency in recall from trial to trial are consistent with the idea that memorizing a list essentially amounts to finding a way to organize it (Martin & Noreen, 1974; Tulving, 1962).

The weight of evidence seems unfavorable to the idea that lists and individual responses are integrated by simple associative connections. (For a contrary conclusion, see Postman, 1972.) However, there do not seem to be strong objections to the idea of contextual associations. Many experimental findings seem to indicate a strong ability by subjects to form sets of items that occurred together in a list; the hypothesis that subjects store information about list membership and other context information appears in every current theory we are familiar with (e.g., Anderson & Bower, 1973; Kintsch, 1974;

Norman & Rumelhart, 1970). Of course, if it is accepted that responses are organized into a structure, rather than connected by undifferentiated associations, the form in which contextual information appears will be affected. It seems more realistic to include context information as a part of the total cognitive structure representing the list, rather than as a stimulus connected to each response item by separate links. However, the basic idea of a connection from the context to the items in a list seems well motivated and reasonable.

Cognitive Interpretation of Response Learning

The questionable aspect of the theory of response learning is the hypothesis that integration consists of forming connections among components. We now will present an interpretation of some phenomena that previously have been considered evidence for the associationistic concept. We will present interpretations of four facts: first, that pairs with meaningful responses are easier to learn; second, that meaningfulness of stimuli has little or no effect on difficulty of associative learning; third, that pretraining a subject to recall a response list facilitates learning of associations; and fourth, that similarity among stimuli causes an increase in response recall when associative learning is interrupted, despite the greater difficulty it produces in learning the associations.

The first fact to be explained concerns the meaningfulness of responses. Familiar words are already represented in the subject's long-term memory. Nonsense syllables, which are not recognized as words, must be treated as combinations of letters; the subject has representations of the letters stored in long-term memory and can construct a syllable from a sequence of those units. Syllables that are not words but remind the subject of words are generally syllables that share phonemic or other features with words that are familiar to the subject.

In memorizing an association, the subject must store a representation of the pair in memory. It is not surprising that subjects can represent a familiar word response more easily than a novel string of letters. An explanation for this is based on the idea that storing the pair requires processing in short-term memory. This idea was discussed in detail in Chapter 3. Especially relevant is Laughery's (1969) and Norman and Rumelhart's (1970) idea that items stored in short-term memory are entered through a naming device, which uses names found in long-term memory. If a nonmeaningful syllable is to be stored, its representation must be a sequence of letters, and Murdock (1961) obtained results suggesting that a three-letter item makes the same demands on the system as a sequence of three short, familiar words. The relative advantage of nonsense syllables that are more meaningful, in that they remind subjects of words, is not explained in any current theory, although ample experimental evidence (e.g., Dallett, 1964; Lindley, 1963) shows that some mechanism is available to subjects for storing syllables that are related to familiar words.

An interesting hypothesis about so-called meaningful nonsense syllables is that the subject organizes them according to schemata based on their similarity to familiar words. The proposal that schemata play an important role in memory is credited to Bartlett (1932), whose experimental support for the idea was convincing, albeit informal. Bartlett's best-known examples involve memory for stories; he observed that the general pattern of a story was remembered well, but details tended to be forgotten or distorted to fit the pattern. More recently, Posner and Keele (1968) have shown the effectiveness of relatively complex relational properties of dot patterns in establishing schemata and have demonstrated that subjects can correctly classify new patterns that are constructed by varying the original pattern. Norman and Bobrow (1976) have given a general discussion that emphasizes the importance of schemata that are stored in memory for processes of identifying patterns. The encoding process that makes the more meaningful nonsense syllables easier to learn than less meaningful syllables probably has much in common with the schema-based encoding and memory processes studied by Bartlett, by Norman and Bobrow, and by Posner and Keele.

The second fact to be explained is negative: it is the relative lack of effect of a stimuli's meaningfulness on the difficulty of learning associations. An explanation for this is in Feigenbaum's (1963) EPAM theory. As Feigenbaum recognized, the subject must store a complete image of each response and a procedure for generating the response. However, a partial representation of each stimulus is sufficient as long as enough information is stored to distinguish the stimulus from the other stimulus cues used in the experiment. The effects of response meaningfulness and pronounceability are consistent with the idea that an advantage in learning comes when the materials used can be generated by mechanisms already known. The advantage is greatest when the responses are words that are already known, but some advantage is also gained when the response is phonemically similar to a word, or uses some known phonemic components. On the other hand, because there is no requirement to perform the stimulus term, a fragmentary representation is often sufficient; therefore, variables that would aid integration and production of stimuli give little or no advantage in associative memorizing.

The third fact to be explained is that pretraining on response recall aids learning of associations. If responses are not meaningful, pretraining permits integration of responses. Our interpretation here agrees with the associationist view, although we believe the process of integration is more properly viewed as an organizational process.

When responses are familiar words, pretraining for response recall has much less effect than when responses are not meaningful, as would be expected from either associationistic or cognitive theory. We agree that contextual associations play a role in acquisition of paired-associate lists, and prior knowledge of the set of responses used could have a facilitating effect. On the other hand, when subjects study a list for free recall, they acquire an organized structure that makes retrieval of the responses possible. When items from this list appear later as responses in a list of paired associates, the subjects must alter the original structure so that the paired-associate stimuli can be used as specific retrieval cues for their respective responses. Whether the availability of an organized set of responses should facilitate learning of a list of pairs should depend on the compatibility of the organization needed for the learning of associations and that needed for learning the response list. Although it is not inconsistent with our interpretation that pretraining on word responses can facilitate paired-associate memorizing, it would not be surprising if the opposite effect were to be found in some cases.

The fourth fact to be explained is Underwood, Runquist, and Schulz' (1959) finding: Although learning of associations is made slower when response terms are similar to each other, if subjects are stopped after a number of trials and asked to recall responses, they will give more of the words. The interpretation in associationist theory is that response learning is facilitated by similarity of responses, but association learning is retarded by difficulty in discrimination. An alternative hypothesis is that, in paired-associate training, subjects store representations of the stimulus-response pairs, rather than representations of responses, stimuli, and connections. If a subject has been working on memorizing associations for a while, the request to recall responses calls for retrieval of part of each stored record—a retrieval task for which the representations in memory are not ideally suited. However, when responses are similar, more information linking responses with other responses is available in memory, and this feature could be responsible for the advantage in response recall produced by similarity. The greater difficulty of associative learning with similar responses may be due to greater difficulty of discrimination, as supposed in associationist theory. But the greater ease of recalling similar responses may not indicate an advantage in response learning as much as an advantage in retrieving the stored information about responses.

STIMULUS ENCODING

Underwood (1963) called attention to the need for analysis of stimulus encoding by distinguishing between the nominal stimulus (the physical event presented by the experimenter) and the functional stimulus (the mental representation of that event). Of course, the stimulus that is associated with the response is the functional stimulus, and Underwood concentrated on situations where the functional stimulus apparently is a selected partial representation of the nominal stimulus, such as the first letter of a three-letter nonsense syllable or the color of a compound in which there is both a nonsense syllable and a block of color.

Given that subjects select some aspects of a stimulus as functional cues, there will be failures of retention if the aspects noticed on a test do not match aspects stored during study. This idea has been developed by Martin (1968), who emphasized that a part of the subject's task in memorizing an association is to develop a stable encoding of the stimulus so that on tests the memory of the association will be activated.

Bower (1972c) has further developed the theory of encoding variability, including formal development of assumptions in the framework of the theory of fluctuation of stimulus elements (Estes, 1955). In Bower's theory, the representation of a stimulus depends on an encoding operation. A subject has several alternative operators and selects one on a probabilistic basis. Bower developed assumptions about the dependency of encoding on context in a way that explains a variety of phenomena concerning both memory of items from different lists and effects of varying time intervals between practice and events that interfere with retention.

Each stimulus must be encoded distinctively, and the difficulty of forming distinctive stimulus encodings is an important factor in difficulty of learning paired associates. Although the meaningfulness of stimuli makes little difference, similarity among stimulus terms greatly affects the difficulty of learning lists of associations (e.g., Underwood, 1953).

The importance of storing a stable and retrievable encoding of the stimulus was illustrated in an experiment by Martin (1967), who presented pairs with letter trigrams as stimuli and the numbers 1, 2, and 3 as responses. There were test trials in which new letter trigrams were presented, as well as tests on which trigrams from the original list were presented. Each time a trigram was presented, the subject was asked to judge whether it was an old or new trigram. Then, regardless of whether the subject thought the trigram was old or new, the subject was also asked to choose the response that had been paired with the trigram if it was from the original list. Martin's main result was that on items from the list that the subject mistakenly called new, performance on response selection was at chance. The point illustrated is that if the subject fails to recognize the stimulus term of an association, then any stored information about the association or the response is not useful in selecting a response.

The representation of a stimulus in memory need not be complete, and it appears that subjects often use partial representations in memorizing paired associates (Underwood, 1963). The partial quality of subjects' stored representations is seen in experiments using compound stimuli; each stimulus may be a pair of words, or a word with a colored background, or some other combination of distinctive cues. After learning a list with such a set of compound stimuli, subjects are shown the individual stimulus components and are asked to give the response that was paired with the stimulus containing the component. Subjects frequently fail to give the correct response for some components.

An important set of findings by Harrington (1969) showed that the selection of stimulus components takes place in a systematic way. As in most studies using compound stimuli, Harrington's experiments presented stimuli whose components fell into two distinct categories. In one experiment, each stimulus was a pair of short words, typed on a single line. The components could be classified according to their position. In another experiment, each stimulus contained a meaningful word and a nonsense trigram. In this case, components could be classified by position (left or right) or by meaningfulness. Some subjects in this second experiment had lists in which one component in each stimulus was emphasized by use of a colored background. This permitted a third basis of classification: each component was either the emphasized or nonemphasized member of its pair.

The important finding from Harrington's study was that subjects showed a significant tendency to select elements in a single category. In the experiment where stimuli were word pairs, each individual subject apparently represented most of the stimuli with the component seen on one of the sides, either left or right. When stimuli combined words and nonsense trigrams without any emphasis, nearly all subjects used the words. But when one of the components of each pair was given perceptual emphasis, some subjects used the strategy of coding with the more meaningful component; others used the strategy of coding the emphasized component.

Another finding of some interest regarding stimulus selection was obtained by James and Greeno (1967). Groups of subjects studied paired-associate lists with compound stimuli. Training was stopped at varying points for different groups and they were given tests on stimulus components. Subjects whose training was stopped at or before the point of learning the list failed to give the correct response to many of the stimulus components, thus giving evidence that they had stored partial representations of the stimuli. However, subjects whose training continued beyond a criterion of learning the list gave correct responses to a substantially greater number of individual components, indicating that during overtraining subjects had stored additional information about many stimuli.

Both Harrington's (1969) and James and Greeno's (1967) results point to the idea that stimulus selection occurs because of a deliberate learning strategy by the subject. Harrington's finding indicates that stimulus components are selected on the basis of some identifiable classification that can be made. And James and Greeno's results are most easily explained by assuming that the subject restricts attention to a minimal set of stimulus components during the time the list is being learned but, after the list is learned, the restrictive attention is relaxed because the demands of the task are no longer as severe.

Critique of Associationist Interpretation

There is serious question whether any process of selective encoding is compatible with the basic ideas of associationist theory. Earlier versions of stimulus-response associationism (Spence, 1936) assumed that the stimulus impinges on the subject and that learning affects only what is done in response to the stimulus. The subject could learn a specific orienting response in the situation, such as always looking on the right side of a stimulus display, and this could explain selective effects based on physical position. However, selective attention to perceptual cues seems problematic on the stimulus-response view, as does selection of components based on their meaningfulness.

In a more general associationist framework, selective encoding can be analyzed as the result of perceptual learning. Lawrence (1963) and Postman (1955) have argued that perceptual learning can be analyzed as a process of acquiring new stimulus-response connections involving perceptual or encoding responses. On this view, distinct stimuli can be made more similar by connecting the same encoding response to them, and similar stimuli can be made more distinct by connecting them to different encoding responses.

A theoretical response to the associationist view was given by Gibson and Gibson (1955). It is generally reasonable to view perception as the result of an active process in which the individual seeks information, rather than a simple impinging of energy on the organism (Gibson, 1966). In this framework, it is natural to consider perceptual learning as a change in the sensitivity of the individual to various kinds of information, rather than in the perceptual responses of the individual to specific stimuli. Selective attention occurs because in specific stiuations the individual identifies certain kinds of information as being especially important, and seeks those kinds of information particularly, perhaps by use of specific stimulus analyzing mechanisms (Sutherland, 1959). If the hypothesis of active stimulus analysis is accepted, then changes in stimulus encoding result from structural changes in the perceptual system rather than in responses to stimuli, and thus are hard to reconcile with the associationist position.

Cognitive Interpretation of Encoding

In the theory of associative learning that we presented in Chapter 2, encoding of stimuli results from analysis by the retrieval network that is acquired. This is a form of the theory of active stimulus analysis. The stimulus features noticed are those for which tests are specified in the retrieval network. The main requirement for retrieval is that there be a sufficiently detailed analysis to distinguish each stimulus from all the others. It would be expected, then, that features of the stimuli not needed for discrimination often will be omitted from the representation.

It would also be expected that, when possible, selected components would tend to be in some easily identified category. The retrieval system, which must begin by testing some feature of each stimulus that appears, will be more efficient if the test can be carried out on a component that is easily identified. For example, if each stimulus is a pair of words, as in Harrington's (1969) first experiment, a retrieval network using features of the left word for some items and the right word for others would be quite inefficient. Each time a stimulus is presented, one word or the other must be examined by the system; consistently checking the features of the word on one specific side of the stimulus pair makes matters much simpler.

We suspect that the preference for selecting meaningful components when both meaningful and nonsense elements are included reflects the greater ease in finding a relational encoding of the meaningful component with the response. Apparently, this is not a large advantage; a list containing only nonsense stimuli is not much harder to learn than a list with only word stimuli. However, because a meaningful word corresponds to an entry in the subject's long-term memory, it provides a relatively rich set of possible relationships with other elements that are available for use in memorizing a new association.

SEQUENCE OF STAGES

We do not disagree with the assertion that both response learning and learning to encode stimuli are processes that occur when subjects memorize paired associates. We believe, however, that associationist analysis of response learning probably is incorrect. And we believe that the need to postulate selective perception of stimuli seriously weakens the argument that learning is basically a process of forming stimulus-response connections.

But the involvement of response learning and stimulus encoding in some form is undeniable and can be deduced from the nature of the experimental task of memorizing associations. In a test of a subject's memory of an association, the stimulus term is presented and the subject tries to remember the response term. In order to give the response correctly, the subject must have a representation of the stimulus stored in memory, including enough distinctive properties to avoid confusion with other stimuli in the list. The subject also must have information specifying which of the responses goes with the presented stimulus. Moreover, relatively complete information about the response must be stored, allowing the subject to perform the response term. Of course, other kinds of information may also be stored, including relations among response terms or among stimulus terms (cf. Battig, 1968), but there certainly must be information about the stimulus, information about the response, and information that connects the two elements.

Any theory of paired-associate memorizing must make some provision for the acquisition of all the information needed to perform in the task. Both the associationist theory and the cognitive analysis we have developed here include processes that can explain the main facts of performance in paired-associate memorizing experiments. However, a deep conceptual difference separates the two viewpoints.

Associationist theory views the processes of stimulus encoding and response learning as auxiliary processes, brought about by the demands of the task, and capable of being understood in terms of undifferentiated connections between mental elements. Learning to distinguish among stimuli is a process of associating distinctive meaning responses to physically similar stimuli (Lawrence, 1963; Postman, 1955). And learning a response involves overcoming interfering associations when the components are combined in unusual ways and forming a connection between the response and general context stimuli (Underwood & Schulz, 1960). In associationist theory, there are many kinds of associative learning in a paired-associate experiment, and formation of a connection between the stimulus and response seems to play a relatively minor role in the whole process.

On the other hand, the cognitive analysis that we favor gives central importance to the process whose properties the paired-associate experiment is intended to investigate. According to the Gestalt concept, the main process in paired-associate memorizing is learning to associate the stimuli and the responses. This Gestalt idea is at the base of our cognitive theory, in which we assume that the main information stored about an association is a new cognitive unit involving some relation that integrates the stimulus and response terms. The hypothesis that the stimulus-response association is stored as a new mental unit, rather than as a connection, has been discussed in the literature on associative symmetry (e.g., Asch, 1968; Horowitz & Prytulak, 1969) and has also been used in a recent theoretical analysis by Estes (1976).

In the Gestalt view, association is not an elementary process, but is a form of cognitive organization. Consideration of requirements for retrieval and response production lead to further assumptions about the information that is stored. The requirement of retrieval based on stimulus terms leads us to hypothesize a retrieval network containing tests of features of the stimuli that will provide an organized representation of the whole list. The requirement that responses be performed on tests suggests that response integration must occur, but we assume that this is another instance of cognitive organization and that subjects will make strong use of available schemata in organizing novel responses.

Because the concepts in the associationist and cognitive theories are very general, it is not surprising that much of the empirical content that is interpretable by one of the theories is also interpretable by the other. Nonetheless, the difference in emphasis between the two approaches leads to different expectations about some kinds of empirical effects. One possibility for distinguishing between the points of view involves identification of processes that occur at different stages of the learning process.

In the cognitive view we favor, a major component of a subject's task in associative learning is to organize the stimulus and response into an integrated unit. This might be preceded or followed by other processes required by the task, but it would not be surprising if the process of storing relational information about the stimulus-response pair were to occur early in the process. The sequence of relational storage followed by learning to retrieve would agree with conclusions by Estes and DaPolito (1967) and by Kintsch and Morris (1965), who found evidence that learning to recognize corresponds to a first stage of learning, and learning to recall corresponds to a later stage. It also would agree with Polson, Restle, and Polson's (1965) conclusion that acquiring the association precedes stimulus discrimination.

On the other hand, in associationist theory acquiring the connection between stimulus and response has generally been expected to occur rather late during learning. The feeling that response learning probably precedes learning a connection has been made quite explicit, on grounds that a response cannot be connected to a stimulus if the response has not yet been learned. From the general view that learning involves storage of information, the question is whether early stages of learning focus primarily on the encoding of information about the response, or whether information about the stimulus-response pair is involved in the learning process from the outset.

An experimental design that provides information about this question was used in a study carried out by Michael Humphreys. Humphreys taught paired associates to subjects; the lists of stimulus-response pairs that he used are in Table 4-1. The point of the experiment was a simple one—to vary the difficulty of learning by manipulating both the stimuli and the responses. In this case, response difficulty related to the ease of pronouncing the nonsense trigrams used. The stimulus difficulty involved similarity among the stimuli used. The experimental variables were effective. The mean number of

Table 4-1   Lists Used in Humphreys' Experiment

Easy Stimuli *Easy Responses*	*Easy Stimuli* *Hard Responses*	*Hard Stimuli* *Easy Responses*	*Hard Stimuli* *Hard Responses*
1—HAZ	1—HPF	11—RAS	11—GPS
2—MAK	2—IPW	12—MAK	12—HPF
3—GAW	3—NPE	13—JAV	13—BPC
4—RAS	4—GPS	21—BAQ	21—IPW
5—BAQ	5—JPV	22—HAZ	22—NPE
6—LAN	6—MPA	23—FAC	23—XPO
7—DAP	7—BPC	31—DAP	31—RPK
8—JAV	8—XPO	32—GAW	32—MPA

Source: From Humphreys & Greeno, 1970.

errors per item in each group was easy stimuli and responses (EE), 4.3; easy stimuli and hard responses (EH), 6.6; hard stimuli and easy responses (HE), 7.1; hard stimuli and hard responses (HH), 9.5.

This experiment was conducted to obtain empirical evidence about the effects of stimulus and response difficulty in the two stages of paired-associate memorizing. If the first stage of learning is mainly a process of acquiring responses, then difficulty of learning in the first stage should be due primarily to the differences between the two kinds of responses used in the experiment. That is, Groups EE and HE, both having easy responses, should have a rather easy task in accomplishing the first stage of learning; moreover, the first stage should not be much harder for Group HE than for Group EE, because these groups differ only in the stimuli to which the responses are to be connected. For the same reasons, Groups EH and HH should find the first stage of learning difficult, but both should find it equally difficult. On the other hand, if the first stage involves storing information about the stimulus-response pair, then it would be expected that both stimuli and responses would influence the difficulty of accomplishing the first stage.

Evidence on the issue can be obtained only if it is possible to measure difficulty of learning in the two stages separately, a technical problem that may not be solvable. One technique, based on the idea that first-stage learning is response acquisition, is to count the trials before a response is given by the subject, regardless of whether it is given to its correct stimulus. Of course, the subject must learn a response before it can be performed, so this observation must be correlated with the difficulty of response learning. On the other hand, in the paired-associate task subjects are trying to give the correct response for each stimulus, and as Ekstrand (1966) pointed out, probably do not give just any response that comes to mind unless they have some basis for giving it to the stimulus being presented. Thus, the number of trials before first occurrence of a response almost surely overestimates the number involved in learning that response, if in fact response learning as such is occurring.

A second technique used in some studies is to stop paired-associate training after a few trials and ask the subject to recall as many responses as possible. Again, observations will be correlated with amount of response learning, since subjects must acquire responses in order to perform them. But difficulty of retrieving response terms that subjects have been studying in the context of paired-associate training probably is affected by variables such as similarity among the responses that may not be related to the difficulty of learning the responses; therefore this technique may also give a distorted and misleading set of results, as we have mentioned earlier in this chapter.

Aside from the technical drawbacks, an additional disadvantage of these methods from our point of view is their assumption that response acquisition is the main process involved in the first stage of learning. It would seem more appropriate to test this theoretical assumption using a method of obtaining measurements that is neutral with regard to the theoretical question at issue.

MARKOV ANALYSIS OF STAGES

A method used by Humphreys and Greeno (1970) in analyzing the results of Humphreys' experiment seems to have some advantages over the earlier techniques, although it too has drawbacks. The method uses measurements obtained by estimating the parameters of a Markov model that assumes two stages of learning. The main stages of the model are graphed in Figure 3-8, and several applications of the model are discussed in the accompanying text.

The Markov model involves no commitment to a theoretical position. It merely says that learning involves two stages, and the two stages occur in a specified way. The strong assumptions are that (1) accomplishment of each stage is an all-or-none event, and (2) the stages are sequential and independent; therefore, the second stage cannot occur before the first stage, and the probability of accomplishing the second stage in any given number of trials is unaffected by the number of trials it took to accomplish the first stage. Investigators who use such techniques as analysis of variance make assumptions that are different in content, but equivalent in their status in the analysis, when they assume that variances within experimental conditions are equal, and that scores are distributed normally. An important difference is that, in using a Markov model, the distribution of scores obtained in the experiment is used as data to check the assumptions of the analysis, rather than as something about which an assumption is made. Also, the variances of scores obtained in different experimental groups should not generally be equal; distributions for each experimental condition can be compared with predicted distributions derived from the model to see whether the assumptions of the analysis can be rejected for any of the experimental groups.

To allow for some irregularities that can occur at the beginning of the experiment and on trials when a transition occurs, the model used is slightly more complicated than Figure 3-8 shows. State *U* and State *L* are the initial and terminal learned states of an item, corresponding to Figure 3-8. State *I* in Figure 3-8 is the state of an item after the first stage of learning has been accomplished. According to the model, correct responses never occur as long as an item is in State *U*; correct responses always occur after an item has reached State *L*. But in State *I*, the correct response occurs with some degree of probability. It is convenient for analysis and necessary for some versions of the model to specify two states corresponding to the intermediate stage of learning: the state called *I* in Figure 3-8 is divided into two states, called *E* and *C*. State *E* applies when an item has left State *U* and an error occurs.

State C applies when an item has not yet reached State L and a correct response occurs. More formally, the states of the model are as follows:

> U—the state of an item at the beginning of an experiment, before the first stage of learning has been accomplished;
>
> E—the state of an item after the first, but before the second, stage of learning has been accomplished, on trials when errors occur;
>
> C—the state of an item after the first and before the second stage, on trials when correct responses occur;
>
> L—the state of an item after both stages of learning have been accomplished.

It is assumed that only errors occur in States U and E, and only correct responses occur in States C and L.

In an experiment, the items are all shown to the subject before the subject has to respond. Thus, the first observation occurs after a study trial, and some learning should occur on that trial. The probabilities of learning on the initial trial are given in the vector of initial probabilities for the Markov model:

$$P(L_1, E_1, C_1, U_1) = [t, (1 - s - t)r, (1 - s - t)(1 - r), s] \qquad (4\text{-}1)$$

In this equation, t is the probability of being in State L after the initial study trial, s is the probability of being in State U after the initial study trial, and r is the probability of an error on the first test if just the first stage of learning was accomplished on the initial study trial.

After the initial study trial, learning of an item is assumed to be governed by the matrix of transition probabilities:

$$P = \begin{array}{c} \\ L_n \\ E_n \\ C_n \\ U_n \end{array} \begin{array}{|cccc} L_{n+1} \quad E_{n+1} \qquad C_{n+1} \qquad\qquad U_{n+1} \\ \hline 1 \quad\quad 0 \qquad\qquad 0 \qquad\qquad\quad 0 \\ d \quad\quad (1-d)q \quad (1-d)p \qquad\quad 0 \\ c \quad\quad (1-c)q \quad (1-c)p \qquad\quad 0 \\ ab \quad a(1-b)e \quad a(1-b)(1-e) \quad 1-a \end{array} \qquad (4\text{-}2)$$

a is the probability of accomplishing the first stage of learning, as in Figure 3-8, and b is the probability that the second stage of learning is accomplished on the same trial with the first stage. If the second stage is not accomplished along with the first stage (probability $= 1 - b$), then on the first trial in the intermediate states the probability of an error is e.

Once the first stage of learning has been accomplished, c and d are the probabilities of accomplishing the second stage: c applies when the item has been given correctly on a trial, and d is the probability of completing learning when an error has been given. On trials after the first stage has been accomplished, if learning is not completed on a trial, then q is the probability of an error on the next trial, and $p = 1 - q$ is the probability of a correct response.

When the model is used to obtain measurements of difficulty of the two stages, the information needed is in the values of parameters. To measure the difficulty of the first stage we need values of $1 - s$ and a; $1 - s$ is the probability of accomplishing the first stage on the initial trial, and a is the probability of accomplishing the first stage on trials after the initial trial. If the first stage is easy, these parameters will be large and few trials will be needed for most items to accomplish the first stage.

To measure the difficulty of the second stage values of b, c, d, and $t/(1 - s)$ are needed. The probability of accomplishing the second stage on the initial study trial, if the first stage was accomplished on that trial is $t/(1 - s)$. The probabilities of accomplishing the second stage on trials later in learning are b, c, and d. If the second stage is easy, then b, c, d, and $t/(1 - s)$ should be large; if the second stage is hard, these quantities should be small.

The task of obtaining numerical values for the quantities in the model is the problem of estimating parameter values. Various methods of estimation are possible. One that meets nearly all the desirable statistical criteria is the method of maximum likelihood (see Restle & Greeno, 1970, chap. 9 for a general discussion). It is necessary to express the likelihood of the data as a function of the parameters of the model. Recall the discussion for the all-or-none model in Chapter 3. To see how the ideas apply to the two-stage model, consider the likelihood of a specific sequence for illustration:

$$X = 1\ 1\ 0\ 1\ 1\ 0\ 0\ 0\ 0 \ldots$$

where 1 stands for an error and 0 stands for correct response. The sequence of observed responses could have been produced by any of several different sequences of theoretical states:

$$Y_1 = E\ E\ S\ E\ E\ L\ L\ L\ L \ldots;$$
$$Y_2 = U\ E\ S\ E\ E\ L\ L\ L\ L \ldots;$$
$$Y_3 = U\ U\ S\ E\ E\ L\ L\ L\ L \ldots;$$
$$Y_4 = E\ E\ S\ E\ E\ S\ L\ L\ L \ldots;$$
$$Y_5 = U\ E\ S\ E\ E\ S\ L\ L\ L \ldots;$$
$$Y_6 = U\ U\ S\ E\ E\ S\ L\ L\ L \ldots;$$
$$Y_7 = E\ E\ S\ E\ E\ S\ S\ L\ L \ldots;$$

and so on. Each sequence Y_i has a likelihood that can be calculated directly from the initial and transition probabilities of the Markov model. For example,

$$L(Y_2) = sa(1 - b)e(1 - d)p(1 - c)q(1 - d)qd$$
$$= sa(1 - b)e(1 - c)(1 - d)^2pq^2d.$$

Since X could have been produced by any of the Y_i, the likelihood of X is just the sum of the likelihoods of the Y_i. In this case,

$$L(X) = [(1 - s - t)r(1 - c)p(1 - d)^3q^3 + sa(1 - b)e(1 - c)p(1 - d)^2q^2$$
$$+ s(1 - a)a(1 - b)(1 - e)(1 - c)(1 - d)q^2]\left[d + \frac{(1 - d)pc}{q + pc}\right].$$

(Restle & Greeno, 1970, chap. 2, gave a general discussion of derivations like this one.) The likelihood of the data from an experiment is the product of the likelihoods of all the individual sequences observed in the experiment, assuming that the various sequences were independent events. Note that this uses the simplifying assumption that all sequences were obtained with the same parameter values. Thus, individual differences among subjects and different difficulties of items are ignored for simplicity.

The likelihood function provides the basis for the estimation procedure. Any set of numerical values assigned to the parameters would correspond to a numerical likelihood of the data. To estimate parameters by the method of maximum likelihood, we select those values of parameters that make the likelihood as large as possible. Well known theorems in statistics show that the estimates obtained in this way use all the information in the data that is relevant to the value of the parameters (technically, the maximum likelihood estimates are functions of the sufficient statistics), and the estimates are as efficient as possible, in the sense of having as small a standard error of estimate as possible. The maximum value of the likelihood function can not be found by solving equations; therefore we use a numerical method. Our estimates are obtained using Subroutine STEPIT (Chandler, 1965).

There are nine parameters in the model as it is stated in Equations 4-1 and 4-2. However, only seven parameters can be estimated from the data of an experiment. One of the identifiable parameters is the value of a, useful because a can give a direct measurement of the difficulty of the first stage when $s = 1 - a$. The other eight parameters are not identifiable, which means that numerous possibilities have to be considered in making inferences, especially about the second stage of learning. (For a general discussion of the problem of identifiability, see Restle & Greeno, 1970, chap. 10. A complete discussion of identifiability for this model was given by Greeno, 1968.)

Some hypotheses that simplify the model can be tested in data. One such hypothesis is the idea that the initial study trial has effects exactly like those of later trials. If all items start in State U, and if the initial study trial is the same as later trials, then the probability of being in State U after the initial study trial should be $1 - a$, the probability of being in State L after the initial study trial should be ab, and the probability of an error if the item is in the intermediate states should be e. This can be stated as a relationship among the parameters

$$t = ab, r = e, s = 1 - a. \tag{4-3}$$

Other simplifying hypotheses that are testable include $e = q$, and if that is accepted, then $b = d$ is also testable. These two equations express the idea that the probabilities of completing the second stage of learning and of giving a correct response are the same on the first trial after an item leaves State U as they are on later trials.

To determine whether one or more simplifications of the model are acceptable, likelihood ratio tests are used. The procedure involves finding maximum likelihood estimates of the parameters of the general model, and then finding maximum likelihood estimates of the parameters with a restriction imposed. The value of the likelihood obtained with the restriction will be lower than the maximum likelihood obtained without the restriction, and the ratio of the two values (restricted over general) is called λ. If the restricted version is correct, the value of $-2 \log_e \lambda$ is asymptotically distributed as chi square with degrees of freedom equal to the number of restrictions. (General discussion of this likelihood ratio test is found in many statistics texts, such as Wilks, 1962.) Note that restrictions have to be imposed on identifiable parameters for an hypothesis to be testable in this or any other way, and the degrees of freedom in the chi square test equals the number of restrictions on identifiable parameters. For example, the restriction given as Equation 4-3 involves three of the parameters of the model, but only two of the model's identifiable parameters are restricted by Equation 4-3. Thus, in testing that hypothesis, the distribution consulted in evaluating the value of $-2 \log_e \lambda$ is χ^2 (2). Another example involves the hypothesis $b = d$. If $e \neq q$, then no restriction in the identifiable parameters is implied by $b = d$, and that restriction is then not testable. But a restriction in identifiable parameters is implied by $e = q$, and if $e = q$ is accepted, then $b = d$ does impose a restriction on identifiable parameters.

Tests of simplifying restrictions such as Equation 4-3, $e = q$, and $b = d$ represent preliminary work with the model. The main analyses involve tests of significance comparing different experimental conditions in the difficulty of the two stages of learning. Likelihood ratio tests are also used in these analyses. Suppose, for example, that we want to test whether two groups differ in the value of a. A maximum likelihood value is obtained for all the data of both groups, with all parameters free to vary. A second maximum likelihood value is obtained with a single value of a used for both sets of data. The restricted value of the likelihood divided by the maximum likelihood without the restriction gives a likelihood ratio λ. In this case $-2 \log_e \lambda$ is asymptotically distributed as chi square with one degree of freedom if the two groups really have the same value of a. Tests can be carried out using more than one parameter, and the degrees of freedom for the chi square distribution equal the number of parameters involved in the test. In this way, we can test whether two groups differed in the difficulty of the first stage of learning, or in the difficulty of the second stage of learning, or in performance during the intermediate stage of the learning process, or in some combination of these characteristics. It should be noted that these tests, like the tests of simplifying assumptions, are possible only when the hypotheses being tested impose restrictions on the identifiable parameters of the groups being tested, and the appropriate degrees of freedom of a test equal the number of restrictions imposed on identifiable parameters.

ANALYSIS OF HUMPHREYS' EXPERIMENT

Each of the lists shown in Table 4-1 was learned by 18 subjects, giving 144 sequences in each condition for analysis. Each item was considered learned if a criterion of five consecutive correct responses was given.

Simplifying assumptions

The first question is whether the model must be applied in its general form, or whether simplifications are possible. Table 4-2 shows the results of testing Equation 4-3, $e = q$, and $b = d$. The latter two hypotheses were tested against the alternative with Equation 4-3 incorporated, since that hypothesis was acceptable for all groups. The results show that Equation 4-3 was acceptable in these data, which means that we can consider the initial study trial as having effects equivalent to those of later trials. The further hypothesis is that $e = q$ was acceptable for three of the four groups, and in those groups $b = d$ was also acceptable. Group HH's data were inconsistent with the hypothesis $e = q$, which means that the hypothesis $b = d$ can not be directly tested in the data for that group. The results in Table 4-2 permit use of the model with six parameters (a, b, c, d, e, q), for which there are five identifiable parameters, in all groups. Although a model with four parameters (a, c, d, q), corresponding to three identifiable parameters, could be used in all but group HH, Humphreys and Greeno carried out all the analyses with the largest number of free parameters needed for any group. However, note for future reference that $b = d$ was an acceptable restriction for all the groups in whose data that assumption could be tested.

Table 4-2   Results of Testing Simplifying Assumptions

Stimuli	Responses	Hypothesis: $t = ab$, $r = e, s = 1 - a$		Hypothesis: $e = q$		Hypothesis: $b = d$	
		$-2 \log_e \lambda$	p	$-2 \log_e \lambda$	p	$-2 \log_e \lambda$	p
Easy	Easy	1.30	.25	.81	.37	.17	.65
Hard	Easy	3.11	.07	1.21	.27	1.79	.18
Easy	Hard	1.99	.16	1.07	.29	2.44	.12
Hard	Hard	1.81	.18	10.13	.002	—	

Source: From Humphreys & Greeno, 1970.

Goodness of fit

The next question is whether the model fit these data well enough for the parameter values to be meaningful. As was mentioned earlier, goodness of fit can be checked using the distributions of statistics taken from the data. Several statistical properties of data were examined by Humphreys and Greeno. Two that are easy to understand intuitively are the number of trials and the number of errors occurring after the first correct response. In the model, the first correct response can not occur until the item has left State U. This means that when the first correct response occurs, the item either is in State L already, or there is just one stage of learning left to be accomplished. This leads to the rather strong prediction that if only data after the first correct response are considered, these data will have properties like those of all-or-none learning. Let X be the number of errors after the first correct response, and let Y be the number of trials between the first correct response and the beginning of the criterion string of correct responses at the end. From the model, it can be shown that X and Y have the same form as the number of errors and trial of last error in all-or-none learning, given in Equations 3-1 and 3-2. That is,

$$P(X = j) = \begin{cases} z & j = 0 \\ (1 - z)(1 - u)^{j-1}u & j \geq 1. \end{cases} \tag{4-4}$$

$$P(Y = k) = \begin{cases} z & k = 0 \\ (1 - z)(1 - uv)^{k-1}uv & k \geq 1, \end{cases} \tag{4-5}$$

where $u = (pc + qd)/(q + pc)$, $v = q + pc$, and z is a rather complicated function of all the parameters of the model. (See Greeno, 1968, for details.)

The distributions of X and Y for the four experimental groups are shown in Figures 4-1 and 4-2. The data are given as histograms, and the theoretical distributions based on parameters estimated separately for the four groups are given by the connected dots. A suitable statistical test of goodness of fit uses the chi square statistic. Frequencies were pooled in adjacent points of the distribution to obtain cells that have theoretical frequencies of at least 5.0. Then the goodness-of-fit chi square statistic was calculated in the usual way. Degrees of freedom for the test are not well defined, because estimates of parameters are taken from all of the data, rather than from the specific frequency distributions used in the tests. However, a theorem given by Chernoff and Lehmann (1954) states that the distribution of the chi square statistic is bounded by $\chi^2(n - 1)$ and $\chi^2(n - 1 - m)$ where n is the number of cells in the distribution (after pooling) and m is the number of parameters estimated. To compute the theoretical distribution of X, two quantities are needed, z and u. Similarly, calculation of the distribution of Y uses two theoretical values, z and uv. Thus, for these two statistics, the bounds on the distribution

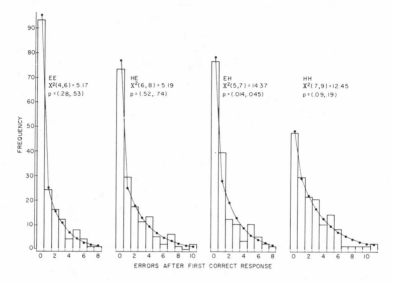

Figure 4-1 Theoretical and empirical distributions of the number of errors after the first correct response in Humphreys' experiment (Humphreys & Greeno, 1970).

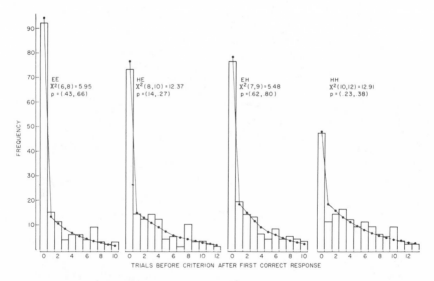

Figure 4-2 Theoretical and empirical distributions of number of trials between first correct response and criterion in Humphreys' experiment (Humphreys & Greeno, 1970).

of the chi square statistic are $\chi^2(n-1)$ and $\chi^2(n-3)$, where n is the number of cells in the pooled frequency distribution. As Figures 4-1 and 4-2 show, the data agreed quite well with the theoretical distributions for both X and Y. In only one of the eight distributions tested was the discrepancy large enough to produce statistical significance, and even in that case the form of the empirical distribution seems to follow the general pattern of decreasing frequencies predicted by the all-or-none model. It seems reasonable to conclude that learning that occurred after the first correct response can be described well as an all-or-none process.

Figure 4-3 shows the distributions obtained for errors before the first correct response. The upper panel shows frequencies of sequences having no errors after the first correct response, and the lower panel shows frequencies of sequences with one or more errors after the first correct response. The goodness-of-fit chi square statistics were calculated by first pooling adjacent cells to obtain distributions that had theoretical frequencies of at least 5.0, and then summing the terms of the chi square statistic based on deviations in both of the component distributions. Note that the data agreed well with the theoretical distributions for groups HE, EH, and HH. For group EE the discrepancy between empirical and theoretical distributions may have been large enough to reject the null hypothesis at the .05 level, but it is not definite because of the uncertainty about degrees of freedom.

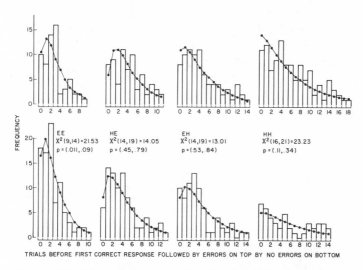

Figure 4-3 Theoretical and empirical distributions of number of errors before first correct response in Humphreys' experiment (Humphreys & Greeno, 1970). Upper panels show frequencies where at least one error followed the first correct response; lower panels show frequencies where no errors followed the first correct response.

Figures 4-4 and 4-5 show theoretical and empirical distributions of total errors and trial of last error. These distributions combine information about errors before the first correct response (Figure 4-3) with information about performance after the first correct response (Figures 4-1 and 4-2). None of the distributions apparently differed sufficiently from predictions to warrant rejecting the null hypothesis that the theory fit the data. It seems reasonable to conclude that there was sufficient agreement between the data and the predictions based on the model to make it reasonable to use the model in measuring the difficulty of the two stages of learning.

Tests of Parameter Invariance

Preliminary tests considered hypotheses that parameters were invariant between pairs of experimental groups, differing either in difficulty of stimuli or difficulty of responses. Since a is an identifiable parameter, testing its invariance is straightforward. The first line of Table 4-3 shows the values of $-2 \log_e \lambda$ obtained with the null hypothesis that a was the same in two groups against the alternative that all five identifiable parameters were free to vary between the groups. The numbers in parentheses are the significance levels at which the null hypothesis of equal parameter values could be rejected, based on the chi square distribution with 1 degree of freedom. The evidence is quite clear that between all four pairs of groups there were different values of a.

Testing invariance regarding second-stage learning parameters is considerably more complicated, because the five theoretical parameters b, c, d, e, and q determine the values of four identifiable parameters, and only the values of the identifiable parameters are determinable from data. It is a simple matter to find optimal estimates of the parameters and compute the values

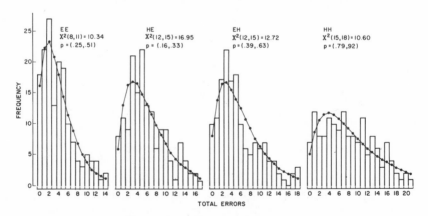

Figure 4-4 Theoretical and empirical distributions of the total number of errors in Humphreys' experiment (Humphreys & Greeno, 1970).

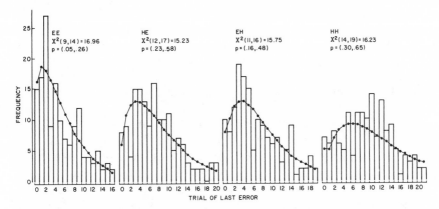

Figure 4-5 Theoretical and empirical distributions of the trial of last error in Humphreys' experiment (Humphreys & Greeno, 1970).

of $-2 \log_e \lambda$, but the degrees of freedom for the tests are not well understood because the exact restrictions imposed on identifiable parameters by the assumptions of invariance have not been worked out. A test for invariance of just one of these parameters could not be carried out. Any one of these parameters could be set arbitrarily for one of the groups, within limits, and the remaining parameters could be adjusted to compensate. The numbers given as degrees of freedom in rows of Table 4-3, other than the first row, are one fewer than the number of parameters tested, and this probably is a reasonable guess as to the appropriate degrees of freedom. The general conclusion is that most hypotheses involving invariance of b, c, and d between these pairs of groups apparently are acceptable by the usual statistical criteria.

Since little or no difference appeared between pairs of groups in the second-stage learning parameters, Humphreys and Greeno tested invariance of these parameters across all groups. The hypothesis that b, c, and d were all constant over all four groups probably involves 5 degrees of freedom. There are 20 identifiable parameters for the four groups, and under the restriction there are three parameters with four values each (a, e, and q), along with

Table 4-3 Tests of Parameter Invariance between Pairs of Groups

Invariant Parameters	Degrees of Freedom	EE, HE	EH, HH	EE, EH	HE, HH
a	1	5.97(.015)	6.69(.010)	14.23(.0002)	16.23(.0001)
b,c	1	1.21(.28)	.09(.77)	.47(.50)	.00(1.0)
b,d	1	.98(.33)	.01(.93)	.25(.62)	.00(1.0)
c,d	1	.02(.89)	5.34(.021)	.00(1.0)	.30(.59)
b,c,d	2	1.21(.55)	5.38(.08)	.74(.70)	.69(.71)

Source: From Humphreys & Greeno, 1970.

single values of *b*, *c*, and *d*. The hypothesis can be rejected ($\chi^2(5) = 14.14$, $p < .02$).

When pairs of the second-stage parameters were held constant, the hypotheses were all acceptable in the data. Partial results are given in Table 4-4, which shows the values estimated for the parameters held constant in each test, the values of the test statistics, the significance level at which the hypotheses could be rejected, and the estimates obtained for the remaining second-stage learning parameter. The fact of interest in Table 4-4 is that when any two second-stage parameters were held constant, the estimates obtained for the remaining parameter were relatively close to each other for groups having the same stimuli (EE-EH and HE-HH), but differences were somewhat larger for groups differing in stimuli (EE-HE and EH-HH). Since the estimates for these parameters interact, the result in Table 4-4 suggested that the second-stage parameters may have depended mainly on the stimuli, being fairly constant over the groups differing only in responses. Further findings making this reasonable are in Table 4-3, where all hypotheses involving second-stage parameters across groups EE, EH and groups HE, HH were acceptable. In contrast, at least one hypothesis involving groups differing only in responses was rejected (*c* and *d* invariant across groups EH, HH).

To examine the idea that second-stage parameters depended only on the stimuli, Humphreys and Greeno tested the hypothesis that *b*, *c*, and *d* were all determined solely by the difficulty of stimuli. This is a testable hypothesis; with four values of *a*, *e*, and *q* and two values of *b*, *c*, and *d*, there are 18 free parameters under the hypothesis and 20 identifiable parameters. However, Humphreys and Greeno chose to test a stronger hypothesis, using the fact that $b = d$ was an acceptable hypothesis in the three experimental groups for which that hypothesis was testable (recall Table 4-2). Using the hypothesis that *b* and *d* are the same, that their common value depended only on stimuli, and that *c* depended only on the stimuli, there are 16 free parameters. However, *c* was also restricted in ways that have been studied in connection with other questions about the learning process (see Greeno, 1967). If it is assumed that the second stage only occurred when the subject failed to respond correctly in the intermediate stage, then $c = 0$. If completion of the second stage occurred with equal probability on all trials in the intermediate state, then

Table 4-4 Tests of Parameter Invariance over All Groups

Invariant Parameters	$-2 \log_e \lambda$	*p*	Varying Parameter	Estimated Value			
				EE	*HE*	*EH*	*HH*
b(.26), *c*(.00)	3.95	.14	*d*	.36	.28	.33	.25
b(.16), *d*(.22)	2.03	.37	*c*	.19	.10	.18	.06
c(.18), *d*(.17)	5.62	.06	*b*	.24	.06	.14	.00

Source: From Humphreys & Greeno, 1970.

Table 4-5 Parameter Estimates Assuming $b = d$ and Second Stage Dependent Only on Stimuli

Hypothesis	Parameter	EE	EH	HE	HH
$b = c = d$	a	.29	.18	.22	.13
$b = c = d$	$b = c = d$	.20	.20	.15	.15
$b = c = d$	e	.55	.34	.68	.00
$b = c = d$	q	.43	.55	.52	.57
$b = d, c = 0$	a	.29	.18	.21	.13
$b = d, c = 0$	$b = d$	.34	.34	.26	.26
$b = d, c = 0$	e	.68	.38	.66	.10
$b = d, c = 0$	q	.54	.64	.60	.64

Source: From Humphreys & Greeno, 1970.

$c = d$. Either of these hypotheses makes the model identifiable for a single group, when it is added to the restriction $t = ab, r = e, s = 1 - a$.

Results for both tests were positive. With either identifying restriction there are 14 free parameters, giving 6 degrees of freedom. With $b = c = d$, the value of $-2 \log_e \lambda$ was 8.44, which corresponds to a probability of .21 in $\chi^2(6)$. Testing $b = d$ with $c = 0$ gave $-2 \log_e \lambda = 4.37$, $p = .62$. Table 4-5 gives the parameter values estimated under the hypotheses. (Recall that only two values of $b = d$ were allowed under the hypotheses.)

THEORETICAL IMPLICATIONS

The purpose of obtaining measurements of difficulty in the two stages was to obtain evidence on the question of what the main processes are that occur in each of the two stages of learning. Keep in mind that a "stage" in the Markov model involves a series of trials in which the probability of correct response remains relatively constant. The probability of correct response starts at zero, then at some later time changes to p, an estimated parameter. The measurement obtained by estimating a and s (the first-stage parameters) is the difficulty of accomplishing that change in response probability. The measurement obtained by estimating b, c, d, and $t/(1 - s)$ (the second-stage parameters) is the difficulty of accomplishing the change in probability from p to 1.0.

The experimental result was that both stimulus and response variables affected the difficulty of the first of these operationally defined stages of learning. On the other hand, the results were consistent with the hypothesis that the second stage depended only on properties of the stimuli.

The simplest interpretation of the finding would be that storage of stimulus-response pairs occurred in the first stage of learning, and that the associations were made reliably retrievable, mainly through stimulus discrimination, in the second stage. This interpretation fits well with the Gestalt idea that associative learning is mainly a process of forming a new mental unit, with storage of relational information occurring first and with a further assumption that additional learning occurs later if it is needed to make the information easy to retrieve. We assume that learning to retrieve an item consists of incorporating it into a retrieval network of the kind discussed in Chapter 2.

In carrying out their analysis, Humphreys and Greeno had expected a result consistent with a simple application of associationist theory. It was expected that the first-stage parameters would largely reflect the process of response learning, and that the second-stage parameters would be related to the process of learning associative connections. According to this view, it was expected that a would depend mainly on the response variable, perhaps being equal in groups EE and HE, and having a different single value in groups EH and HH. The second-stage parameters were expected to depend on both the stimulus and response variables, since both elements are involved in the formation of a connection. Of course, this expected pattern of results was not obtained.

Although an interpretation of the results can be given in relation to processes of response and connection learning, it is not as simple as the one originally expected by Humphreys and Greeno. It could be assumed that response acquisition occurs early in the learning process, as associationist theorists have hypothesized. But the accomplishment of response learning need not in itself produce a change in response probability. It can be further assumed that a certain amount of associative strength needs to be built up before the probability of correct response changes from zero. According to this view of things, the learning that occurs in the first stage of the Markov model would include response acquisition and the beginning of associative learning. The second stage of the Markov model would correspond to the completion of associative learning. If this interpretation is adopted, the data in this experiment indicate that the difficulty of associative learning depended mainly on stimulus similarity and did not seem to depend on response difficulty.

This associationist interpretation of Humphreys and Greeno's results is inconsistent with the model used in analyzing the data. According to the model, learning occurred in two discrete and sequential steps. The associationist interpretation given here says that in the first stage at least two things are happening: acquisition of response and acquisition of some associative strength. While this theory is contradicted by the model used to analyze the data, it is not necessarily contradicted by the data. Even though the data were consistent with the discrete two-stage model, it is known that more complicated processes can generate data in approximate agreement with predictions from a Markov model (Heine, 1970), especially if provision is made for differences in learning difficulty among subjects and items (Restle, 1965).

The findings that contradicted the simple associationist idea about stages of learning also contradicted the expectations with which Humphreys and Greeno began their analysis. The interpretation they developed, which involved storing representations of pairs followed by learning to retrieve, was a response to the empirical findings. The advantage of the stages specified in the cognitive interpretation is that they correspond in a rather direct way to the states of a statistical model that agrees well with data and whose parameters can be estimated for measurement of the difficulty of stages of learning. This technical advantage probably should not be interpreted as evidence for the cognitive view or against the associationist interpretation, except insofar as the cognitive view seems to provide a simpler analysis of the results.

REPLICATION OF HUMPHREYS' EXPERIMENT

An experiment was conducted by Greeno with the assistance of Herbert Marsh, to check the pattern of results obtained in Humphreys' experiment. In the replication, stimuli were either letters (easy) or overlapping letter pairs (hard), and responses were either high-frequency words (easy) or low-frequency words (hard). The lists are shown in Table 4-6. In this study, the stimulus variable had a greater effect on overall difficulty than the response variable. The mean total errors per item in the four groups were: EE, 4.25, EH, 5.09, HE, 10.63, and HH, 11.02.

Tests of simplifying assumptions led to acceptance of $b = d$ and $e = q$ for groups EE and EH, although the assumption about the initial study trial, Equation 4-3, could not be accepted for these groups. On the other hand, Equation 4-3 was acceptable for groups HE and HH, while $b = d$ was not. The fit of the model to these data was not as good as with Humphreys' study, but it seemed tolerably good for purposes of a replication.

Because different simplifying assumptions were acceptable for the various groups, direct comparisons of parameter values do not give a very meaningful picture of the relative difficulty of states. For example, in group EE, the parameter a was estimated to be .11, while in group HE a was .26. However,

Table 4-6 Lists Used in Replication of Humphreys' Experiment

EE	*EH*	*HE*	*HH*
P—Touch	P—Delft	FQ—Touch	FQ—Delft
V—Night	V—Blear	VF—Night	VF—Renal
F—Grain	F—Renal	VQ—Grain	VQ—Anode
C—Stand	C—Houri	QV—Stand	QV—Houri
L—Earth	L—Ingot	QF—Earth	QF—Ingot
S—Offer	S—Anode	FV—Offer	FV—Blear

Source: From Greeno, 1970.

it would be a mistake to conclude that the first stage was harder for group EE, because $1 - s$, the probability of accomplishing the first stage in the initial study trial, was .94 in group EE, while $1 - s$ was .26 in group HE under the simplifying assumption used for that group. Summary measures of difficulty of the two stages can be obtained by calculating from the theoretical parameters. Let $E(Z_1)$ be the mean number of trials before the first stage of learning is accomplished, and let $E(Z_2)$ be the mean number of trials after the first stage is accomplished but before the second stage is accomplished. In terms of the states of the model, $E(Z_1)$ is the mean number of trials (including the initial study trial) spent in State U, and $E(Z_2)$ is the mean number of trials spent in the intermediate States E and C. The value of $E(Z_1)$ is straightforward:

$$E(Z_1) = 1 + s/a. \tag{4-6}$$

The value of $E(Z_2)$ depends on the initial probabilities and on weighted averages of the second-stage learning parameters. Let $R = rd + (1 - r)c$, $E = ed + (1 - e)c$, $Q = qd + pc$. Then

$$E(Z_2) = (1 - s - t)R + s(1 - b)E$$
$$+ \left(\frac{1 + Q}{Q}\right)[(1 - s - t)(1 - R) + s(1 - b)(1 - E)]. \tag{4-7}$$

Use of Equations 4-6 and 4-7 requires that identifying restrictions be employed to allow empirical estimates to determine parameter values. Greeno (1970) used the assumption $c = 0$ in calculating values from the data of this replication. The results are shown in Table 4-7, and they seem to confirm the pattern of results from Humphreys' study quite nicely, in that the estimated difficulty of the first stage is affected by both stimulus similarity and response frequency, and the difficulty of the second stage essentially is dependent only on the stimulus variable.

PAGEL'S MEASURES OF EFFECTS OF MEANINGFULNESS AND SIMILARITY

Pagel (1973) studied the effects of varying stimulus meaningfulness and intrastimulus similarity, mainly the effects of these variables on negative transfer, and these data will be discussed in Chapter 6. But the data she obtained in the first list learned by subjects provide further information about how the stages of learning are affected by stimulus variables.

Pagel examined the hypothesis that learning was all-or-none in her experiment. A likelihood ratio test is possible, since the all-or-none model is a special case of the two-stage model. Thus, the all-or-none hypothesis can be used as the null hypothesis of a statistical test, with the two-stage model being

Table 4-7 Measures of Difficulty for Stages of Learning in Replication of Humphreys' Experiment

Measure	Group			
	EE	EH	HE	HH
$E(Z_1)$—First Stage	1.49	2.55	3.90	5.51
$E(Z_2)$—Second Stage	3.00	3.34	9.75	8.51

Source: From Greeno, 1970.

the alternative hypothesis. Pagel tested this assumption in its most general form, using the unrestricted form of the two-stage model which has seven identifiable parameters, and a general form of the all-or-none model which has free initial probabilities of the states giving four identifiable parameters. The results showed clearly that the all-or-none model should be rejected as a description of learning in Pagel's experiment. There were four experimental groups, and the values of $-2 \log_e \lambda$ for the likelihood ratio test summed to 402.45. With 3 degrees of freedom per group, that statistic should have been distributed approximately as $\chi^2(12)$ if learning had really been all-or-none. The smallest of the four values was $\chi^2(3) = 10.31, p < .05$.

The fact that learning required two stages fits nicely with the hypothesis that the main stages are storing pairs and learning to retrieve the stored representations. The stimulus materials used by Pagel made discrimination quite difficult in some of the conditions, and would be expected to require a second stage of some difficulty. Pagel's result thus agrees with Polson, Restle, and Polson's (1965) finding of two-stage learning in conditions where stimulus discrimination is difficult. As a general rule, the conditions needed to give data in agreement with the all-or-none model include having a small number of responses (two or three), as well as a relatively short list of stimuli that are quite distinctive. With only a dozen or so items, and with just two or three responses, the task is quite similar to a sorting task, in which the subject must learn only in which category each stimulus belongs. It seems intuitively reasonable that problems of information retrieval would be minimal in that kind of task, therefore, it seems consistent with storage-and-retrieval notions that all-or-none learning should occur in the kinds of experiments where it has been found, and not in situations like Pagel's, where response learning as such is no problem but where stimulus conditions produce difficulty in retrieving stored information.

The four groups in Pagel's experiment involved factorial variation of stimulus meaningfulness and similarity; examples of the stimulus lists are given in Table 4-8, along with the theoretical measurements of difficulty. $E(Z_1)$ and $E(Z_2)$ are given (from Equations 4-6 and 4-7), because some simplifying assumptions were not acceptable in all groups. Note that both stages were apparently affected substantially by the varied stimulus properties.

Table 4-8 Lists and Measurements of Difficulty from Pagel's Experiment

	High Meaning Low Similarity	*Low Meaning Low Similarity*	*High Meaning High Similarity*	*Low Meaning High Similrity*
	Law	Gac	Ban	Yaj
	Jam	Laj	Bin	Yij
	Get	Yeb	Pan	Zaj
	Bed	Xed	Pin	Zij
	Six	Kih	Bat	Yaf
	Kin	Riw	Bit	Yif
	Fur	Zuf	Pat	Zaf
$E(Z_1)$	1.16	1.44	2.26	5.26
$E(Z_2)$	1.71	2.59	7.73	14.66

Furthermore, when stimuli were highly similar, meaningfulness played an important role in difficulty of both stages. Recall from discussion earlier in this chapter that the usual small effect of stimulus meaningfulness can be explained by assuming that subjects encode partial representations of stimuli. With highly similar stimuli like those used by Pagel, partial encodings are not sufficient to distinguish the stimuli. In this case, when more complete representations of stimuli must be stored, meaningfulness of stimuli apparently plays a strong role in determining how easy it is both to store and to make retrievable representations of the associations.

HUMPHREYS AND YUILLE'S MEASURES OF EFFECTS OF CONCRETENESS

Another set of measurements of difficulty in two learning stages was obtained by Humphreys and Yuille (1971). The variable manipulated was the concreteness of words—the ease with which words can be related to a pictorial image. Lists were constructed using nouns rated for concreteness by subjects of Paivio, Yuille, and Madigan (1968). In the experiment, concreteness of stimuli and responses was varied factorially, with 25 pairs being learned by each subject.

An important result obtained by Humphreys and Yuille was that with concrete stimuli, learning occurred in essentially an all-or-none fashion, with a very low probability of correct response (about .10) for unlearned items. The two-stage model was required for lists having abstract words as stimuli. One interpretation is that concrete stimuli, once a subject succeeds in storing a representation of the item, are easy to retrieve, and further learning is not needed. On this interpretation, the items with concrete stimuli had only one stage of learning because the second stage occurred with probability close to 1.0 when the first stage was accomplished. The inference that retrieval is particularly easy with concrete stimuli is a comfortable one since a concrete word on the stimulus side would be expected to make easy contact with a relational encoding of the pair.

The parameters estimated from Humphreys and Yuille's data are given in Table 4-9. Values of a estimated for groups with concrete stimuli are the estimated learning rates obtained from the all-or-none model. The effects of concreteness on the first stage were small and not significant. But strong effects of both stimulus and response concreteness were obtained in the second stage. On the interpretation given here, concreteness of stimuli had a very large effect, raising the probability of accomplishing the second stage essentially to 1.0. A significant effect of response concreteness was also obtained when stimuli were abstract. (The parameters given in Table 4-9 were obtained with the identifying restriction $c = d$, which seems reasonable since, in Humphreys and Yuille's experiment, subjects studied all the pairs, then were tested on all the pairs; they did not have a study trial on each item immediately after its test as they would in the anticipation procedure. The significant effect that was obtained involved the quantity $u = c/(q + pc)$, which was different in groups Abstract-Concrete and Abstract-Abstract, $-2 \log_e \lambda = 13.63$, $df = 1$, $p < .001$.

Manipulations of response difficulty by Humphreys and Greeno (1970) and in Greeno's replication of Humphreys' experiment failed to produce changes in difficulty of the second stage of learning, and this lack of effect seems to support the idea that the second stage of learning is a process of making stored representations more retrievable. Humphreys and Yuille's result is consistent with that interpretation, especially if it is accepted that stimulus concreteness had a stronger effect on the same process. Here the involvement of response concreteness occurred when stimuli were words, rather than numerals or letters and letter pairs, whereas in the earlier studies, response difficulty had effects only in the first stage. A major assumption of the cognitive analysis of association is that the encoded representation of a stimulus-response pair is relational, affected by properties of both terms. The finding that concreteness of responses affects ease of retrieval can be interpreted as an indication that abstract stimulus words were encoded in ways that made them better retrieval cues when the subject was encoding

Table 4-9 Parameter Values Estimated from Humphreys and Yuille's Experiment

Parameter	Concrete Stim. Concrete Resp.	Concrete Stim. Abstract Resp.	Abstract Stim. Concrete Resp.	Abstract Stim. Abstract Resp.
a (First Stage Learning)	.34	.30	.31	.27
c (Second Stage Learning)	$\simeq 1.0$	$\simeq 1.0$	.42	.33
p (Intermediate State Performance)	—	—	.45	.33

them in relation to concrete responses than when the subject was encoding them in relation to abstract responses.

EFFECTS OF STIMULUS AND RESPONSE MEANINGFULNESS

A large study has been conducted by Greeno with assistance from Jane Hoffman, Christine Shaffron, and Annette Menuhin, to provide measurements of difficulty in the two stages of learning in situations involving negative transfer. These results will be presented in Chapter 6. However, the data obtained from the first lists learned by the subjects provide information about effects of meaningfulness of responses and of stimuli. Materials used in the experiment were common four-letter words and consonant-vowel-consonant trigrams that were easy to pronounce but had very low association value. Lists of eight items were constructed, with minimal intralist similarity. Four kinds of lists were used: one with words as both stimuli and responses; one with words as stimuli and nonsense trigrams as responses; one with nonsense trigrams as stimuli and words as responses; one with nonsense trigrams as both stimuli and responses. Eight different sets of items were used in each condition, to completely balance the specific materials used as stimuli and responses. One of the lists used in the nonsense-word condition was the following: Tyz-Nail, Daq-Flag, Vec-Dish, Byl-Goat, Gax-Pipe, Ruq-Wing, Hyj-Leaf, Mef-Yard.

In the experiment, subjects sat at computer-controlled display/keyboards. Up to five subjects were run at the same time in separate booths. The pairs were each shown for 2.5 seconds. Then the items were presented by the anticipation method; that is, the stimulus was shown while subjects typed responses on the keyboards to enter them into the computer, or merely pressed the "enter" key to indicate they did not know. After all subjects had made some response, the stimulus and response were shown for 1.5 seconds, then the next stimulus appeared. Learning was continued to a criterion of two perfect cycles through the list, with a maximum of 30 trials.

Because the experiment was aimed at the transfer conditions, a very large number of subjects was run in each condition of initial learning. The numbers of sequences for analysis in the four conditions were 1208, 1240, 1168, and 1224. These numbers are sufficient to ensure that any simple statistical model will be rejected by a goodness-of-fit test, and when the two-stage model was applied to the data, tests indicated significant discrepancies. However, the discrepancies were not unusually large or systematic, and the parameter estimates probably give a fairly accurate reflection of relative difficulty in the two stages of learning.

The large number of cases also made the tests of simplifying assumptions of the model very powerful. We will present estimates obtained under some simplifying assumptions that were statistically unacceptable, but none with $p < .001$. The simplifying assumptions used were (1) $t = ab$, $s = 1 - a$, $r = e$, and (2) $b = d$, $e = q$. In two of the groups estimates will be presented under both of these restrictions. In the group with word stimuli and word responses, both restrictions were acceptable, $p > .10$, while in the group with nonsense stimuli and word responses, both restrictions were statistically unacceptable, $.001 < p < .01$. The results are shown in Table 4-10. All the estimates shown use the identifying restriction $c = d$.

The outcome appears to show that meaningfulness of both stimuli and responses had effects on first-stage difficulty, although the effect of response meaningfulness appears to have been somewhat greater. This agrees with the idea that subjects must encode the entire response but they can use a simpler encoding for nonsense stimuli, perhaps using only one letter instead of remembering the entire trigram. On the other hand, these data show a somewhat greater effect of stimulus meaningfulness on the first stage than Pagel's results did in the condition where stimuli were dissimilar. Effects on the first stage were approximately additive—that is, using nonsense responses rather than words added about as many trials to the first stage when stimuli were words as when stimuli were nonsense trigrams.

Meaningfulness appears to have a much different kind of effect on the second stage. Differences between conditions having words either as stimuli or responses or both were small but, when both stimuli and responses were nonsense, the time needed to accomplish the second stage was approximately doubled. The point taken from Humphreys and Yuille's study—that difficulty of learning to retrieve can be a joint function of stimuli and responses—is made stronger by these estimates. One interpretation is that when either of the terms of an association is a meaningful item for the subject, subjects can form an organized system for retrieving the items, based on the meanings of the items and associations involving other words in memory. Only when both items are meaningless does the effect on difficulty of retrieval become strong.

Table 4-10 Estimates of Difficulty in Stages of Memorizing Associations

Stimuli	Responses	First Stage: $E(Z_1)$		Second Stage: $E(Z_2)$	
		$t = ab$ $s = 1 - a$ $r = e$	$b = d$ $e = q$	$t = ab$ $s = 1 - a$ $r = e$	$b = d$ $e = q$
Word	Word	1.42	1.51	2.24	2.45
Nonsense	Word	3.01*	2.14*	2.46*	2.81*
Word	Nonsense	4.50*		2.75*	
Nonsense	Nonsense	7.30		5.49	

*denotes a simplifying restriction with $.001 < p < .01$.

SUMMARY AND CONCLUSIONS

This chapter has discussed the process of learning new associations. First, we discussed the formation of complex ideas, an important issue in motivating the development of associationist theory. We believe that complex ideas are probably relational structures, rather than bundles of component ideas linked by undifferentiated connections, a view that is inconsistent with the classical associationist analysis, which required that complex ideas develop through the simple connection of elementary components. We then conclude that the associationist analysis fails to accomplish the goal of explaining the development of complex ideas from a system in which only sensory elements are available initially and only undifferentiated connections are built among them. A more sophisticated system, capable of comprehending relations and generating relational structures, is apparently needed.

Although rote memory was originally studied by Ebbinghaus to analyze the association between ideas, recent analyses have been influenced by behaviorist concepts, and psychologists have considered associations as connections between stimuli and responses. In this framework, the process of association has been studied by using the laboratory task of paired-associate memorizing. It has been recognized that this is not usually a single process, and we have reviewed hypotheses about components of paired-associate memorizing that have been added to associationist theory in recent years.

We considered the process of response learning. An associationist analysis of response learning is conceptually possible; however, given the known importance of organizational factors in the rote memorization of lists, it seems implausible. Because memorizing an association requires complete knowledge of the response, the task is easier when the responses are already familiar to the subject, or when there is opportunity for practice on the responses before the paired associates are presented. However, these facts do not imply that learning a response and learning a connection between that response and a stimulus are separate processes. A more plausible alternative is that the main task is to store in memory a representation of the pair that includes sufficient information to produce the response when it is needed.

Next, we discussed stimulus encoding. Experiments using compound stimuli have indicated that subjects often store partial representations of stimuli in memory and, like other phenomena of selective attention, this fact is problematic for associationist theory. We have proposed that retrieval of associations occurs through an analysis of stimulus features, such as an EPAM net. In this kind of system it is natural to expect partial representations of stimuli, omitting stimulus features not needed for discrimination. It would also be expected that selected components would tend to come from a single, easily identified category, making retrieval much more efficient.

A major effort in this chapter was the presentation of results obtained when a two-stage Markov model is used to analyze acquisition of paired associates. According to the model, the process of learning each individual item consists of two transitions. When the first transition occurs, the probability of a correct response changes from zero to p, a parameter that is estimated from data. When the second transition occurs, the probability of correct response becomes unity.

We have interpreted the findings as supporting the idea that in the first stage a representation of the stimulus-response association is stored in memory; further learning that is accomplished in the second stage supports reliable and efficient retrieval of the association. The main assertion of the Gestalt analysis of association is that the process involves formation of new mental units consisting of relational structures having the associated elements as components. We identify this process of finding a relation that integrates the stimulus and response terms as the first stage of learning. The representation of the association must include a complete representation of the response term, sufficiently organized to permit production of the response. However, we view the integration of the response not as a process separate from association, but as a part of the subject's task in forming an organized representation of the stimulus-response pair.

We suppose that once a representation of the association is stored in memory, there is some probability that the items can be retrieved on a test. This probability depends on the situation. It can be very nearly 1.0, and when it is, learning is approximately an all-or-none process.

More often, the probability of retrieval after storage of a representation is substantially below 1.0, and further learning is required before the item becomes sufficiently retrievable to meet the experimental criterion of learning. We assume that the second stage of learning consists of incorporating the item into a network of feature tests that eventually permits efficient retrieval of all the items in the list.

The major findings obtained by applying the Markov model to paired-associate data seem quite compatible with this interpretation of the stages represented in the model. First, the difficulty of accomplishing the first stage of learning was strongly influenced by properties of both the stimulus and response terms, supporting the hypothesis that the first stage in learning a new association involves storing a relational representation of the stimulus-response pair. Next, large differences in the difficulty of the second stage were produced by varying stimulus similarity, in agreement with the idea that the second stage consists of learning to retrieve stored items reliably, especially if retrieval learning is assumed to consist of incorporating an item into an efficient retrieval network composed of tests of stimulus features. In Humphreys and Yuille's experiment, pairs with concrete words as stimuli were apparently retrieved with sufficient ease so that a second stage of learning was not required. Apparently the semantic features of concrete words provide for efficient retrieval—either because they are trivially easy to form into a retrieval network or because the individual associations are distinctive and accessible enough so that little or no interitem structure is needed for retrieval.

Meaningfulness of stimuli usually has very small effects on difficulty of paired-associate memorizing, but in Pagel's experiment, stimulus meaningfulness, when stimuli were very similar, had a substantial effect on difficulty of the second stage. We interpret this to indicate that when a nearly complete representation is needed to make stimuli distinguishable, there is a strong advantage in having stimuli familiar enough to allow the subject to recognize them as units. Features of a familiar word have previously been used by the subject to identify the word in many contexts; therefore, it should not be surprising that the subject can more easily incorporate those features into a retrieval network than the features of an unfamiliar string of letters.

Two variables concerning response difficulty that had marked effects on the first stage of learning had little or no effect on the second stage. The pronounceability of nonsense responses in Humphreys' experiment and the word frequency of the relatively abstract responses used in Greeno's replication of Humphreys' study had negligible effects on the second stage, and these results agree with the idea that difficulty of learning to retrieve should depend mainly on characteristics of the stimuli. However, in Humphreys and Yuille's study, concreteness of responses had a small effect on the second stage and in Greeno's transfer experiment, meaningfulness of responses in the first lists learned made a sizable difference in the second stage of learning when stimuli were nonsense, but not when stimuli were words.

We believe that an interpretation can be given for the effects of response meaningfulness and concreteness on the ease of learning to retrieve. The effect of response meaningfulness in Greeno's experiment interacted strongly with the effect of stimulus meaningfulness. Compared with pairs of words, neither word-nonsense pairs nor nonsense-word pairs were substantially harder in the second stage; nonsense-nonsense pairs, however, were a great deal harder. Our conjecture would be that when a pronounceable trigram was paired with a word, the initial encoding of the pair might more likely involve matching the trigram with a word physically similar to the trigram, due to activation of semantic features of the words that were presented in the situation. If in storing the trigram-word pairs substantially greater contact between trigrams and word schemata were made, then the stimuli in that condition would be effectively more meaningful, and their advantage over trigram-trigram pairs in the second stage could be explained by the availability of semantic features or by the subject's familiarity with retrieval of the words that are incorporated in the associative representation. Response concreteness had much less effect on retrievability, and also could be indirectly produced by a difference in the relational encodings caused by the nature of the responses.

chapter 5

Abstraction and Positive Transfer of Association

This chapter is concerned with categorical concepts as analyzed in associationist theory. We begin with a brief discussion of the general problem of abstract ideas, then deal with positive transfer when different associations include members of the same categorical concept and when new associations are learned more easily because the learner can identify the concept the various items share.

ABSTRACT IDEAS

The traditional associationist theory explained how persons acquired abstract concepts with two ideas. According to one idea, an abstract concept is simply a super-complex concept made up by combining complex concepts. For example, the concept "dog" is the combination of many properties; so too are the concepts "cat," "squirrel," and "lion." Beyond this level, the concept "animal" combines all the properties in the concepts of its subsets. In this combination, or bundle, theory, abstract ideas occur through a process of still further association—association among properties that have already been associated in concepts at a lower level.

The other idea assumes a process of generalization: an abstract concept consists of those properties that are shared by the ideas that are its special cases. In the generalization theory, an inverse process of association occurs, in which the relevant properties of a concept are identified and separated from the respective lower-level concepts to form more abstract ideas.

An analysis of acquisition of abstract ideas was given by Hull (1920). Hull trained subjects on a series of lists containing several paired-associate items. Each stimulus term was a form similar to a Chinese ideogram; each response was a nonsense syllable. The items in successive lists were related; successive items that had the same response also had some component of the stimulus in common. It should be possible for a subject to use the similarity among stimuli to make the learning easier, generalizing the nonsense labels learned in earlier lists to the new stimuli on the basis of the shared components. This occurred, and Hull's experiment provides an illustration of how an abstract concept is acquired. The subjects learned to identify a stimulus category that they had not been familiar with, and the induction occurred because, through generalization, a set of stimuli all were given the same label.

An analysis given by Underwood (1952) provides a more recent associationist analysis of abstraction. Underwood's theory considered a task called verbal concept formation, in which stimuli are words that can be classified by a common characteristic. For example, "barrel," "doughnut," and "moon" all refer to round things and can be classified on that basis. Underwood's theory is based on the fact that properties of named objects are associated with the objects' names. In the verbal concept task the various associates of each word are assumed to occur with some strength and, because the basis for grouping the stimuli is associated with all the members of its category, strengthening of the association occurs more than other responses, and eventually the association occurs with enough strength that the subject recognizes it as a valid basis for classifying the stimuli.

Critique

It is important to note that in Underwood's theory the property names used to classify stimuli must be associated with the stimuli before they can be used for classification. In Hull's analysis, subjects do not learn to perceive the features of stimuli that are used to form the categories—perception of those features is assumed in the learning process. Thus, in an important sense the associationist theory, rather than showing how abstract concepts are formed, explains how subjects use properties they already know. Many abstract concepts, such as the concept of electrical current or the concept of due process under law, seem to depend on complex relational features, rather than on simple perceptual attributes. To apply the associationist analysis to abstraction in cases where the defining features include relations seems to assume prior knowledge of the relations. Thus, we find it problematic whether the hypothesis of associationism really solves the problem of abstract ideas, just as we are dubious whether it solves the problem of complex ideas.

Abstract Ideas in Cognitive Theory

Systems that form abstract ideas have been developed rather fully in domains where the abstraction consists of a single perceptual attribute or a set of attributes combined by conjunction and disjunction. Hunt's Concept Learning Systems (Hunt, Marin, & Stone, 1966), cited in Chapter 2, are examples of one kind of a number of artificial-intelligence systems that induce categorical concepts that consist of combinations of defining features. Another form of categorical information is simple knowledge of objects that belong to categories. This kind of information is represented in semantic networks such as Quillian's (1968) model. It has been shown now, notably by Rosch (e.g., 1973), that both these forms of categorical knowledge are important in the way human knowledge is organized. A model that represents categorical knowledge as a network of relations can explain some facts about the answering of questions—for example, it takes less time to verify "a robin is a bird" than to verify "a robin is an animal" (Collins & Quillian, 1969). However, knowledge about the typical features of objects in a category also affects our performance in answering questions, as is seen by the fact that it takes less time to verify "a robin is a bird" than to verify "a penguin is a bird" (Rips, Shoben, & Smith, 1973).

Inducing relational patterns is also important in acquiring abstract ideas. An important contribution to the theory of pattern induction was given by Simon and Kotovsky (1963), who studied the process of solving series-extrapolation problems. This process apparently requires background knowledge about the normal order of symbols used in the task (the alphabet of letters or the sequence of numerals) as well as ability to identify rules for applying relations in a complex sequence.

Another induction task was studied by Huesmann and Cheng (1973), who presented sets of numbers and required a subject to induce a mathematical formula that connected all the sets. Induction in this task seemed to depend strongly on the subject's prior knowledge of a well-specified set of relations (adding, subtracting, multiplying, and so on) and a systematic strategy for generating and testing possible rules. There has also been some preliminary study of the principles needed to identify the grammatical rules that generate a body of sentences (Anderson, 1975; Hamburger & Wexler, 1975). All these cases seem to require of the learner considerable background knowledge of a relational kind as a prerequisite for acquiring new abstract concepts and patterns. Although our objection to the associationist analysis of acquiring abstract ideas is informal, as we noted our doubts regarding the acquisition of complex ideas, we also consider it implausible that the mechanisms for acquiring categorical concepts and relational patterns are generated from simple connections among elementary sense impressions.

CONCEPTS IN ASSOCIATIVE LEARNING

Experimental analyses of categorical concepts by associationists have used items that can be classified into a few categories; the subjects' success in the task depends on identifying those categories and using them to classify the items. When the task involves learning of associations, as in Hull's (1920) experiment, the categorical relations among items bring about positive transfer, in that previous learning has a facilitating effect on learning in subsequent situations.

Our view of positive transfer is an extension of our hypothesis about memorizing individual associations. We say that a major process in learning an association is finding a relational property that makes a cognitive unit, or Gestalt, of the pair of items. We propose that a major process leading to transfer of association is finding relational properties involving groups of associations. We say, in other words, that transfer depends on association at a higher level, and we presume that the principles of relational association that operate to form pairs are probably the same as the principles involved in forming the higher-order groupings involved in transfer.

The simplest case of positive transfer involves pairs with similar stimuli and the same response. Let A–B and A'–B denote two such pairs, and suppose that A–B has already been learned. The association between A and B transfers to A'–B if the subject notices the similarity between A and A' and groups the two items together. When the stimuli are similar because they share many physical properties, the subject's memory of A may not even include the distinguishing features, and A' may be treated as another presentation of the first item. (Recall Polson, Restle, & Polson's, 1965 experiment, requiring subjects to give different responses to similar stimuli, in which a distinct second stage of learning was involved in learning not to treat the two similar items identically.) Of course, similar stimuli might be distinguished as being different in appearance, but still grouped together for the purpose of responding in the task. The effort to find such groupings and the kinds of properties used for grouping would undoubtedly depend on factors of set and learning strategy used by subjects as well as interpretations of the task induced by instructions.

Transfer also occurs on the basis of groupings of stimuli not similar in appearance, but similar in meaning. A subject may learn to say "gex" to the stimulus word "table." Then, when the word "chair" is presented, a basis exists for the subject to group the association "chair-gex" with "table-gex," because "table" and "chair" are associated in the subject's semantic memory. More indirectly, if "butter" and then "canary," are associated with the same response, subjects can group the two stimuli because both name yellow things.

The hypothesis we take regarding positive transfer, then, is that when pairs with the same response have stimuli that can in some way be grouped, subjects can associate the response with those properties or meanings shared by the stimulus group. Consequently, associations need not be learned and remembered individually, but may be treated as a set. Tasks involving positive transfer will generally involve a mixture of learning events that occur at two or more levels. Individual associations will be learned; rules involving relations among associations will also be learned. Analysis of these situations involves identifying and describing the learning that occurs at the different levels.

In associationist theory the concept of generalization explains positive transfer between associations. Again, the simplest case involves two associations having the same response and physically similar stimuli. Once a response has been associated with one of the stimuli, if the other similar stimulus is shown, a subject is likely to give the same response to this second stimulus as well. In associationist theory, there is some strength of association that generalizes to the new item, and the strength of the generalized association depends on the degree of similarity between the stimuli. In the system of concepts used by associationist theory it is quite reasonable to postulate that stimuli that look alike or sound alike will give rise to stimulus generalization. For example, the activity in the nervous system generated by a particular pattern of sound waves becomes connected to a certain response. When another stimulus is presented, involving a very similar pattern of sound waves, the neural activity generated by this second stimulus probably has much in common with the neural activity that is associated with the response —so much so that the response is likely to occur when the new but similar pattern of sound waves energizes the subject's ear drum.

But what of generalization that occurs because of meanings? Recall that a major point of classical associationist theory was to show that complex cognitive structures, including complex and abstract concepts, could be generated within a system whose only raw material was disorganized sensory experience. This gives strong motivation for postulating mechanisms that could produce basic cognitive achievements such as transfer of response based on meanings of stimuli. The mechanism used in recent associationist theories is a process of mediation.

When transfer occurs between words that are associated, the postulated mechanism involves forming an associative chain. Suppose a subject has learned "table-gex," then a new item, "chair-gex," has to be learned. An association, "chair-table," already is known by the subject, and this gives rise to a chain of associations, "chair-table-gex." By utilizing the association already established, the subject only needs to learn to suppress the middle item, "table," rather than to learn a new association from "chair" to "gex."

What if the stimulus members of two associations are not as directly linked in the subject's memory as are "table" and "chair," but do have similar meanings, as do "butter" and "canary"? Mediation gives a possible, though less direct, basis for this case also. For associative transfer to occur, say, from "butter-mur" to "canary-mur," there must be some associative linking from "canary" to "mur," providing some initial associative strength to make the learning easier. It could occur from "canary" to "yellow," and then to "butter," giving a four-item chain "canary-yellow-butter-mur," with two mediating links. Or it could occur if in learning "butter-mur" some associative strength was implicitly given to "yellow-mur," perhaps because strong associates of "butter" occur implicitly as responses whenever "butter" is seen.

The cognitive and the associationist views of transfer have much in common. According to both, transfer depends on shared properties of stimuli or shared associations in memory. However, they differ in conception in an important way. In the cognitive view, transfer occurs because of a subject's ability to organize experience and depends on finding appropriate relational properties for grouping associations into higher-level units. In the associationist view, transfer occurs because of generalized strength of association, either directly or through mediation.

The two ideas suggest different implications about the process of transferring a response to a new stimulus. The hypothesis of generalized strength suggests that entirely new items will require learning from zero strength, while items that are related to previously learned items begin with some amount of strength, depending on their similarity to already learned items. On the other hand, the cognitive view suggests that transfer to new items should occur in an all-or-none fashion. If the subject recognizes a relationship between the new item and one or more items previously learned, then the response should be known on the basis of that grouping. If a relationship is not seen, then the new item should be no different from an item that has no relationship to previously learned items.

TEST OF ALL-OR-NONE TRANSFER

The idea that transfer of associations might occur in an all-or-none fashion was tested in an experiment by Greeno and Scandura (1966). The materials used involved categories based on verbal concepts, in the sense mentioned earlier in this chapter. Table 5-1 shows one of the lists of materials learned in training and one of the lists given in transfer.

Subjects in this experiment first memorized a list of seven associations, as shown in List 1 in the table. Subjects were told that items having the same response could be related to one another, and that these relationships would help in a later task. Subjects studied the items in List 1, and then were given a brief test to assure that the items had been memorized. Next the items in List 2 were presented, one at a time, and the subject was asked to respond on each trial; the experimenter then gave the correct response.

The inclusion of items in the transfer lists that would be expected to pro-

Table 5-1 Items Used in Transfer Experiment

List 1		List 2	
Stimulus	*Response*	*Stimulus*	*Response*
Freckle	Pel	Atom	Pel
Earthworm	Pel	Sulphur*	Pel
Tweezer	Pel	Ivory	Mur
Grasshopper	Pel	Alley*	Mur
Paste	Mur	Globe	Dix
Sheep	Mur	Beak*	Dix
Knuckle	Dix		

*denotes control words, unrelated to the category concepts which in this list were small (Pel), white (Mur), and round (Dix).
Source: From Greeno & Scandura, 1966

duce varying amounts of transfer was important because the two views about transfer give different expectations about the way in which transfer facilitates learning. According to the all-or-none idea, different lists of items may include different proportions of items that benefit from transfer but, for any single item, transfer either occurs completely or not at all. According to the idea that transfer involves some quantity of associative strength, each item benefits from transfer to some extent, and different sets of items will have different average amounts of transfer. The analysis of results allows a decision as to which kind of effect produced the differences in the amount of transfer that occurred.

The main difference in amount of transfer was between transfer items and control items, which were selected to involve little or no relationship with the categories used in List 1. A second variable, illustrated in Table 5-1, was the number of examples in List 1 for each category: of the three categories used, one was represented by four examples, one by two examples, and the third by a single example. A third variable used to produce different amounts of transfer is called the dominance of category examples. The materials were selected using measurements taken by Underwood and Richardson (1956). To obtain measurements, words were shown to subjects, who were asked to respond with associations in the category of sense impressions. For example, an appropriate association for "table" might be "flat" or "square" but the usual free association, "chair," was not appropriate in this task because "chair" is not a descriptive term applying to tables. In selecting materials for an experiment, words for which subjects gave the same response are put together in a category. For example, "barrel," "doughnut," and "moon" are all words to which many subjects respond by saying "round." They are then used together in a category as examples of the concept "round." The dominance of an example for a concept is defined as the percentage of subjects who gave the concept in Underwood and Richardson's association test. Thus, examples with high dominance involve categories that are quite obvious; examples with low dominance involve categories that are difficult to form. Items of high dominance were selected for this experiment with association frequencies above 50%, and items of low dominance were selected with association frequencies between 10% and 20%. The examples shown in Table 5-1 have low dominance in List 1 and high dominance in List 2.

To summarize the experimental design, each subject learned a transfer list containing six items, three of which were control items. For each subject, the transfer items were either all of high dominance or all of low dominance, and the training items learned previously had been either all of high dominance or all of low dominance. In other words, both training dominance and transfer dominance were varied in a 2 × 2 factorial design. There were 24 subjects in each of four groups. Of the three transfer items in each list, one was an example of a concept that had four examples in the training list, one was an example of a concept that had two examples in the training list, and one was an example of a concept that had just one example in the training list.

The question whether transfer was an all-or-none process can be framed in relation to a Markov model of the learning process. Figure 3-7 shows the states of the model used, with transition probabilities. The discussion up till now has not involved initial probabilities of the states—in ordinary learning experiments it is natural and reasonable to assume that all items begin in the unlearned state. However, the possibility of transfer introduces the possibility of an item in State L at the beginning of the transfer task. The initial probabilities of the states are

$$P(U_1, S_1, L_1) = (1 - t, 0, t);\qquad(5\text{-}1)$$

that is, t is the probability that an item starts in State L. This event corresponds to knowing the item's response when it is first seen. Assume that the probability of transition into State L is a constant, c, on all trials. From Figure 3-7, $c_u = c_s = c$. The remaining parameter is f, the probability of losing an item from short-term memory between trials. For this analysis, assume that d, the probability of transiting to State L while other items are presented, is zero.

The issue of whether transfer is all-or-none is an issue about parameters of learning. Specifically, the issue involves which parameter or parameters are affected by the variables influencing transfer. If transfer is an all-or-none affair, then all of the difference between conditions will appear as difference in the values of t—that is, the difference would consist only in different proportions of items known at the start. If transfer involved generalization of associative strength, then either the learning probability c, or the short-term retention parameter f, or both, should also be involved in transfer effects. Of course, an important possibility is that the learning process would be more complicated than the one described in the all-or-none model. However, if it appears that learning is all-or-none, then the question about transfer takes the precise form stated above.

Goodness of Fit

First, we must determine whether the learning process can be described adequately by the all-or-none model. The distributions used to test goodness of fit were the number of errors and the trial of last error. The exact expressions for these statistics are generalizations of Equations 3-1 and 3-2. The important new feature is seen in the probability of no errors:

$$P(L = 0) = P(T = 0) = t + (1 - t)\frac{gc}{1 - (1 - c)(1 - f + fg)}. \qquad (5\text{-}2)$$

Note that the probability of no errors depends strongly on t, the probability of transfer. Other terms of the distributions have formulas that include effects of short-term retention as well as transfer, but have the same form as Equations 3-1 and 3-2.

$$P(L = k) = \begin{cases} \dfrac{(1 - t)(1 - g)c}{1 - (1 - c)(1 - f + fg)}, & k = 1 \\[3mm] \dfrac{(1 - t)f(1 - g)c}{1 - (1 - c)(1 - f + fg)}(1 - c)^{k-1}, & k \geq 2. \end{cases} \qquad (5\text{-}3)$$

$$P(T = j) = \frac{(1 - t)(1 - g)c[1 - (1 - c)(1 - f)]}{[1 - (1 - c)(1 - f + fg)]^2}$$
$$\cdot \left[\frac{(1 - c)f(1 - g)}{1 - (1 - c)(1 - f + fg)}\right]^{j-1}, \qquad j \geq 1.$$

The comparison between theoretical and empirical proportions is given in Figures 5-1 and 5-2. These theoretical distributions were obtained using maximum likelihood estimates of the parameters, which were $\hat{t} = .197$, $\hat{c} = .227$, $\hat{f} = .693$. The fit appears to be satisfactory, and the conclusion seems to be warranted that learning was approximately all-or-none.

Invariance of Parameters

The question of all-or-none transfer can be answered by examining invariance of parameters between groups having different amounts of transfer, as mentioned previously. To test the hypothesis using the greatest amount of information possible, all the transfer items were combined in one set of items and compared with the entire set of control items. Three tests are of main interest. First, consider the transition parameters of the model, c and f. A likelihood ratio test for invariance of both these parameters has two

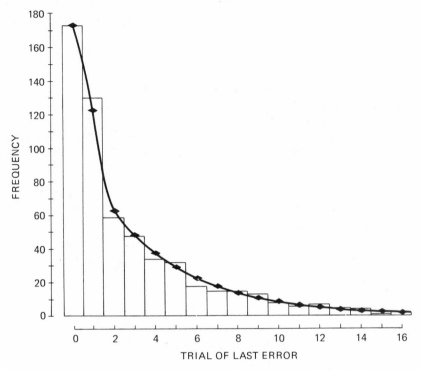

Figure 5-1 Theoretical and empirical distributions of trial of last error from Greeno and Scandura's (1966) experiment.

degrees of freedom; the test statistic was 1.92, which is well below the level indicating significance in the chi-square distribution. Second, a test for invariance of t between control and transfer items gave a highly significant test statistic: $\chi^2(1) = 59.60, p = $ nil. A third test was for the hypothesis that t was equal to zero in the control items. That hypothesis was acceptable in the data: $\chi^2(1) = 1.09, p > .20$. The conclusion favors the idea that transfer occurred in an all-or-none fashion, with the effect of generalization all located in the values of t.

Another analysis was carried out, showing the result in another way. According to the hypothesis of all-or-none transfer, any item for which there is one or more errors can be identified as an item for which transfer failed to occur. All such items should be alike, whether they were transfer or control items. This can be examined by looking at conditional distributions; that is, if items having zero errors are removed, the remaining items should give identical distributions, whether control or transfer items are considered. Figure 5-3 shows conditional distributions of the number of errors, given at least one error. Note that in each panel, the distributions are virtually identical for items having corresponding responses from List 1.

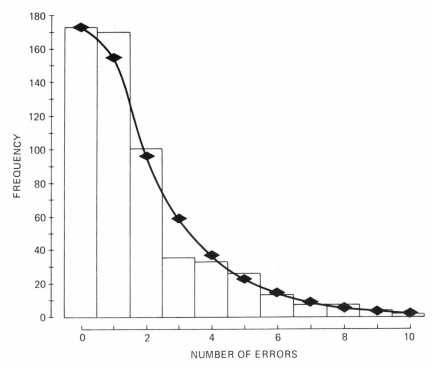

Figure 5-2 Theoretical and empirical distributions of number of errors from Greeno and Scandura's (1966) experiment.

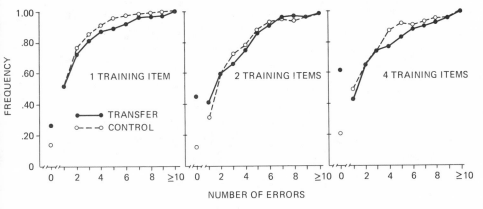

Figure 5-3 Proportions of items with zero errors, and cumulative proportions of imperfect items with k errors, starting with $k = 1$, on transfer and control items for which the response had been paired with one, two, or four examples during training in Greeno and Scandura's (1966) experiment.

The evidence obtained by comparing transfer and control items gives quite strong support for the idea of all-or-none transfer. In our view, the result favors the cognitive idea that transfer depended on a subject's having in mind an appropriate relationship that permitted grouping of the new transfer item with the correct item or items from List 1. The idea of generalized response strength seems hard to justify, considering the apparent all-or-none character of transfer that was observed.

Theoretical Analysis of Values of t

A final analysis was concerned with the varying amounts of transfer that were related to the different degrees of dominance of the examples of concept categories, and with the different numbers of examples used in List 1 for the concept categories. A very simple model was used in this analysis, and while some weaknesses in the assumptions appear to be shown in the data, the results were not sufficiently far from the data to give strong reasons for modifying the model. The assumptions used include the view that individual items are learned in an all-or-none fashion. When an individual item is learned, it is encoded in memory in some way. The assumption is that each possible encoding either is or is not related to the other items in the concept category—that is, there is a certain probability that a successful encoding for learning will provide the basis for transfer. Let c be the probability of learning an item. The value of c is the probability of achieving an encoding of the item that will be sufficiently permanent in memory to allow good performance of the item in the experiment. We assume that some of those sufficient codes represent the property that is used as the basis of a conceptual category in the experiment. Thus, there is some probability a that a concept will be acquired when an individual item is learned. Assume that a takes two values: a_H for high-dominance examples and a_L for low-dominance items. Let k be the number of examples of the concept in the training list. Then the probability of acquiring the concept when List 1 was memorized would be

$$A_{ik} = 1 - (1 - a_i)^k,$$

where $i = H$ or $i = L$, and k is the number of training examples.

Now let b equal the probability that a subject recognizes a new member of a concept category, given that the concept was acquired. b takes two values, b_H for transfer examples with high dominance and b_L for transfer examples with low dominance. The probability of transfer then is

$$t_{ijk} = A_{ik}b_j = [1 - (1 - a_i)^k]b_j, \tag{5-4}$$

where $j = H$ or $j = L$.

Parameters were estimated and Equation 5-4 was used to obtain values of t; these were in turn used in Equation 5-2 to predict frequencies of items with

Table 5-2 Theoretical Values of *t* and Predicted and Obtained Frequencies of Zero Errors

Training dominance	*Test dominance*	*No. of examples*	*t*	*Predicted frequency*	*Obtained frequency*
High	High	4	.858	21.05	17
High	High	2	.624	16.15	21
High	High	1	.387	11.20	10
High	Low	4	.566	14.95	14
High	Low	2	.412	11.72	9
High	Low	1	.255	8.45	12
Low	High	4	.472	12.97	15
Low	High	2	.273	8.83	7
Low	High	1	.147	6.21	2
Low	Low	4	.311	9.63	13
Low	Low	2	.180	6.89	6
Low	Low	1	.097	5.16	2

Source: From Greeno and Scandura, 1966.

no errors in the 12 transfer conditions in the experiment. The results are shown in Table 5-2. The predicted frequencies came from the estimates

$$a_H = .387, \quad a_L = .147,$$
$$b_H = 1.000, \quad b_L = .600.$$

The results show some reasons for suspicion of some of the assumptions. With low training dominance, relatively large overpredictions were made for the cases having only one training example, and this causes suspicion that acquisition was probably facilitated by the simultaneous presence of more than one example. However, with only 24 cases per cell, the predictions were not significantly discrepant from the data by a chi-square test ($\chi^2(7) = 13.75$, $p > .05$).

ACQUISITION OF RULES FOR GROUPING

Greeno and Scandura's evidence was quite strong on the issue of how transfer occurred—that is, it was all-or-none. However, strong evidence was not obtained about how the learning that provided the basis for transfer occurred. The hypothesis used to analyze different amounts of transfer was that properties corresponding to the conceptual categories were or were not encoded, on an all-or-none basis. However, this was tested only weakly in Greeno and Scandura's experiment. We now turn to an experiment by Polson (1972), in which the process of acquiring conceptual categories was studied in detail.

When transfer occurs, we assume it is because the subject discovers a property or rule that allows the transfer item to be grouped with the appropriate previous items. The process by which relational groupings are acquired has been discussed in some detail by many Gestalt psychologists, notably Katona (1940), Köhler (1927), and Wertheimer (1959). The idea of learning through insightful discovery (Yerkes, 1927) and the acquisition of relational principles (Judd, 1908) have been considered as characteristic views of Gestalt psychologists in the area of learning theory (e.g., Hilgard & Bower, 1966).

The experiment that Polson designed involved subjects memorizing a series of five lists. The five lists given to the first two groups had items that could be related on the basis of conceptual categories. The five lists given to the other two groups had unrelated items. One of the concept-acquisition conditions, called CA, Noun, had categories based on superordinate concepts. The categories were kinds of furniture (chair, table, and so on), parts of the body, insects, fruits, articles of clothing, geographical features, means of transportation, and animals. The examples used were taken from normative data obtained by Cohen, Bousfield, and Whitmarsh (1957), in which subjects were given the names of categories and wrote down examples of the categories. The other concept acquisition condition, called CA, Sense, had categories based on concepts involving sense impressions (Underwood & Richardson, 1956). The categories were "soft," "red," "round," "dark," "white," "small," "smelly," and "green." The measured dominance of the examples used in the CA, Sense condition was above 50%.

Each list in the CA conditions included one example of each category, with each word paired with one of the numbers 1–8. The five members of each category were all paired with the same numeral response in the five lists. That is, all the items of furniture might be number 1, all the parts of the body might be number 2, and so on. (Different subjects had different assignments of responses to the categories.) The lists given to the control groups had words that were phonemically similar, but unrelated in meaning, to those in the CA lists. For example, in the control list for LL, Noun, the word "plume" was used in place of "plum," a member of the category "fruit." Care was taken to balance the conditions in word length and word frequency of the items used.

Each subject was given the items of each list in turn using the anticipation method. The items of each list were presented until the subject gave only correct responses for three successive presentations of the list. Twenty-four subjects were run in each of the four experimental conditions.

All-or-None Learning and Transfer

The main question in this experiment is the process by which the categorical groupings are acquired. However, this question is precise only in relation to a definite model of the process of learning and transfer. The simplest case for analysis has both learning and transfer that are all-or-none, and Polson tested these ideas in his experiment.

The hypothesis of all-or-none learning was tested using the predicted distributions of errors and trial of last error (Equations 5-2 and 5-3) and other theorems that are implied by the Markov model of all-or-none learning with short-term retention. The agreement of the data with the model was quite good; satisfactory agreement was found with distributions of the number of errors, the trial of last error, and some sequential statistics. There was evidence that performance prior to learning was not stationary, as the model stipulates, but this was largely confined to the first list learned in the experiment. However, the extent of the discrepancy in Polson's results did not seem sufficiently large to justify analysis using a more complex model, especially since the main questions of the investigation involved the later lists, where transfer was possible.

The hypothesis of all-or-none transfer was examined by estimating the values of parameters in the model of all-or-none learning. Figure 5-4 shows

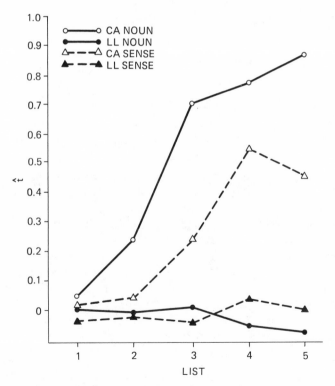

Figure 5-4 Estimated probabilities of transfer in different lists in Polson's (1972) experiment.

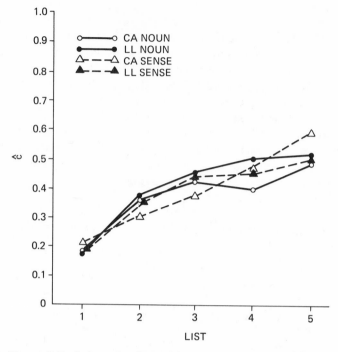

Figure 5-5 Estimated values of learning parameters in different lists in Polson's (1972) experiment.

values of t estimated in each of the four conditions for the five lists.[1] The graph shows that values of $\hat{t}$ were near zero for both learning-to-learn control groups, and increased substantially across lists in both concept-acquisition groups. This was expected; the idea of all-or-none transfer says that the effect of transfer should appear in values of t, and as more concept categories are acquired by the subjects, there should be increasing values of t in the transfer conditions.

Figures 5-5 and 5-6 show the estimated values of c and $1 - f$. The behavior of c probably is more critical in judging the all-or-none transfer hypothesis, since values of c correspond to probabilities of learning untransferred items. Values of $1 - f$ are probabilities of holding unlearned items in short-term memory between trials. Thus, $1 - f$ is an indicator of performance prior to learning. As Figure 5-5 shows, there was no indication of any systematic

[1]The method of estimation allows negative values, in case of relatively low proportions of items with zero errors. A more appropriate method would restrict parameters to the (0, 1) interval; this was not done because it involves considerably more complicated calculations, and none of the estimates obtained here were very far negative. (Only one value was less than −.05.)

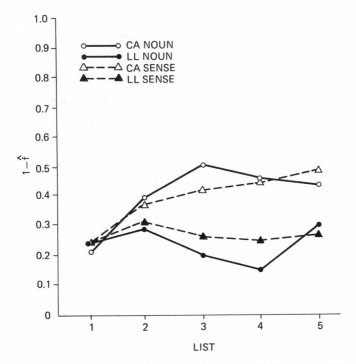

Figure 5-6   Estimated prelearning performance in Polson's (1972) experiment.

difference between conditions in the learning parameters for the various lists. The estimates of c increased across lists, indicating that subjects became more skillful in memorizing items as the experiment proceeded. However, this generalized transfer was just as great in the control conditions as it was in the concept-acquisition conditions. This result corresponds to the finding of Greeno and Scandura: that items in a transfer condition on which the subject did not perform perfectly did not differ from comparable control items.

As Figure 5-6 shows, there was an increased probability of holding unlearned items in short-term memory in the concept-acquisition conditions relative to the control conditions. This means that there was a transfer effect influencing performance prior to learning, in addition to the transfer of association that is measured by the transfer parameter t.

We do not have a satisfactory explanation of this transfer effect on performance before learning. One possibility is that short-term retention is facilitated if the list contains a number of items that have already been learned. If, say, one-half the items were known by a subject on the basis of transfer, then that subject would have a list containing only four unlearned items. A comparable subject with a control list would have eight unlearned items at the beginning. It is reasonable to suppose that presentation for study and test of a learned item produces less interference with short-term retention than does presentation of an unlearned item, and Calfee and Atkinson (1965) have used this idea in analyzing effects of list length on learning parameters. On the other hand, this argument would lead to a prediction about mixed lists that was not confirmed in results obtained by Polson (1967) In a mixed list, some transfer and some control items are included in the san.e list, as was the case in Greeno and Scandura's (1966) experiment. Polson (1967) included mixed-list conditions in his original study, and obtained a similar difference in values of $1 - f$ between transfer and control items to the one shown in Figure 5-6.

Of course, an alternative explanation of the transfer effect is that it indicates a transfer of associative strength. We think it does not, because we have not been able to think of a way in which transferred associative strength could produce a decrease in f without at the same time producing an increase in c.

We conclude that the hypothesis of all-or-none transfer was supported reasonably well in Polson's (1972) results. The outcome is not as clearly supportive as was Greeno and Scandura's (1966), in that Polson's data showed a transfer effect on performance prior to learning on untransferred items. However, that effect was relatively small—a difference of .20 to .25 in the performance parameter compared to effects of .50 to .80 in the transfer parameter. And the result of measuring the probability of learning for untransferred items was very clear—there was no evidence of any difference between control and transfer items in the learning parameter. While we do not know why the transfer effect on performance occurred, the absence of any effect on the learning parameter seems a more cogent datum, and we conclude that the idea of all-or-none transfer represents the best available general conclusion to be taken from available results.

Theory of Acquisition

The theoretical analysis of the transfer parameter t given by Greeno and Scandura (1966) was tried also by Polson. The result was close, but differed from the data in an important way. We present the simple theory here, for the successful analysis carried out is a generalization of it. Recall that in the simple hypothesis, there is a probability a that the concept-category is acquired when any single item is learned. It is further assumed that when a new member of the category is presented, there is a probability b that the relationship is recognized and thus transfer occurs. Polson added the assumption that if a transfer item is not recognized, the concept will be reacquired with probability a when the item is learned.

There was only one member of each concept-category in each list. The question is whether the theory can give an account of the value of t in each list. Let t_i be the value of t in the ith list. The assumptions given above imply the following:

According to this theory, each item in a list has four states: State U, where the item is not known at all; State S, where the item is in short-term memory; State L, where the response for the item has been learned, but where the concept-category is not known; and State A, where the concept-category has been acquired. At the beginning of the ith list, an item is in State A with probability t_i, otherwise it is in State U. The probabilities of transition among the states are

$$
P = \begin{array}{c|cccc}
 & A & L & S & U \\
\hline
A & 1 & 0 & 0 & 0 \\
L & 0 & 1 & 0 & 0 \\
S & ca & c(1-a) & (1-c)(1-f) & (1-c)f \\
U & ca & c(1-a) & (1-c)(1-f) & (1-c)f
\end{array}
\tag{5-5}
$$

Each list was presented until the subject learned all the items; thus, each item is absorbed either in State A or State L at the end of each list. The probability of absorbing in State A at the end of the ith list is

$$P(A_i) = t_i + (1 - t_i)a.$$

Recall that the probability of transfer is the probability of knowing the concept, times b, the probability of recognizing a new example. That is,

$$t_{i+1} = P(A_i)b = [t_i + (1 - t_i)a]b = ab + t_i(1 - a)b. \tag{5-6}$$

The initial value of t, t_1, is zero, since the subject cannot transfer until at least one chance has been given to acquire the concept. For List 2, the probability of transfer is $t_2 = ab$, and in general,

$$t_i = \frac{ab}{1 - (1-a)b}[1 - (b - ab)^{i-1}] \qquad i \geq 2. \tag{5-7}$$

Equation 5-7 can be proved by induction using the recursion given in 5-6.

The parameters of Equation 5-7 were estimated and used to predict the proportions of items with zero errors using Equation 5-2. Estimates for the superordinate concepts were $\hat{a} = .488$, $\hat{b} = .935$; for the sense-impression concepts, $\hat{a} = .343$, $\hat{b} = .632$. The values of t_i obtained when these parameters were used to predict the proportions of items with zero errors, using

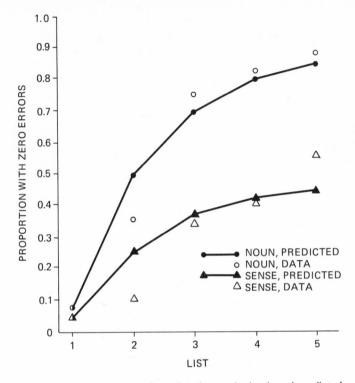

Figure 5-7 Proportions of errorless items obtained, and predicted using equation (5.4).

Equation 5-2 are shown in Figure 5-7, and the apparent sizable discrepancies were significant. The statistical test used each subject's sequences of items across lists as the data—for each concept every subject gave a sequence in which each item either had errors or was performed without error. Thus, each concept from each subject gave a four-tuple, having as entries zeros and ones. For example, the four-tuple 0100 would mean that no errors occurred for the examples of a concept in Lists 2, 4, and 5, but one or more errors occurred for the example of the concept in List 3. The parameter estimates were obtained to minimize the chi-square statistic comparing predicted frequencies of these four-tuples with the data. The results showed that the null hypotheses had to be rejected; for superordinate concepts $\chi^2(13) = 45.01$, $p < .01$, and for sense-impression concepts, $\chi^2(13) = 45.43$, $p < .01$. (Details of this analysis are in Polson, 1967.)

The way in which the data departed from the theory in Figure 5-7 is helpful in developing an alternative analysis. The theory predicts a negatively accelerated function, and the data for List 2 have too small proportions of items with zero errors. This is the kind of discrepancy that would occur if the process of acquiring concepts had two stages, and Polson developed a two-stage model that agreed with the results satisfactorily. In the two-stage model, subjects are assumed to begin in a state where they do not know what kind of relationships to look for in the materials. In this state of uncertainty about the kind of groupings to look for, the probability of acquiring a concept is relatively low. However, when transfer occurs for a concept, the subject is assumed to transit to a state in which she or he knows the general kind of relationship that is involved in the groupings, and the probability of acquiring concepts increases.

Polson's theory is conceptually straightforward, but it involves a considerable technical development, involving analysis of the state of a subject, as well as the states of the individual items being studied. The subject has two states S_0 and S_1, and each item has States A, L, S, and U, as before. When the subject is in State S_0, the transitions among states for an item have probabilities given in Equation 5-5, with $a = a_0$. When the subject transits to S_1, the transition probabilities for items change, being the probabilities in Equation 5-5 but with $a = a_1$.

As Polson formulated the theory, a subject would not stay in State S_0 unless no concept categories were known. This implies that the following states are sufficient to characterize subjects:

$$S_0, S_{1,0}, S_{1,1}, \ldots, S_{1,M},$$

where $S_{1,m}$ means that the subject is in State S_1 and transfer occurs on m of the items, and M is the total number of concept-categories. Let $q_{r,N,p}$ be the binomial probability of r events in N independent trials, where the probability of the event is p; that is,

$$q_{r,N,p} = \binom{N}{r} p^r (1 - p)^{N-r}.$$

The list-to-list transition probabilities are p_{jk}, the probability of state k on List $i + 1$ given state j on List i.

$$
p_{jk} = \begin{cases}
(1 - a_0 b)^M & j = k = S_0 \\
0 & j = S_0, k = S_{1,0} \\
\sum_{h=1}^{M-k+1} (1 - a_0 b)^{h-1} a_0 b q_{k-1, M-h, a_1 b} & j = S_0, k = S_{1,1}, \ldots, S_{1,M} \\
0 & j = S_{1,0}, \ldots, S_{1,M}, k = S_0 \\
\sum_{h=\max(0, j-k)}^{\min(j, M-k)} q_{k-j+h, M-j, a_1 b} q_{h, j, 1-b} & j, k = S_{1,0}, \ldots, S_{1,M}.
\end{cases}
$$

$$(5\text{-}8)$$

Since Polson's theory considers the subject as a unit of analysis, it leads to strong and interesting predictions about the performance given by a subject, rather than just about individual items. Polson's test of the idea was based on analysis of the random variable X_i, the number of items for a subject in the ith list that had no errors. Let z_i be defined as

$$z_i = \frac{gc_i}{1 - (1 - c_i)(1 - f_i + f_i c_i)},$$

the probability of zero errors for an item that did not transfer. (Recall that the parameters c and f were not constant across lists.) Define $P_i(S_0)$ and $P_i(S_{1,m})$ as the probability of state S_0 or $S_{1,m}$ on the ith list. Then the probability distribution of the variable X_i is

$$P(X_i = x) = P_i(S_0)q_{x,M,z_i} + \sum_{h=0}^{x} P_i(S_{1,h})q_{x-h,M-h,z_i}. \qquad (5-9)$$

Polson obtained maximum-likelihood estimates of the parameters of the model, using as data the empirical distributions of X_i, $i = 2, \ldots, 5$. The possibility of starting in state $S_{1,0}$ was allowed in the analysis, but the estimated probability of this event was zero. Thus, the parameters of the model of acquiring the concepts are a_0, a_1, and b. The estimated values were

Superordinate: $\hat{a}_0 = .127$, $\hat{a}_1 = .779$, $\hat{b} = .950$;

Sense-Impression: $\hat{a}_0 = .067$, $\hat{a}_1 = .555$, $\hat{b} = .751$.

The cumulative distributions of X_i obtained with these parameters are given in Figure 5-8 for the superordinate concepts, and in Figure 5-9 for the sense-impression concepts. The agreement of the data with the model was satisfactory in all cases.

Figure 5-10 shows the theoretical and empirical proportions of items with zero errors, with the theoretical values obtained from the two-stage theory. The comparable function from the single-stage theory of concept acquisition is in Figure 5-7. Note that the two-stage theory has successfully accounted for the relatively low proportions of errorless items on List 2.

BATCHELDER'S ANALYSIS OF INTRALIST TRANSFER

The analyses given by Greeno and Scandura (1966) and by Polson (1972) apply to transfer from associations that have been learned previously and that are not presented during the transfer task. A more complicated situation was studied by Batchelder (1970, 1971), who considered learning tasks that include pairs of items, each consisting of an association with the same response and with similar stimuli. When the subject learns one of the associations, performance or learning of the other association may be facilitated.

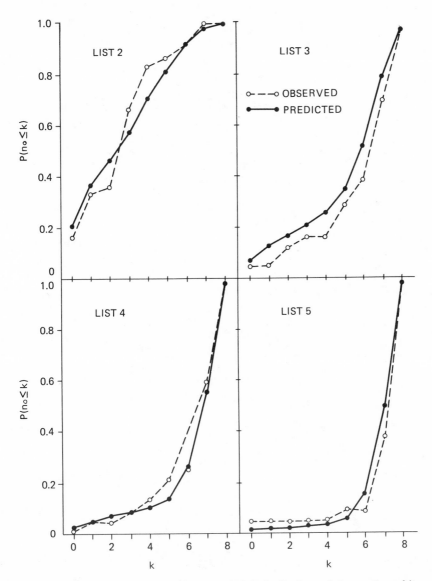

Figure 5-8 Observed and predicted cumulative distributions of the number of items with zero errors (n_0) on list i $(X_i, i = 2,3,4,5)$ for the noun concepts in Polson's (1972) experiment.

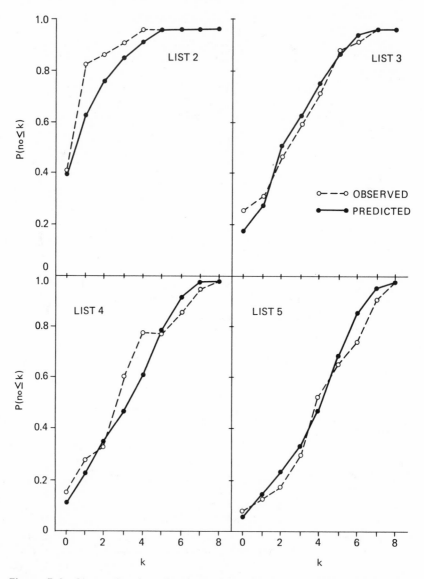

Figure 5-9 Observed and predicted cumulative distributions of the number of items with zero errors (n_0) on list i (X_i, i = 2,3,4,5) for the sense concepts in Polson's (1972) experiment.

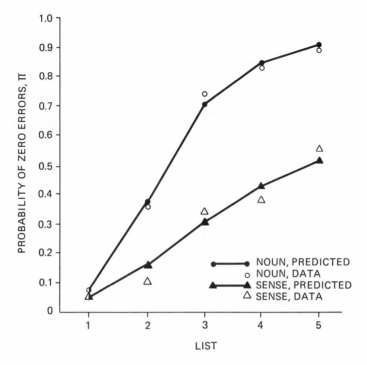

Figure 5-10   Proportions of errorless items obtained, and predicted by the two-stage theory.

Batchelder considered two assumptions about the interaction between learning of two related items. One model uses the assumption that interaction between the items depends on the subject's acquiring a rule involving use of a property or properties shared by the stimuli. This rule-acquisition model uses the same idea as was used by Greeno and Scandura and by Polson in accounting for transfer. The other model Batchelder considered is based on ideas developed in stimulus sampling theory (Atkinson & Estes, 1963). Because it assumes a mixture of processes involving association to stimulus patterns and transfer based on components of stimuli, it is called the mixed model. According to this model, learning of one item does not affect learning of the other item; however, when one of the items is learned there is an increased probability of the correct response on tests of the other item.

A strong feature of Batchelder's analysis was use of the pair of related items as the unit of analysis. Each state of the system specifies the condition of a pair of items; thus, the states are U, U; U, L; L, U; L, L; and A; U denotes an unlearned item, L denotes an item that has been learned, and A denotes the state where the subject has acquired a rule relating the two items. A change in state can occur when either of the two items is presented. Thus, the learning theory is specified as a pair of operators, one giving the transition probabilities when the first item is presented, the other giving transition probabilities when the other item is presented. According to the rule-learning theory, the transition probabilities are

$$
P_1 = \begin{array}{c} \\ A \\ L,L \\ U,L \\ L,U \\ U,U \end{array}
\begin{array}{c|ccccc}
& A & L,L & U,L & L,U & U,U \\
\hline
& 1 & 0 & 0 & 0 & 0 \\
& a_2 & 1-a_2 & 0 & 0 & 0 \\
& ca_1 & c(1-a_1) & 1-c & 0 & 0 \\
& a_2 & 0 & 0 & 1-a_2 & 0 \\
& ca_1 & 0 & 0 & c(1-a_1) & 1-c
\end{array}
$$

$$
P_2 = \begin{array}{c} \\ A \\ L,L \\ U,L \\ L,U \\ U,U \end{array}
\begin{array}{c|ccccc}
& A & L,L & U,L & L,U & U,U \\
\hline
& 1 & 0 & 0 & 0 & 0 \\
& a_2 & 1-a_2 & 0 & 0 & 0 \\
& a_2 & 0 & 1-a_2 & 0 & 0 \\
& ca_1 & c(1-a_1) & 0 & 1-c & 0 \\
& ca_1 & 0 & c(1-a_1) & 0 & 1-c \ .
\end{array}
$$

(5-10)

It is assumed that on a test, if an item is in State U, the subject will guess, and be correct with probability g. If an item is in State L, the subject will give the correct response on a test. And if the pair of items is in State A, the subject gives the correct response to either item.

The pattern-components mixed model has the transition operators

$$
P_1 = \begin{array}{c} \\ L,L \\ U,L \\ L,U \\ U,U \end{array}
\begin{array}{c|cccc}
& L,L & U,L & L,U & U,U \\
\hline
& 1 & 0 & 0 & 0 \\
& c & 1-c & 0 & 0 \\
& 0 & 0 & 1 & 0 \\
& 0 & 0 & c & 1-c
\end{array}
$$

$$
P_2 = \begin{array}{c} \\ L,L \\ U,L \\ L,U \\ U,U \end{array}
\begin{array}{c|cccc}
& L,L & U,L & L,U & U,U \\
\hline
& 1 & 0 & 0 & 0 \\
& 0 & 1 & 0 & 0 \\
& c & 0 & 1-c & 0 \\
& 0 & c & 0 & 1-c \ .
\end{array}
$$

(5-11)

In this model, if the pair is in State U, U, the subject guesses on either item that is tested. If the pair is in State U, L or L, U, the subject will be correct on a test of the item in State L, and on the item in State U the probability of correct responding is $b + (1 - b)g$, giving the transfer effect on performance.

The two models were used to analyze the results of five experiments. In all the experiments, stimuli were nonsense forms originally constructed by Gibson (1940). Responses were English words on which subjects were given pretraining, and a card showing all the responses was available to the subject throughout the experiment. The lists contained pairs of associations having similar figures as stimuli, associated with the same response. Four of the experiments used the anticipation procedure, with the total list divided into two sublists, each containing one of the two related members of each pair of associations. In each cycle of presentations of the list, all the items in the first sublist were presented, followed by all the members of the second sublist, with the orders of items within sublists randomized on different presentations. The fifth experiment also divided the items into sublists, but gave all the items for study, followed by tests on all the items, then another study cycle, and so on.

The results of the experiments are given in Tables 5-3 and 5-4. Estimated values of c varied from .22 to .46 in the five experiments. The values of b for the mixed model ranged from .63 to .81. Values of a_1 in the rule-learning model were estimated between .53 and .77. Batchelder found that the assump-

Table 5-3 Predicted and Observed Values of the Mean and Variance of the Total Error Distributions

Experi-		x_1		x_2		z	
ment		$E(T)$	$V(T)$	$E(T)$	$V(T)$	$E(T)$	$V(T)$
I	Mixed	—	.74	—	.79	.33	.31
	Rule	—	.77	—	.75	.35	.32
	Data	.97	.77	.72	.75	.38	.33
II	Mixed	—	1.47	—	1.66	.66	.70
	Rule	—	1.72	—	1.75	.71	.74
	Data	1.51	1.79	1.24	1.96	.73	.90
III	Mixed	—	.91	—	.98	.53	.54
	Rule	—	.97	—	1.09	.54	.54
	Data	1.22	1.09	.86	.98	.58	.70
IV	Mixed	—	3.41	—	3.26	1.08	1.65
	Rule	—	2.27	—	3.30	1.08	1.65
	Data	2.09	2.34	1.63	1.96	1.05	1.17
V	Mixed	—	.77	.52	.77	—	.40
	Rule	—	.81	.52	.81	—	.40
	Data	.52	.66	.52	.70	.30	.38

Source: From Batchelder, 1971

Table 5-4 Predicted and Observed Values of the Mean and Variance of the Last Error Trial Distribution

Experi-ment		x_1		x_2		z	
		$E(L)$	$V(L)$	$E(L)$	$V(L)$	$E(L)$	$V(L)$
I	Mixed	1.26	1.88	1.03	1.98	.41	.58
	Rule	1.16	1.34	.87	1.26	.43	.58
	Data	1.15	1.29	.87	1.25	.44	.53
II	Mixed	2.02	4.12	1.81	4.40	.84	1.37
	Rule	1.82	2.80	1.49	2.79	.92	1.49
	Data	1.80	3.16	1.56	3.59	.85	1.30
III	Mixed	1.52	2.20	1.18	2.39	.63	.94
	Rule	1.41	1.47	.97	1.43	.66	.96
	Data	1.41	1.79	1.00	1.55	.67	1.05
IV	Mixed	3.35	5.68	3.08	7.52	1.55	3.97
	Rule	2.51	5.43	2.08	5.39	1.55	3.97
	Data	2.57	5.80	2.04	3.11	1.50	1.86
V	Mixed	.75	1.86	.75	1.86	.35	.61
	Rule	.58	1.07	.58	1.07	.35	.61
	Data	.63	1.20	.63	1.04	.35	.44

Source: From Batchelder, 1971

tion $a_2 = ca_1$ gave a satisfactory fit to the data, and did not use the data for estimation of an additional parameter. In the tables, x_1 refers to the data from the first members of the related pairs, x_2 refers to the data from the second members, and z refers to sequences of double errors—that is, z is a random variable with the value 1 if both members of a pair were given incorrectly, and 0 if either or both answers were correct. The missing predictions for total errors are cases where the empirical values were used in estimating parameters, guaranteeing that the theories would agree with the data exactly for those cases.

One point of major interest involves the success of both models in accounting for the performance on pairs, as measured in the distributions of double errors. The substantive target of the analysis is an understanding of relationships in the learning of pairs having similar stimuli, and these are reflected in correlations of performance such as those involved when double errors are counted. It happens that the two models are indistinguishable regarding these data, and both models appear to have fit the observed distributions quite well.

The main distinguishing characteristic of the models appears to be in the predicted variances of distributions of trial of last error on single items. The theoretical variance of that statistic is less according to the model hypothesizing rule learning than it is according to the mixed model of association to patterns and transfer to components; the data appear to favor the model of rule learning. However, the overall picture shows fairly good agreement with the data for the predictions of both models.

SUMMARY AND CONCLUSION

We have considerable skepticism regarding the success of associationism in explaining the acquisition of abstract ideas. It appears that associationist analyses have explained only identification of concepts that were known previously. Thus, emergence of an abstract category seems to require prior knowledge of the property or relation used to identify members of the category, and induction of a relational pattern requires prior knowledge of the relations and general structural features of the pattern.

Apart from these general difficulties, our results raise serious doubts about the validity of associationist explanations of phenomena that occur in the specific kinds of transfer experiments that have been designed to illustrate associative mechanisms in concept formation. We have described three investigations involving positive transfer of association. All of these have been based on the idea that learning and transfer involve discrete events in a subject's state of knowledge: transfer in these analyses consists simply of an item's being known because another item had been learned and the two items could be grouped according to some shared property or meaning. The results do not constitute a hard refutation of associationist ideas; concepts of a threshold and of variability in initial response strength undoubtedly could be developed to make association theory compatible with these findings, just as they were in the case of all-or-none results regarding memorizing of individual items (Restle, 1965). On the other hand, these analyses treating transfer as an all-or-none event based on success in finding relational properties fit naturally in the cognitive framework, and thus support the plausibility of that view.

An important technical feature of these analyses is the development of methods for analyzing learning that occurs at more than one level and for measuring the parameters of that learning. The general problem of analyzing the acquisition of knowledge surely involves investigation and analysis of complex structures, including structures of rules and individual associations as well as more intricate relational patterns. The successful application of rigorous analytical methods to systems involving as many as three levels of learning, as in Polson's (1972) analysis, argues well for the continued development of methods for testing definite and productive hypotheses about significant learning processes.

chapter 6

Negative Transfer

Suppose a subject has learned a list of associations—denote the list A–B. Now a new list is presented; stimuli and responses may be all new items (C–D), or stimuli may be the same and the responses new (A–C), or new stimuli may be paired with the old responses (C–B), or the old stimuli and responses may be used, with the B terms rearranged to create new pairings (A–B$_r$). A–C is a harder transfer list than C–D. The relative difficulty of C–B and A–B$_r$ to C–D depends on the kind of responses used. If responses are hard (for example, nonsense syllables), then it is an obvious advantage to be able to use the same responses in the transfer list as in the initial training list. But A–B$_r$ is always harder to learn than C–B.

COGNITIVE THEORY OF NEGATIVE TRANSFER

These main facts about negative transfer can be interpreted in terms of the cognitive theory of association developed in Chapter 2 and specified further in Chapter 4. Recall that in this theory, the process of learning a new association can be divided into two main component stages: storing a representation of the pair of elements to be associated, and learning to retrieve the pair reliably when the stimulus is presented on a test. Negative transfer could be expected in either of these stages.

Consider the process of storing representations of the pairs to be learned in the transfer list. First, note that when responses are not meaningful for the subjects, if responses from the first list are also used in the second list, there should be an advantage in the first stage of transfer learning. The reason for this was mentioned in Chapter 4, where a cognitive theory of response learning was sketched. That is, storage of a stimulus-response pair will be harder if the response must be stored as a string than it will be if the response can be stored as a single element, because it is easier to build a new associative structure with a unitary response than it is to build a new associative structure with a response that must be integrated. Therefore, when nonsense syllables are used as responses, there should be an advantage in the first stage of transfer learning for C–B and A–B$_r$ conditions, relative to C–D and A–C, respectively.

The negative transfer that can occur in the first stage of transfer is due to the presence of the same stimuli as were used in List 1. Recall that the stored representation is a structure involving a relation between the stimulus and response, suggesting a bias toward encoding features of the stimulus that are relevant to a relationship with the response. Evidence of such bias has been obtained in experiments (Ellis & Shumate, 1973; Voss, 1972; Weaver, 1969). In A–C or A–B$_r$ transfer, the stimulus term in each transfer pair has previously been encoded as part of a different association. This means that the stimulus term has features represented in memory that were selected in the context of storing and retrieving the initial A–B association.

When the subject has to store a representation of the transfer pair, three possibilities may occur. First, the features used to represent the stimulus in the A–B association may fit easily into a relation involving the new response, so that the subject may simply encode the new association representing the stimulus in the same way as it was represented in List 1. Although that event would probably cause some difficulty in retrieval, there is no reason to expect a disadvantage in storage of the association. In fact, the opportunity to use a stimulus representation that had been developed previously might conceivably facilitate storage of new associations in some circumstances.

A second possibility is that the features initially used to represent the stimulus do not fit easily into a relational structure, but the subject ignores the initial representation and recodes the stimulus using new features. It is not obvious that subjects could easily ignore representations developed earlier for stimulus terms unless they had some systematic basis for classifying stimulus components. However, if representations can easily be found involving new stimulus features, then the storage of a representation could occur as easily in A–C or in A–B$_r$ transfer as in the C–D control condition.

The third possibility is that there would be interference in the storage phase of transfer learning. This final case would involve an initial representation of the stimulus that does not easily form a relationship with the second-list response, and a tendency by the subject to use the initial stimulus representation in storing the new association. We have called a tendency for subjects to continue using old representations, *persistence in encoding* (Greeno, James, &

DaPolito, 1971). There is some experimental evidence that subjects often persisit with initial stimulus representations, even when this causes increased difficulty in learning List 2 and retaining List 1. (See Martin, 1972, for a thorough discussion and review of experimental findings.) If the subject encodes the stimulus in List 2 in the same way as in List 1, but that encoding was biased toward providing a relation with the List-1 response, then it is reasonable to expect encoding of pairs in List 2 to be more difficult.

In an earlier form of this theory (Greeno, James, & DaPolito, 1971), we speculated that the effect of persistent encoding would be symmetrical, retarding storage when either the response or the stimulus was carried from initial training to a transfer list. The data that supported that assumption were rather scant; data to be presented below make it much more likely that effects of response encoding are located entirely in the second stage of transfer learning. In retrospect, the hypothesis of symmetrical effect of persistent encoding seems weak on theoretical grounds as well. The encoding of the stimulus can be partial and still be used to retrieve the association. The encoding of the response must be complete to allow performance of the response. It seems that possible encodings of the stimulus are more variable than the possible encodings of the response, and that stimulus encoding must be more sensitive to influence by the nature of the response than vice versa. For these reasons, in addition to the data we will present later, we now suppose that negative transfer in the first stage of learning will be due to use of stimuli from the first list. Use of responses from the first list should have a facilitating effect on second-list learning when responses are not meaningful and must be integrated by the subject.

In the second stage, prior learning that involves the same stimuli used in transfer may either facilitate or interfere with second-list learning. We assume that the learning that occurs in the second stage has two major aspects. One involves noticing distinguishing features of individual stimuli; the other involves noticing features of the pairs that provide organization, including relations that produce groupings. We expect that differentiation of stimuli will generally be facilitated by prior use of the stimuli in the first list. We agree with Battig's (1966) proposition that the more similarity among stimuli in the first list, the more likely subjects are to have acquired strong distinctive representations to use in the second list. (There is a considerable literature concerning the effects of stimulus pretraining on overall difficulty of associative learning; see Ellis, 1968, for a discussion. The effect of predifferentiation depends on what the subject is required to do in the pretraining task—facilitation apparently is more likely if the pretraining task requires the subject to attend to distinctive features of the stimuli, see Ellis & Muller, 1964.)

We suppose that the organizational aspect of learning to retrieve will usually be more difficult if the stimuli have been used before. Groupings of stimuli that are helpful in retrieving the responses of one set of pairs may be quite unhelpful in retrieving pairs after the responses have been changed. Of course, it should be possible to arrange pairings that would make use of the same groupings; an example might be a first list with the responses A, B, C, D, E, F, and G and a second list with the responses 1, 2, 3, 4, 5, 6, and 7 assigned to the stimuli in the same order. However, in the conditions generally used in transfer experiments we suppose organization acquired in the first list usually makes it harder to acquire an efficient retrieval system for the second list.

Now consider effects in Stage 2 produced by having the same responses that were used in the first list. The contrast is between A–C, where new responses are used, and A–B$_r$, where the List-1 responses are re-paired with the List-1 stimuli. We should expect that interference during Stage 2 should be strongest in the A–B$_r$ situation. For each item, a new stimulus-response unit has been formed that must be fit into the retrieval system. If different features of the stimulus are involved in the second encoding from the first one, and if the new features overlap with those used to encode other items, then some rearrangement will be needed for successful retrieval of List-2 items. In addition, relationships between different responses used in A–B$_r$ may have induced some groupings of items in List 1 that interfere with retrieval in the A–B$_r$ list. Two similar responses might be paired with stimuli having some shared feature, and this feature would most likely be included in the retrieval network for the items. But the responses assigned to those similar stimuli after re-pairing might be quite dissimilar, and the interpair grouping that was useful in List 1 could lead to confusion in organizing List 2.

By comparison, the situation in A–C could be relatively less difficult in the second stage. The subject has two alternative strategies available for building a new retrieval system, and both of them should be easier to carry out if new responses are used. One strategy for the subject is simply to set aside the retrieval system used in List 1 more or less intact. This would seem especially likely in a situation involving compound stimuli with easily classified components—for example, colors and words. Subjects could choose one kind of component in List 1 and shift to the other in List 2. This would make the task of building a new retrieval system essentially independent of the existence of the network acquired for List 1.

A second strategy available for acquiring a retrieval network for List 2 is to keep the List-1 network active, modifying it as needed to allow retrieval of the items in List 2. Subjects could incorporate new features not used in retrieval for List 1, or could modify the structure so that new items would be retrieved on the basis of the same feature tests.

The hypothesis that subjects set aside the List-1 retrieval system in A–C learning is similar to Postman's (1963a) and Underwood and Schulz' (1960) idea of response-set selection, mentioned in Chapter 4. Conceptually, the ideas differ because the hypothesis of a new retrieval system involves a recoding of the stimuli, while response-set selection involves only the availability of responses. However, both ideas would explain less severe negative transfer in A–C on the basis of greater independence between List 1 and List 2. In our earlier theorizing (Greeno, James, & DaPolito, 1971), we proposed the hypothesis of an independent retrieval system to explain the empirical finding of less negative transfer in A–C than in A–B$_r$ in the second stage. An independent retrieval system would be easier to construct in A–C because a new set of responses are involved.

Further thought has led us to believe that it is probably much more common for subjects to adopt the second strategy for dealing with the transfer list—that is, we now believe that subjects generally keep the first-list retrieval system active and modify it to retrieve the List-2 items. For one thing, use of the second strategy conforms to the principle of persistent encoding, which is necessary in our framework for explaining negative transfer in the first stage of List-2 learning. Another consideration is empirical; Goggin and Martin (1970) and Schneider and Houston (1969) obtained evidence that subjects usually used the same components of stimuli to encode items in List 2 as they had in List 1.

If subjects modify their first-list retrieval system, rather than set it aside, what implications are there regarding the relative difficulty of A–C and A–B$_r$ transfer in the second stage? The principle of persistent encoding implies that subjects will use as much of the first-list retrieval network as they can. In A–C transfer with new responses, it might be possible to use most or all of the same stimulus features in retrieving the second-list items as were used in the first list. However, this would require fitting the second-list items into relational units involving the same stimulus features as were used initially, and this Procrustean difficulty would produce some interference, primarily in Stage 1 learning. On the other hand, to the extent that the retrieval network from List 1 could be preserved, negative transfer in the second stage of learning would be decreased. We assume that the use of first-list responses in List 2 for A–B$_r$ causes modification of the retrieval network at relatively higher nodes, involving a greater change in the features used in retrieving List-2 items. First, the features used to encode each first-list item support retrieval of the first-list response *rather than* the other responses, including the one paired with the stimulus in List 2. It would not be surprising if it were more difficult to maintain retrieval using most of the same features when the initial response is still in the list and when the new response is one that had to be avoided in the initial situation. Second, whatever groupings of stimulus-response pairs may have developed because of stimulus similarities that in List 1 were paired with responses that share features would probably produce confusions in List 2 after the items are re-paired; therefore the retrieval network would probably be modified so as to avoid use of those stimulus features. We would expect the modification of a retrieval network during A–B$_r$ learning to involve a relatively greater number of features at relatively high levels in the network, and would expect a tendency in A–C learning to modify the network at lower levels, closer to the representations of the individual pairs. The changes required to support retention of A–B$_r$ would be expected to create more difficulty in second stage learning, since they involve more extensive recoding of stimuli including greater change in the organization of the list than would be produced by relatively lower-level changes that we suppose are typical in A–C learning.

ASSOCIATIONIST THEORY OF NEGATIVE TRANSFER

In the associationist theory, negative transfer is explained by interference with new learning caused by existing associations. When A and B terms have been associated in the first list, it is assumed that three kinds of connections have been formed. First, there are forward associations, from A to B. Second, there are backward associations, from B to A, although it is expected that these are ordinarily weaker than the forward associations. And finally, there are contextual associations, from the general stimulus situations to the B responses. In addition to these associations, the subject has acquired a stable encoding of the A stimulus and has integrated the B response.

The application of these ideas to analysis of transfer was given by Martin (1965). When responses in the two lists are the same, the process of response integration need not be carried out in learning the second list, and contextual associations that result in response pool formation will already be in place. Thus, in C–B and A–B$_r$ the occurrence of the first-list responses gives a source of positive transfer, and this factor has more importance if responses are difficult. On the other hand, backward associations learned in the A–B task provide a source of negative transfer in C–B and A–B$_r$. Whether there is negative or positive transfer in C–B and A–B$_r$ compared to C–D depends on the relative importance of response learning and backward associations. When meaningful responses are used, it is reasonable to expect that backward associations could be more important, and produce negative transfer.

When stimuli from the first list are present in transfer in A–C and A–B$_r$, forward associations from the first list will interfere with second-list learning. There are possible facilitating effects as well. Battig (1966) has suggested that when there is strong interference within the initial learning task, retention and transfer may be enhanced. One possible mechanism consistent with Battig's hypothesis is stimulus differentiation. With very similar stimuli in the first list, the subject will learn to discriminate the stimuli and this learning could be helpful in the A–C and A–B$_r$ transfer tasks.

In a recent discussion, Martin (1972) has given a careful analysis of implications of the hypothesis of stimulus-encoding variability concerning transfer. In a number of his conclusions, Martin has sided with the kind of cognitive theory that this book is presenting. However, Martin also discusses mechanisms that are consistent with the form of encoding variability hypothesized earlier by associationist theorists (see Martin, 1968). Martin has noted that if the subject uses the same encodings of stimuli in A–C and A–B$_r$ as in the initial list, forward associations will be elicited and interfere with second-list learning. But if subjects can encode the stimuli differently for the second list than they did initially then associations in the second list should be relatively easier to form. Martin (1972) reported an experiment conducted by Polzella involving compound stimuli, with a test for backward associations given on both A–B and A–C items following learning of the transfer task. For items in which recalled stimulus components were the same for both the B and the C responses, second-list learning was substantially slower than in the C–D control condition. But for items in which different components of the A stimulus were given when B and C response terms were used as cues, second-list learning occurred just as rapidly as in the C–D control condition.

Martin (1968) also noted that if the stimuli used are relatively easy to recode, negative transfer should be relatively less severe than if encodings of the stimuli are limited. Martin hypothesized that low-meaningful stimuli such as nonsense syllables probably are more variable in their encodings than familiar and meaningful words. This implies that there should be less negative transfer when nonmeaningful stimuli are used in A–B, A–C transfer experiments. Some support of this prediction has been obtained, although the empirical situation is not completely consistent (see Martin, 1972, for more thorough discussion of this).

ASSOCIATIONIST CONCEPTS AND STAGES OF LEARNING

The hypothesis that negative transfer is caused by interference between associations does not, in itself, identify the stage of learning in which we might expect negative transfer to be located. On the other hand, it is not clear that the hypothesis in the form stated gives an adequate explanation of negative transfer. Nor is it clear why the mere presence of associations from earlier learning should make new learning more difficult. Some more specific assumptions are needed to explain how interfering associations have an interfering effect.

Perhaps the simplest assumption would be to use the idea common in stimulus-response behaviorism that the response with the strongest associative connection to a stimulus is the one that will be given by the subject. It is not assumed that a stimulus is connected to only one response, but rather that there is a habit-family hierarchy (Hull, 1952) based on differing response strength, and the strongest response is the one that occurs. If this assumption is made in the associative theory, then the cause of negative transfer is clear; because of previous learning, the correct response starts lower in the habit-family hierarchy for its stimulus than it would without the previous learning. Without the initial learning, association to the correct response has to be strengthened until it exceeds the strength of other associations that the subject happened to have for the stimulus when the experiment began. The complete process involves increasing the strength of the correct association and decreasing the strength of other associations whose responses occur but are not reinforced. If there has been previous training for a response that is not now correct, then the old response starts with much higher associative strength than the correct association. During practice, the old association will be weakened, as will any other incorrect associations that manage to recover strength or that happen to arise in the new context. And the new correct association will, of course, be gaining in strength as a result of the pairings provided in the experiment. Eventually, the new correct association will rise to the top of the habit-family hierarchy where it will dominate performance, as it must for the subject to achieve the experimenter's criterion of correct performance. (We have discussed only the interfering effects of forward associations that occur in A–C and A–B$_r$ transfer. A similar story could be developed regarding backward and contextual associations, although it would be somewhat more complicated for backward associations because their influence on forward stimulus-response performance must be indirect.)

According to the hypothesis of learning as acquiring the greatest strength for the correct response, the process of weakening the initial A–B associations will occur mainly during the early stages of second-list learning in A–C and A–B$_r$, since at these stages the first-list associations are still stronger. It would not be necessary or even very natural to assume that weakening of the A–B association must occur before the A–C or A–B$_r$ association could start to be strengthened. On the other hand, some trials would occur in which A–B had sufficiently greater strength than the new association so that the correct response would have virtually zero probability of occurrence. Only when the new association was strengthened and the old association weakened to the point where their strengths were in the same neighborhood would the new correct response be expected to have substantial nonzero probability. (Response strengths are assumed to vary; thus, the term, the same neighborhood, refers to a situation in which the distributions of strength for the two associations have a substantial amount of overlap. In this case, the correct response would be stronger on some trials; the old response, stronger on other trials; as a result the probability of correct response would be greater than zero, but less than one.)

It seems to us that this theory quite clearly implies that the major observable effect of negative transfer should be a delay of the acquisition of nonzero probability of the correct response.[1] Once the correct association has achieved a strength in the same neighborhood as the association from the first list, the situation would seem comparable to the one that occurs when any association is being learned. The statistical methods derived from the two-stage Markov model enable us to estimate the mean number of trials occurring before the probability of correct response changes from zero to some intermediate value, p, as well as the mean number of trials between that transition and the time when the probability of correct response becomes approximately 1.0. We derive the expectation from the theory of associative strength that the major effect of negative transfer should occur in the first of these stages, and little or no effect of negative transfer should be found in the measurements of trials needed to complete learning once the probability of correct response has become nonzero.

While the theory of learning as acquiring the strongest associative strength provides one clear explanation for negative transfer, other mechanisms could possibly operate to produce the effect. If the first-list associations were recalled on some trials, these reminiscences would take time that would otherwise be available for study of the new associations. This could reduce the rate at which the new associations gained strength over trials. (This hypothesis was suggested by Anderson & Bower, 1973.) A related hypothesis is that the mind is limited in the total amount of change in associative strength that will occur in a small amount of time. On this hypothesis, reductions as well as increases in response strength use some of the limited capacity for modification. In conditions where either individual associations or whole sets of responses are found to be erroneous, the subject would be learning to inhibit these errors and would have less capacity for modification to increase the strength of the new associations.

All of the mechanisms that we have been able to think of for producing negative transfer based on interference between associations imply that the interfering effect of strong associations will be greater, at least on the average, than the interfering effect of weak associations. If negative transfer occurs because of recall of the first responses, then such recall is more probable when

---

[1] In earlier discussion we have given a simpler and, we now see, inadequate version of associationist theory in which the first stage involves "unlearning of the first associations clearing the way for the learning of new pairings," and the second stage, "replacement of [the old associations] by the new pairings" (Greeno, James, & DaPolito, 1971). Postman and Underwood (1973) have correctly pointed out that no such simple notion of breaking off the A–B and replacing it with A–C was ever assumed by proponents of associationist theory. We hope that the present discussion gives a fairer picture of at least one viable form of associationist theory. The assumptions we now attribute to associationist theory have the same implication regarding the locus of negative transfer effects as the simplistic view we addressed earlier. On the other hand, they seem to provide realistic expectations for retention of first-list responses after second-list learning, the possibility of probabilistic multiresponse learning, and maintenance of both A–B and A–C associations under appropriate conditions, such as instructions to use B responses as mediators.

the first responses are strong. If negative transfer occurs because capacity for learning is shared between increasing the strengths of new associations and decreasing the strengths of old ones, then the amount of decrease is greater when the current level of associative strength is high. If negative transfer occurs because the new associations must exceed the strength of old associations before new responses can be performed, then more delay will occur when the old associations start at high strength. Perhaps there is an associative mechanism that can cause negative transfer but that lacks the property of having greater effect when the interfering associations are stronger. As far as we can determine, though, no such mechanism has been proposed, and because we also cannot think of one, we remain convinced that associationist theory predicts that the major effect of negative transfer should occur early in learning, when the associations learned in List 1 are the strongest, and where it would appear as an increase in the mean number of trials needed to raise the probability of correct response above zero.

COMPARISONS OF C–B AND A–B$_r$

We have several experimental comparisons involving the paradigms C–B and A–B$_r$. The advantage of such comparisons is that they should not be complicated by effects of response familiarity, since in both the C–B and the A–B$_r$ conditions the same responses used in the transfer list were learned in initial training.

James and Greeno's Experiments

The first data are from two experiments reported by James and Greeno (1970). The main results of the analysis of stages have been given in brief form earlier (Greeno, 1970; Greeno, James, & DaPolito, 1971). This presentation will give fuller information regarding goodness of fit of the model and other statistical matters.

In the first experiment, each list contained ten pairs of two-syllable adjectives, with two groups (one A–B$_r$ and one C–B group) learning the first list to a criterion of one perfect trial with no overtraining (No OT) and the other two groups learning the first list to the one-trial criterion and then receiving 15 additional trials of overtraining (OT). In the second experiment each list contained six pairs of two-syllable adjectives. There were eight groups in a 2 × 2 × 2 factorial design. One factor was the main variable—the difference between A–B$_r$ and C–B conditions. A second factor was the presence or absence of a series of pretraining lists (PT or No PT) each with the same responses as those used in the last two lists but with different stimuli; each pretraining list was studied for six trials. The third factor was the presence or absence of 18 trials of overtraining on the next-to-last list following a criterion of one perfect trial (OT or No OT). The experiments were both carried out

Table 6-1 Tests of Simplifying Assumptions in James and Greeno's Experiments

Number of Items	Condition	Init. df = 2	e = q, b = d df = 1	Init., e = q df = 3	Init., e = q, b = d df = 4
10	A–B$_r$, No OT	1.3	14.0**	13.2**	18.1**
10	C–B, No OT	.8	.5	3.2	8.8
10	A–B$_r$, OT	.7	8.4**	33.7**	37.7**
10	C–B, OT	2.0	.7	6.2	15.3**
6	A–B$_r$, No PT, No OT	1.7	2.2	2.3	4.9
6	C–B, No PT, No OT	1.1	9.1**	12.0**	13.3**
6	A–B$_r$, No PT, OT	5.5	8.8**	9.6**	11.0*
6	C–B, No PT, OT	.5	.2	3.2	3.8
6	A–B$_r$, PT, No OT	2.4	.2	2.9	19.1**
6	C–B, PT, No OT	.3	2.3	.5	9.7*
6	A–B$_r$, PT, OT	.6	6.5*	7.3	10.6*
6	C–B, PT, OT	5.6	.1	14.8**	18.6**

*denotes $p < .05$; **denotes $p < .01$.

using a memory drum, presenting the items in the anticipation procedure at a 2:2 second rate, with 4-second intervals between cycles of the list. In the first experiment, there were 20 subjects in each group, giving 200 items for analysis; in the second experiment, there were 25 subjects in each group, giving 150 item-sequences per condition.

The statistical methods used for estimating duration of stages were the same as those described in Chapter 4. Recall that the first step involves testing various simplifications of the general model given in Equations 4-1 and 4-2. Results for four tests are given in Table 6-1. The figures given in the table are values of $-2 \log_e \lambda$, which would be asymptotically distributed as χ^2 with degrees of freedom as indicated for the various tests, if the respective hypotheses were true. The hypothesis denoted in the table as Init. is that the parameters on the first trial before the subject gave responses were the same as on later anticipation trials—that is, $t = ab$, $s = 1 - a$, $r = e$. The only restriction that was satisfied consistently was the restriction on the initial vector. Therefore, the model was applied under that restriction in all groups. Even though further restrictions could have been used in some of the groups, tests of parameter invariance were made much simpler by using a single version of the model, allowing a single computer program to be used for tests in all conditions. The model used was therefore the same as that used for Humphreys and Greeno's (1970) analysis, described in Chapter 4. There are six theoretical parameters; a is identifiable, as are four functions of the remaining five parameters.

Goodness of fit was evaluated using the same five distributions of statistics considered in Chapter 4. The results are summarized in Table 6-2, which gives the goodness-of-fit chi-square statistics obtained for each distribution

Table 6-2 Goodness of Fit of the Two-Stage Model to James and Greeno's Data

Number of Items	Condition	Errors before First Correct	Errors after First Correct	Trials after First Correct	Total Errors	Trial of Last Error
10	A–B$_r$, No OT	18.37 (18, 13)	5.89 (9, 7)	10.67 (12, 10)	16.49 (16, 13)	28.99 (18, 13) * **
10	C–B, No OT	18.12 (16, 11)	2.12 (7, 5)	5.65 (9, 7)	18.52 (13, 10) *	20.74 (15, 10) *
10	A–B$_r$, OT	8.64 (18, 13)	5.34 (16, 14)	11.49 (20, 18)	16.94 (23, 20)	30.62 (25, 20)
10	C–B, OT	20.08 (14, 9)	7.47 (7, 5)	13.75 (10, 8)	11.07 (12, 9)	20.21 (15, 10) *
6	A–B$_r$, No PT, No OT	13.68 (13, 8)	12.08 (7, 5) *	7.42 (10, 8)	12.92 (11, 8)	17.52 (14, 9) *
6	C–B, No PT, No OT	7.25 (10, 5)	1.64 (3, 1)	0.65 (5, 3)	11.26 (8, 5) *	3.45 (9, 4)
6	A–B$_r$, No PT, OT	14.30 (14, 9)	4.21 (7, 5)	13.08 (9, 7)	22.83 (12, 9) * **	15.62 (14, 9)
6	C–B, No PT, OT	2.61 (10, 5)	2.17 (4, 2)	3.13 (6, 4)	2.33 (8, 5)	13.74 (9, 4) **
6	A–B$_r$, PT, No OT	3.44 (10, 5)	8.48 (6, 4)	3.94 (8, 6)	5.61 (9, 6)	12.07 (11, 6) *
6	C–B, PT, No OT	3.03 (8, 3)	1.99 (4, 2)	6.36 (5, 3)	3.02 (7, 4)	2.65 (8, 3)
6	A–B$_r$, PT, OT	16.04 (11, 6)	1.45 (7, 5)	7.99 (9, 7)	21.44 (10, 7) * **	12.92 (13, 8)
6	C–B, PT, OT	3.68 (9, 4)	7.44 (4, 2) *	5.11 (5, 3)	11.29 (7, 4) *	9.28 (8, 3) *

*denotes $p < .05$; **denotes $p < .01$.

tested. Recall that the degrees of freedom for these tests are not well defined, but bounds can be specified. The numbers in parentheses below each chi square statistic are the degrees of freedom on the lower and upper bounds of the distribution for that test, under the null hypothesis. We have indicated with asterisks those tests that would involve significant discrepancies.

The twelve experimental conditions gave 60 tests of the model. Three tests indicated rejection at .05 or below for the upper bounds on degrees of freedom, while 15 indicated rejection for the lower bounds. In all except three of the rejections, the empirical distributions had considerably more variance than the theoretical distributions, and in only one case was the empirical distribution substantially less variable. Thus, it is a reasonable possibility that the main cause of discrepancies from the model was inaccuracy of the simplifying assumption that all items and subjects had identical parameters.

The model seems to have fit well enough to permit parameter estimates to be used in estimating the duration of stages of learning, and in testing hypotheses about which stage of learning showed the greater effect of negative transfer. An identifying restriction is needed, and we used $c = 0$ in these analyses. Other restrictions are possible, and $c = d$ and $b = 0$ were tried. However, with $c = d$, solutions for the parameters in three A–B$_r$ groups gave some values not in the $(0, 1)$ interval required for values of probabilities, and with $b = 0$, impossible values were obtained for four C–B groups. The estimates obtained for the five unrestricted parameters are given in Table 6-3.

The quantities of main interest are the mean numbers of trials needed for the two stages of learning. Under the restrictions on the initial vector and the identifying restriction $c = 0$, Equations 4-6 and 4-7 simplify to

$$E(Z_1) = \frac{1}{a},$$

$$E(Z_2) = (1 - b)\left(1 + \frac{1 - ed}{qd}\right). \tag{6-1}$$

The values calculated are in Table 6-4.

Table 6-3 Estimated Values of Parameters

Number of Items	Condition	a	b	d	$1 - e$	p
10	A–B$_r$, No OT	.22	.25	.26	.73	.22
10	C–B, No OT	.25	.52	.30	.64	.36
10	A–B$_r$, OT	.15	.19	.13	1.00	.32
10	C–B, OT	.29	.54	.27	.76	.36
6	A–B$_r$, No PT, No OT	.30	.12	.25	.25	.32
6	C–B, No PT, No OT	.33	.64	.56	1.00	.31
6	A–B$_r$, No PT, OT	.31	.24	.26	.57	.28
6	C–B, No PT, OT	.39	.39	.42	.85	.35
6	A–B$_r$, PT, No OT	.58	.12	.33	.34	.29
6	C–B, PT, No OT	.54	.64	.34	.41	.30
6	A–B$_r$, PT, OT	.34	.30	.33	.66	.34
6	C–B, PT, OT	.40	.75	.36	1.00	.29

Table 6-4 Measurements of Difficulty in the Two Stages of Learning

Number of Items	Condition	$E(Z_1)$	$E(Z_2)$
10	A–B$_r$, No OT	4.54	4.12
10	C–B, No OT	3.94	2.76
10	A–B$_r$, OT	6.49	10.05
10	C–B, OT	3.50	2.95
6	A–B$_r$, No PT, No OT	2.58	5.09
6	C–B, No PT, No OT	2.99	1.28
6	A–B$_r$, No PT, OT	3.19	4.35
6	C–B, No PT, OT	2.58	2.70
6	A–B$_r$, PT, No OT	1.74	3.80
6	C–B, PT, No OT	1.87	1.55
6	A–B$_r$, PT, OT	2.92	3.59
6	C–B, PT, OT	2.48	1.22

Source: From Greeno, 1970

In most of the experimental conditions, the measurements obtained for the difficulty of Stage 1 were nearly equal for corresponding A–B$_r$ and C–B groups. However, in the estimates of difficulty of Stage 2, there were large and consistent differences between A–B$_r$ and C–B groups, with A–B$_r$ taking more trials in every case. These impressions can be checked by testing statistical hypotheses about the invariance of parameters across experimental conditions. Testing the significance of difference in Stage 1 is straightforward. Since $E(Z_1)$ depends only on the value of a, the relevant hypothesis for test is that both C–B and A–B$_r$ had the same value of a. Maximum likelihood estimates were obtained with a single value of a, and with the four remaining identifiable parameters allowed to take different values in the C–B and A–B$_r$ conditions. The resulting maximum likelihood value was compared with the maximum likelihood obtained with differing values of all the parameters from the two conditions, giving a likelihood ratio test with one degree of freedom.

The question about the second stage can be asked in a variety of ways, because of the involvement of several parameters. We chose to ask it in a relatively weak form. Let b_1, c_1, and d_1 be the second-stage learning parameters for a C–B group, and let b_2, c_2, and d_2 be the second-stage learning parameters for the corresponding A–B$_r$ group. The hypothesis tested allowed a to vary between conditions, and the remaining eight identifiable parameters were restricted by requiring $b_1 = b_2$, $c_1 = c_2$, and $d_1 = d_2$. The two second-stage performance parameters e and q were allowed to vary freely. Thus, the null hypothesis could be satisfied by any combination of parameter values for a_1, a_2, e_1, e_2, q_1, q_2, and with constant values of b, c, and d. This means that the test did not require assumptions of equivalent performance in the intermediate stage, nor did the test depend on any identifying restrictions

Table 6-5   Tests of Invariance between A–B$_r$ and C–B

Number of Items	Condition	Stage 1	Stage 2
10	No OT	1.4	20.4**
10	OT	29.8**	59.5**
6	No PT, No OT	1.1	19.7**
6	No PT, OT	1.6	9.4**
6	PT, No OT	.1	16.3**
6	PT, OT	1.9	11.0**

**denotes $p < .01$.
Source: From Greeno, 1970

such as $c = 0$, which we used in computing the parameter estimates in Table 6-3. Since we estimated nine parameters for the null hypothesis, and estimated ten parameters in the alternative hypothesis of differing parameter values in the two conditions, this test also should have one degree of freedom.

Table 6-5 has the results of both tests in the six experimental conditions. The values given are $-2 \log_e \lambda$, which should be asymptotically distributed as $\chi^2(1)$ if the null hypothesis were true. Note that for Stage 1, the null hypothesis was acceptable for all but one of the comparisons. However, the results for Stage 2 indicate that for each of the six comparisons, at least one of the learning parameters b, c, or d had different values in A–B$_r$ and C–B groups. We can apparently conclude that the differences in $E(Z_2)$ shown in Table 6-4 represent reliable differences in the difficulty of completing the second stage of learning, while only in the condition involving ten items and overtraining was there a reliable difference in the difficulty of completing the first stage of learning.

The gist of the results is that negative transfer in A–B$_r$ relative to C–B is due mainly to a process that operates relatively late in acquisition of the transfer list. This is not a definite prediction of the cognitive theory we outlined earlier, since that theory assumes the operation of processes that could produce negative transfer in both the first and the second stage of learning. However, considerable negative transfer is expected in the second stage of A–B$_r$ transfer, since considerable modification of the first-list retrieval system should usually be required. On the other hand, the finding seems a direct contradiction of the implication that we believe to follow from associationist theory; namely, that negative transfer should be greatest in situations where the interfering associations are the strongest.

Effect of Overtraining on A–B

A major purpose of James and Greeno's experiments was to explore the effect of overtraining on the initial list prior to transfer. In both the experiments described earlier, there were additional groups in which the stimuli

Table 6-6 Mean Total Errors per Item in James and Greeno's Overtraining Experiments

Number of Items	Responses	Condition	No Overtraining	Overtraining
10	Adjective	A–B$_r$	6.46	11.77
10	Adjective	C–B	4.56	4.20
10	Numeral	A–B$_r$	4.21	4.31
10	Numeral	C–B	2.60	1.54
6	Adjective	A–B$_r$, No Pretraining	5.21	5.16
6	Adjective	C–B, No Pretraining	2.69	2.63
6	Adjective	A–B$_r$, Pretraining	3.43	4.18
6	Adjective	C–B, Pretraining	1.93	2.19
6	Numeral	A–B$_r$, No Pretraining	3.12	2.75
6	Numeral	C–B, No Pretraining	1.62	1.04
6	Numeral	A–B$_r$, Pretraining	2.34	2.15
6	Numeral	C–B, Pretraining	1.16	1.26
8	Adjective (Numeral Stimuli)	A–B$_r$	5.31	4.22

were paired with numeral responses. Table 6-6 shows the mean number of errors in the transfer list for all the groups in both experiments, plus an additional A–B$_r$ condition run with an eight-item list with the stimuli being numerals 1–8 and the responses common two-syllable adjectives.

The main reason for studying negative transfer after overtraining is to provide further evidence on the question of whether negative transfer is greater when the interfering associations are stronger. If learning is a process of strengthening associations, then surely overtraining should have the effect of producing associations that are stronger than those acquired when a modest learning criterion is met. But the results indicate that in six cases out of seven, there is no greater overall negative transfer following overtraining on the initial list than there is when the initial list was learned to a criterion of a single errorless cycle.

Return to Table 6-4, and compare the A–B$_r$ conditions with overtraining to the corresponding conditions without overtraining. Note that there was a larger value of $E(Z_1)$ for the group with overtraining in each case. Statistical tests indicated that these were significant; the results are in Table 6-7, which gives values of $-2 \log_e \lambda$ for all comparisons involving lists with adjective responses from the overtraining experiments. The main finding was greater difficulty in Stage 1 for the overtrained groups in the three A–B$_r$ conditions having adjective pairs. In Stage 2, the overtrained A–B$_r$ group with 10-item lists had more difficulty than the criterion group, but the overtrained A–B$_r$ group with six-item lists and no pretraining had a significantly lower value of $E(Z_2)$ than the criterion group. The overtraining effect for the A–B$_r$ group with eight numeral-adjective pairs involved less difficulty in Stage 1 for the group with overtraining.

Table 6-7 Tests of Invariance between Criterion and Overtraining
(Adjective Responses Only)

Number of Items	Condition	Stage 1	Stage 2
10	A–B$_r$	8.9**	37.8**
10	C–B	.9	.4
6	A–B$_r$, No PT	7.2**	6.6*
6	C–B, No PT	1.0	4.6*
6	AB$_r$, PT	11.3**	1.5
6	C–B, PT	2.7	.1
8	A–B$_r$	10.5**	1.9

*denotes $p < .05$; **denotes $p < .01$.

The major finding in these experiments was the general lack of effect of overtraining on the amount of negative transfer when C–B is compared with A–B$_r$. In all cases where numerals were used either as stimuli or responses, the overtrained A–B$_r$ groups had no greater difficulty in the transfer list than corresponding groups trained to criterion. In the groups with adjective pairs and six-item lists, overtrained A–B$_r$ groups apparently had a small disadvantage in Stage 1, but in Stage 2, where most negative transfer was found to occur, the overtrained groups found learning slightly easier than did corresponding criterion groups. Only in the condition involving 10-pair lists of adjectives was there evidence that overtraining had a substantial effect of increasing negative transfer, including increased difficulty in the second stage. Thus, the overall thrust of the results is to provide further evidence against the implication of associationist theory that negative transfer should be greater when the interfering associations are stronger.

What of the two exceptions to the generalization? The list of 10 paired adjectives was a harder list than any of the others used and, unlike the lists containing numerals as stimuli or responses, presented no natural basis of organization to the subjects. This suggests to us that the additional negative transfer found in that condition may have been produced by organizational processes carried out by subjects during overtraining. With shorter lists and with lists of numerals, the learning that preceded the criterion probably was sufficient to permit easy retrieval of the items. However, with the long list containing no numerals, it would not be surprising if criterion could be reached with some items still in a state where retrieval occurred with some difficulty. This difficulty could be relieved if further relations among items were noticed and stored in memory, providing a stronger organization of the list. And this organization led to increased negative transfer.

The fact that overtrained groups with adjective pairs apparently had more difficulty in Stage 1 might be interpreted as slight evidence for the hypothesis that negative transfer is stronger when interfering associations are stronger.

However, in the light of all the other failures of that hypothesis, we are inclined to look for another interpretation. If we follow the hypothesis that the first stage involves storing an encoded representation of the pair, then we must conclude that overtraining can make that process more difficult. Again, the hypothesis that seems most likely is that during overtraining, subjects better organize their representations of the list, and this interpair grouping causes the increase in Stage-1 difficulty. If we conclude that increased subjective organization of the list can produce increased negative transfer in the process of storing representations of pairs, we imply that there probably is some negative transfer affecting that process in any case of transfer. Considering the results of the previous section, the conclusion has to be that these effects are small relative to the magnitude of negative transfer on the second stage, which we assume is the process of learning to retrieve pairs reliably.

Pagel's Comparisons with Effects of Meaningfulness and Similarity

Pagel's (1973) experiment involving study of meaningfulness and similarity was mentioned and her results regarding initial acquisition were discussed in Chapter 4. The main purpose of her experiment was study of negative transfer, and we now turn to her findings regarding comparison of A–B$_r$ and C–B transfer lists. Recall that in all four experimental conditions, stimuli were consonant-vowel-consonant (CVC) trigrams and responses were the numerals 1–7. In two groups, the trigrams were English words, in the other two they were nonsense. Also, one list of words and one of nonsense trigrams had very dissimilar stimuli, and the other had very similar stimuli, formed by using the same letters in many different trigrams. Illustrative stimulus lists are shown in Table 4-8.

Pagel's estimates of the mean number of trials in each stage of learning during transfer are in Table 6-8. (She presented complete details regarding simplifying assumptions, goodness of fit, and estimated values of parameters

Table 6-8 Pagel's (1973) Estimates of Difficulty in Stages during Transfer

Stimuli	Transfer Condition	$E(Z_1)$	$E(Z_2)$
Dissimilar Words	A–B$_r$	1.45	1.70
Dissimilar Words	C–B	1.18	1.64
Dissimilar Nonsense	A–B$_r$	1.41	3.07
Dissimilar Nonsense	C–B	1.22	1.66
Similar Words	A–B$_r$	1.62	8.09
Similar Words	C–B	1.32	2.46
Similar Nonsense	A–B$_r$	4.00	8.06
Similar Nonsense	C–B	3.57	7.65

in her 1973 article.) Pagel conducted rather strong tests of invariance across conditions. In each case, the null hypothesis tested was that all the parameters involved in the summary statistic were constant across groups. Using these tests, her results indicated rejection of equality of A–B$_r$ and C–B in the first stage for the group with similar words, $p < .01$, and the group with dissimilar words, $p < .05$, and rejection of equality of A–B$_r$ and C–B in the second stage for all groups except that with dissimilar nonsense stimuli, $p < .01$ in all three cases.

Pagel obtained the greatest amount of negative transfer, as measured by difference between C–B and A–B$_r$, in the conditions with similar word and with dissimilar nonsense. In both of these conditions, the findings of James and Greeno were confirmed; there was substantially more negative transfer in the second stage of learning than in the first. In the remaining two groups, those with less negative transfer, Pagel found relatively small amounts of negative transfer in both stages of transfer learning.

We find the relatively small amount of transfer obtained with dissimilar words surprising. As Table 6-6 shows, we have obtained moderate amounts of negative transfer in the second stage with six-item lists of adjective-numeral pairs, and we can think of no reason why Pagel's pairs of three-letter words with numerals should have differed so substantially.

The result obtained with similar nonsense, however, probably represents quite an interesting exception to the generalization that A–B$_r$ produces substantial negative transfer in the second stage. Recall that two kinds of processes are assumed to occur in the second stage of learning, where subjects perfect the retrievability of items. One process is stimulus differentiation— the process of achieving more differentiated representations of stimuli to avoid errors of confusion. The other process involves organizing the representation of the list to make retrieval more efficient. We have assumed that the process of organization is probably important in producing negative transfer. The organization appropriate for retrieving pairs involving one set of responses may be quite harmful in attempts to retrieve pairs with different responses, and the need to replace one retrieval system with another causes negative transfer. Stimulus differentiation, however, would be expected to aid learning in the second list, and thus be a factor contributing positive transfer. Pagel's result showing only a small amount of negative transfer with similar nonsense stimuli could be explained on the ground that stimulus discrimination must have been an important component of learning. In the C–B condition with new stimuli, differentiation would require considerable learning. In the A–B$_r$ condition, the advantage of having already differentiated the stimuli compensated for the disadvantage generally found, which we interpret as being due to inappropriate subjective organization.

We note that Pagel's result is consistent with Battig's (1966) intratask interference hypothesis, in which it is asserted that when learning presents difficulty due to interference, retention and transfer will be facilitated. However, the connection proposed by Pagel between Battig's hypothesis and the result was the process of acquiring interpair groupings, a process essentially identical to our idea of forming a retrieval system. We think that a retrieval system is most likely to be a negative factor in A–C and A–B$_r$ transfer, and we think it more likely that Pagel's result is due to stimulus differentiation. Of course, this conclusion is still consistent with Battig's general view that transfer is facilitated by intratask interference in the initial list, because similarities among the stimuli force subjects to develop strongly differentiated representations.

COMPARISONS OF FOUR PARADIGMS

We now turn to experiments that included all four of the standard negative transfer paradigms—C–D, A–C, C–B, and A–B$_r$.

James' Experiment

One set of data was obtained by James (1968) as the transfer phase of an experiment aimed mainly at studying retroactive interference. The data regarding retroaction will be presented in Chapter 8. James' experiment used lists of 10 adjective pairs, presented on a memory drum with alternating cycles of study trials and tests on all items in the list. Each study presentation and test interval was for 4 seconds, and a 4-second interval separated study and test cycles. Both the initial A–B list and the transfer list were presented to a criterion of one errorless test cycle. All subjects learned the same list of items in transfer; the items in the first lists were varied to produce the relations between lists needed for the paradigms. There were 16 subjects in each group.

The overall measures of difficulty in transfer gave typical results. The mean total errors per item in the four transfer conditions were as follows: C–D, 1.07; A–C, 1.94; C–B, .86; A–B$_r$, 2.14. Analysis of variance and pairwise comparisons of groups were carried out, showing that A–C and A–B$_r$ each differed from both C–B and C–D reliably, but the smaller differences between C–B and C–D and between A–C and A–B$_r$ were not significant.

The two-stage Markov model was applied, and tests of simplifying assumptions indicated that the initial vector could be restricted by $t = ab$, $s = 1 - a$, $r = e$, and in addition, $b = d$ and $e = q$ were acceptable. Together these restrictions impose four restrictions on the identifiable parameters. The test statistics obtained for the four conditions were 1.52, 2.22, 1.53, and 4.12, respectively, for C–D, A–C, C–B, and A–B$_r$. All four values are comfortably within the acceptance range of chi square with four degrees of freedom.

Table 6-9 presents the values of chi square obtained in testing goodness of fit for the restricted model. (For A–B$_r$ one of the parameters had an

Table 6-9   Goodness of Fit of the Restricted Model to James' Data

Condition	Errors Before First Correct	Errors After First Correct	Trials After First Correct	Total Errors	Trial of Last Error
A–C	2.88	3.45	1.58	2.51	4.47
	(9, 6)	(3, 1)	(3, 1)	(6, 3)	(7, 4)
C–D	10.37	.11	1.34	.98	2.77
	(6, 3)	(2, 0^a)	(3, 1)	(3, 0^a)	(5, 2)
	*				
A–B$_r$	7.78	.75	2.48	2.18	1.09
	(9, 5)	(4, 2)	(5, 3)	(7, 3)	(8, 4)
C–B	8.3	.11	.11	6.74	4.46
	(5, 2)	(1, 0^a)	(1, 0^a)	(4, 1)	(4, 1)
	*			**	*

*denotes $p < .05$, **denotes $p < .01$. ^{a} indicates too few cells with theoretical frequency of five or greater to have nonzero degrees of freedom for the liberal bound.

unwieldy value, and it was more convenient to test the model without restricting $b = d$. This improves the agreement but reduces a degree of freedom in three of the tests. It should have no effect on the outcome in the present case.) The fit of the model appears to have been satisfactory.

Under the restrictions employed, the model has three identifiable parameters, and four free theoretical parameters, a, c, d, and p. As an identifying restriction, James used $c = d$; this is particularly reasonable for James' experiment, where tests and study trials occurred in separate cycles. Any dependence of the probability of learning on the subject's test performance must have been very small. The parameter estimates for the four conditions are in Table 6-10.

With the restrictions employed, the mean number of trials in the first stage of learning is $E(Z_1) = 1/a$ and for the second stage, $E(Z_2) = (1 - c)/c$. The values obtained for the four conditions are graphed in Figure 6-1. Significance tests are straightforward, involving a for Stage 1 and c for Stage 2. Significance tests were carried out for all three parameters comparing all

Table 6-10   Estimated Parameter Values for James' Experiment

Condition	a	c	p
A–C	.50	.41	.36
C–D	.68	.45	.73
A–B$_r$	.57	.33	.34
C–B	.64	.61	.53

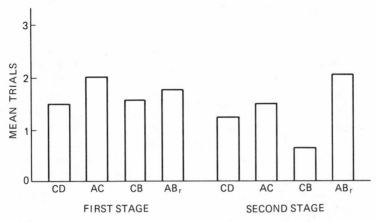

Figure 6-1 Estimated mean number of trials in the two stages of learning for transfer lists in James' experiment.

pairs of conditions. The results are in Table 6-11. In the first stage, the apparent difference between C–D and A–C was reliable. In the second stage, C–B differed significantly from both A–C and A–B$_r$. Reliable differences in performance in the intermediate state were obtained between C–D and both the A–C and A–B$_r$ conditions. The values shown are for the test statistic

Table 6-11 Tests of Parameter Invariance for James' Data

i.	*Invariance of a* (*First Stage Learning*)		

	C–D	A–B$_r$	C–B
A–C	4.42*	.86	3.02
C–D		1.96	.23
A–B$_r$			.99

ii.	*Invariance of c* (*Second Stage Learning*)		

	C–D	A–B$_r$	C–B
A–C	.42	3.58	11.79**
C–D		2.83	3.03
A–B$_r$			27.50**

iii.	*Invariance of p* (*Intermediate State Performance*)		

	C–D	A–B$_r$	C–B
A–C	4.76*	.24	.51
C–D		6.11*	.62
A–B$_r$			.88

* denotes $p < .05$; ** denotes $p < .01$.

$-2 \log_e \lambda$ which should be asymptotically distributed as $\chi^2(1)$ under the null hypothesis in every case.

Greeno's Transfer Experiment

We now present the main results of Greeno's experiment, carried out to provide measures of difficulty of the two stages of learning during transfer under different conditions of meaningfulness. The general procedures for the experiment were described in Chapter 4. Up to five subjects participated at each session, and each subject reached criterion at a different time. When a subject had learned the first list, an instruction was given to remain seated. When all subjects had reached criterion, they were given two review trials on the first list, after which the second list was presented using the same procedure used in the first list.

Table 6-12 shows the test statistics for simplifying assumptions, to determine what simplifications of the two-stage Markov model could be applied. The restriction $e = q$, $b = d$ was acceptable in a majority of cases, and unlike the restriction on the initial vector, it was not rejected by a very large chi square value in any condition. To achieve comparability between conditions, it seems desirable to apply the model under one set of restrictions in all cases being compared; therefore, we will report results obtained with the restriction $e = q$, $b = d$.

Table 6-12 Tests of Simplifying Assumptions in Greeno's Transfer Experiment

Stimuli	Responses	Paradigm	Init., $df = 2$	$e = q$, $b = d$ $df = 1$	Init., $e = q$ $df = 3$	Init., $e = q$, $b = d$ $df = 4$
Words	Words	A–B, C–D	2.62	.02	6.17	19.52**
Words	Words	A–B, A–C	6.92*	1.56	7.31	10.37*
Words	Words	A–B, C–B	7.90*	4.61*	8.25*	11.93*
Words	Words	A–B, A–B$_r$	22.55**	1.34	23.06**	37.11**
Nonsense	Words	A–B, C–D	1.00	3.01	6.80	14.69**
Nonsense	Words	A–B, A–C	74.84**	4.72*	96.61**	107.90**
Nonsense	Words	A–B, C–B	10.07**	.59	10.15*	11.22*
Nonsense	Words	A–B, A–B$_r$	1.84	.80	4.67	4.67
Words	Nonsense	A–B, C–D	22.76**	4.30*	31.85**	37.48**
Words	Nonsense	A–B, A–C	5.90	4.44*	6.82	6.84
Words	Nonsense	A–B, C–B	7.22*	8.94**	8.65*	9.77*
Words	Nonsense	A–B, A–B$_r$	37.53**	3.80	94.85**	105.34**
Nonsense	Nonsense	A–B, C–D	9.77**	.99	13.45**	13.59**
Nonsense	Nonsense	A–B, A–C	11.17**	9.37**	11.45**	16.10**
Nonsense	Nonsense	A–B, C–B	8.28*	.02	14.69**	18.43**
Nonsense	Nonsense	A–B, A–B$_r$	14.19**	7.00**	53.37**	54.88**

* denotes $p < .05$; ** denotes $p < .01$.

Results of testing goodness of fit are shown in Table 6-13. The question is whether the parameter estimates are valid; therefore, the version of the model tested has the restrictions $e = q$, $b = d$, used in obtaining the estimates. There were 80 nonindependent tests. At the upper bounds of degrees of freedom, four indicated rejection at $p < .01$ and two more indicated rejection at $p < .05$. At the lower bounds of degrees of freedom, 10 tests indicated rejection at $p < .01$ and 18 more indicated rejection at $p < .05$.

The goodness of fit was poor enough to raise doubt about the validity of estimates. Therefore, we examined the nature of the discrepancies. Table 6-14 shows theoretical and empirical means and standard deviations of six statistics in all the conditions of the experiment. The column headed "Before First Correct: A" has the distribution of trials before first correct, conditional on there being no errors after the first correct response. "Before First Correct: B" has trials before first correct, given one or more errors after the first correct response. Estimation of seven parameters makes it likely that the theory will agree with the observed means; indeed, only 2 of the 96 predicted means fell outside 90% confidence intervals computed from the data. The question of interest involves the standard deviations. The model assumes homogeneity of parameters for items and subjects; of course, that must be false, but as in nearly all experiments, items were selected in an attempt to produce roughly equal difficulty, and subjects were taken from a fairly homogeneous group. To the extent that the usual experimental efforts to gain homogeneity failed, the variance among subjects and items should lead to larger standard deviations in the data than predicted by the theory. On the other hand, if the learning process were more complex than the one postulated in the model, this could lead to considerably smaller variances than the model predicts. A general property of learning in one or two discrete stages is that performance is highly variable (cf. Restle & Greeno, 1970); if learning occurred in three or more stages, and if parameters were fairly homogeneous across subjects and items, then we would expect the empirical standard deviations to be smaller than the theoretical ones.

In 22 cases, theoretical standard deviations fell outside 90% confidence intervals computed from the data. In 17 of these, the empirical standard deviations were higher than the predicted values. It seems to us that the most plausible conclusion is that the model is a good approximation of the learning process, and the main deviations involved differences among subjects and items not assumed in the model.

Under the restrictions $b = d$, $e = q$, the model has seven theoretical parameters and six identifiable parameters. The identifying restriction chosen was $c = d$. Estimates of the six parameters in each of the twelve groups are given in Table 6-15. It may be noted that the failures of the restriction on the initial vector apparently were due to a greater amount of learning on the initial study trial than on later trials. (As a rule, $1 - s$ was greater than a,

Table 6-13 Goodness-of-Fit Chi-Square Statistics

Stimuli	Responses	Paradigm	Errs. Before First Corr.	Errs. After First Corr.	Trls. After First Corr.	Total Errors	Trial of Last Err.
Words	Words	C–D	8.01 (7, 1) **	2.90 (3, 1)	5.38 (4, 2)	2.94 (5, 0[a])	1.65 (7, 1)
Words	Words	A–C	4.60 (9, 3)	1.69 (3, 1)	8.44 (5, 3) *	5.38 (6, 1) *	2.53 (8, 2)
Words	Words	C–B	3.88 (6, 0[a])	1.80 (2, 0[a])	2.75 (3, 1)	1.30 (4, 0[a])	3.15 (5, 0[a])
Words	Words	A–B$_r$	3.98 (10, 4)	3.28 (5, 3)	3.74 (7, 5)	7.93 (7, 2) *	10.81 (10, 4)
Nonsense	Words	C–D	4.29 (9, 3)	1.10 (3, 1)	3.16 (5, 3)	6.94 (6, 1) **	3.30 (8, 2)
Nonsense	Words	A–C	13.89 (13, 7)	6.04 (6, 4)	4.08 (7, 5)	11.44 (11, 6)	11.95 (11, 5) *
Nonsense	Words	C–B	4.66 (10, 4)	3.02 (4, 2)	2.32 (6, 4)	5.69 (7, 2)	10.59 (9, 3) *
Nonsense	Words	A–B$_r$	13.08 (12, 6) *	12.82 (7, 5) *	13.13 (9, 7)	16.13 (9, 4) **	6.16 (12, 6)
Words	Nonsense	C–D	28.35 (17, 11) * **	6.96 (4, 2) *	8.33 (6, 4)	15.04 (12, 7) *	18.38 (13, 7) *
Words	Nonsense	A–C	23.35 (17, 11) *	7.43 (5, 3)	6.24 (7, 5)	11.38 (11, 6)	13.25 (13, 7)
Words	Nonsense	C–B	8.00 (8, 2) *	4.22 (3, 1) *	6.96 (5, 3)	3.55 (6, 1)	4.37 (7, 1) *
Words	Nonsense	A–B$_r$	11.68 (14, 9)	13.22 (8, 6) *	27.94 (11, 9) ** **	11.92 (13, 8) **	20.17 (16, 10) *
Nonsense	Nonsense	C–D	28.40 (28, 22)	9.96 (8, 6)	11.98 (10, 8)	32.18 (19, 14) ** **	20.04 (20, 14)
Nonsense	Nonsense	A–C	20.29 (25, 20)	14.96 (8, 6) *	17.24 (11, 9) *	13.38 (18, 13)	16.97 (20, 14)
Nonsense	Nonsense	C–B	12.59 (16, 10)	8.14 (8, 6)	7.34 (10, 8)	12.98 (13, 8)	30.28 (15, 9) * **
Nonsense	Nonsense	A–B$_r$	18.49 (17, 11)	34.97 (9, 7) ** **	27.90 (13, 11) ** **	9.80 (16, 11)	19.02 (18, 12)

* denotes $p < .05$, ** denotes $p < .01$. [a] indicates too few cells with theoretical frequency of five or greater to have nonzero degrees of freedom for the liberal bound.

Table 6-14   Theoretical and Empirical Means and Standard Deviations

S/R	Par.		Before First Correct: A		Before First Correct: B		Errs. After First Corr.		Trls. After First Corr.		Total Errors		Trial of Last Error	
			Mean	S.D.	Mean	S.D.	Mean	S.D.	Mean	S.D.	Mean	S.D.	Mean	S.D.
W/W	C–D	Theo.	.76	1.34	.99	1.45*	.22	.66	.33	1.08	1.01	1.54	1.26	1.98
W/W	C–D	Emp.	.72	1.18	1.36	2.18	.22	.67	.34	1.10	1.01	1.61	1.26	2.11
W/W	A–C	Theo.	.88	1.27	1.15	1.34*	.30	.82	.46	1.34	1.23	1.57	1.56	2.15
W/W	A–C	Emp.	.84	1.16	1.42	1.71	.30	.84	.45	1.29	1.24	1.64	1.57	2.20
W/W	C–B	Theo.	.45	.84	.63	.93*	.17	.58	.26	.94*	0.65	1.06	.86	1.52
W/W	C–B	Emp.	.42	.78	.87	1.16	.18	.51	.25	.78	0.66	1.08	.86	1.48
W/W	A–B_r	Theo.	.86	1.58	1.18	1.74	.52	1.26	.77	1.95	1.46	2.12	1.94	2.88
W/W	A–B_r	Emp.	.82	1.61	1.32	1.75	.53	1.26	.76	1.84	1.47	2.24	1.95	2.95
N/W	C–D	Theo.	1.05	1.32	1.44	1.35	.32	.85*	.52	1.50*	1.45	1.64*	1.83	2.34*
N/W	C–D	Emp.	1.06	1.29	1.47	1.43	.32	1.00	.55	1.71	1.45	1.80	1.84	2.58
N/W	A–C	Theo.	1.96	3.78	2.27	3.98	.76	1.67	1.03	2.35	2.80	4.19	3.34	4.68
N/W	A–C	Emp.	1.77	3.65	2.61	3.49	.69	1.60	.96	2.18	2.69	4.12	3.23	4.68
N/W	C–B	Theo.	1.27	1.65*	1.43	1.68	.46	1.12*	.64	1.64	1.77	2.03*	2.17	2.61*
N/W	C–B	Emp.	1.27	1.81	1.49	1.49	.45	1.27	.63	1.71	1.77	2.26	2.17	2.81
N/W	A–B_r	Theo.	1.82	1.89	1.77	1.89*	1.10	2.09	1.52	2.98	2.90	2.81	3.69	3.81
N/W	A–B_r	Emp.	1.65	1.63	2.05	2.27	1.10	2.15	1.50	2.86	2.91	2.92	3.69	3.84
W/N	C–D	Theo.	2.47	3.58	3.12	3.76	.48	1.20	.68	1.76*	3.10	3.88	3.51	4.28
W/N	C–D	Emp.	2.10	3.61	3.50	3.60	.42	1.12	.60	1.49	2.82	4.11	3.22	4.43
W/N	A–C	Theo.	2.57*	2.79	2.78*	2.80*	.66	1.38	1.00	2.22	3.29	3.15*	3.93	3.85*
W/N	A–C	Emp.	2.25	2.44	3.46	3.33	.66	1.32	.98	2.10	3.30	3.40	3.93	4.19
W/N	C–B	Theo.	1.00	1.22	1.03	1.22	.30	.80	.45	1.27*	1.31	1.46	1.64	2.00
W/N	C–B	Emp.	1.00	1.25	1.06	1.20	.31	.70	.43	1.05	1.32	1.46	1.64	1.93
W/N	A–B_r	Theo.	1.88	3.35	2.00	3.42	1.40	2.46	2.07	3.76	3.33	4.19	4.41	5.30
W/N	A–B_r	Emp.	1.71	3.34	2.10	3.00	1.38	2.60	2.03	3.69	3.26	4.41	4.35	5.49
N/N	C–D	Theo.	5.50	5.38	5.82	5.36	1.13	2.11	1.64	3.18	6.75	5.79	7.61	6.41
N/N	C–D	Emp.	4.99	5.72	5.84	5.10	1.11	2.24	1.60	3.06	6.43	5.91	7.30	6.43
N/N	A–C	Theo.	5.03	4.80	5.25	4.79	1.36	2.35	2.08	3.74*	6.48	5.36	7.60	6.27
N/N	A–C	Emp.	4.71	5.05	5.05	4.24	1.34	2.30	1.99	3.19	6.22	5.31	7.34	6.00
N/N	C–B	Theo.	2.52	3.07*	2.68	3.10*	1.24	2.29*	1.76	3.36	3.82	3.87	4.72	4.85
N/N	C–B	Emp.	2.47	3.41	2.42	2.41	1.20	2.69	1.72	3.56	3.66	4.10	4.55	5.04
N/N	A–B_r	Theo.	2.88	4.03	3.18	4.12	1.85	3.06	2.74	4.64	4.87	5.13	6.19	6.40
N/N	A–B_r	Emp.	2.71	4.40	3.16	3.85	1.81	3.09	2.66	4.29	4.76	5.18	6.12	6.17

* denotes theoretical value outside 90% confidence interval computed from data.

Table 6-15 Parameter Estimates from Greeno's Transfer Experiment

Stimuli	Response	Para-digm	N	$1-s$	a	t	$b =$ $c = d$	$1-r$	$p =$ $1-e$
Words	Words	A–C	304	.843	.450	.335	.370	.267	.546
Words	Words	C–D	296	.850	.397	.409	.410	.383	.574
Words	Words	A–B$_r$	312	.793	.411	.395	.298	.518	.455
Words	Words	C–B	296	.822	.727	.495	.434	.583	.578
Nonsense	Words	A–C	280	.914	.092	.200	.271	.142	.364
Nonsense	Words	C–D	296	.649	.541	.302	.344	.265	.588
Nonsense	Words	A–B$_r$	288	.387	.568	.136	.239	.704	.362
Nonsense	Words	C–B	304	.835	.366	.236	.340	.210	.426
Words	Nonsense	A–C	320	.383	.307	.127	.288	.347	.481
Words	Nonsense	C–D	296	.639	.202	.223	.320	.131	.416
Words	Nonsense	A–B$_r$	304	.843	.161	.178	.201	.344	.406
Words	Nonsense	C–B	320	.479	.680	.258	.398	.862	.537
Nonsense	Nonsense	A–C	296	.190	.190	.041	.203	.194	.435
Nonsense	Nonsense	C–D	320	.213	.168	.045	.227	.082	.403
Nonsense	Nonsense	A–B$_r$	280	.654	.183	.122	.170	.259	.395
Nonsense	Nonsense	C–B	328	.647	.247	.118	.217	.207	.376

and t was greater than ab.) By allowing an extra second of study time on the initial trial of each item, we apparently made that trial about equal in effectiveness to later trials for the hardest conditions, but in most conditions the extra second of study time produced an advantage over later trials.

Under the restrictions applied here, the expected numbers of trials in the two stages of learning are

$$E(Z_1) = 1 + \frac{s}{a},$$

$$E(Z_2) = \frac{(1-t)(1-c)}{c}.$$

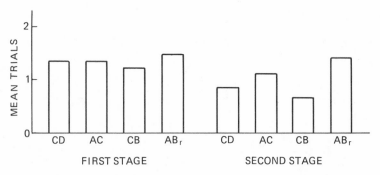

Figure 6-2 Estimated mean number of trials in the two stages of learning for transfer lists composed of noun-noun pairs in Greeno's transfer experiment.

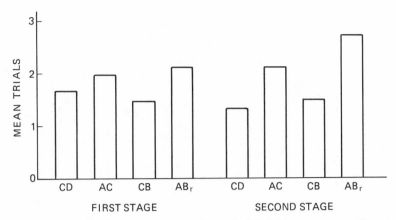

Figure 6-3 Estimated mean number of trials in the two stages of learning for transfer lists composed of CVC-noun pairs in Greeno's transfer experiment.

Values of these expectations calculated from the parameter estimates are in Figures. 6-2–6-5, with each figure showing the data from one of the conditions of meaningfulness.

Reliability of differences between conditions was assessed somewhat less rigorously for these data than in other cases we have presented. The variances

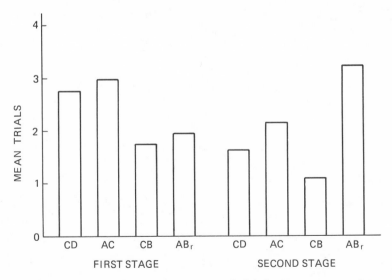

Figure 6-4 Estimated mean number of trials in the two stages of learning for transfer lists composed of noun-CVC pairs in Greeno's transfer experiment.

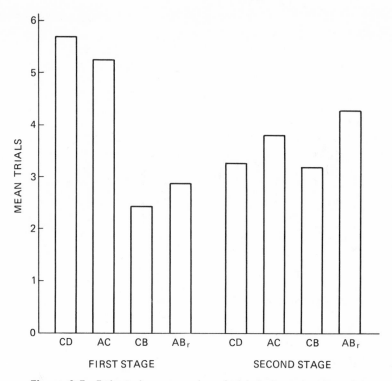

Figure 6-5 Estimated mean number of trials in the two stages of learning for transfer lists composed of CVC-CVC pairs in Greeno's transfer experiment.

of Z_1 and Z_2 are functions of the theoretical parameters; with the restrictions $b = c = d$ and $e = q$,

$$V(Z_1) = \frac{(2 - a - s)s}{a^2},$$

$$V(Z_2) = \frac{(1 - t)(1 - c)(1 + t - tc)}{c^2}.$$

If we could observe the trials of transition between states, then the mean trial in a stage of learning would have the sampling variance

$$V(\bar{Z}) = V(Z)/N,$$

where N is the number of observations. The theoretical values of $V(\bar{Z})$, computed using the empirical estimates of parameters, should give at least a rough approximation of the stability of the estimates of $E(Z_1)$ and $E(Z_2)$. These estimates were calculated for the various experimental conditions, and used to compute the 95% confidence intervals that will be presented below.

We begin our discussion of comparisons by noting that the main results reported in the previous section comparing A–B$_r$ and C–B were repeated here. There were relatively small differences between C–B and A–B$_r$ in Stage 1, but substantial differences in Stage 2.

$E(Z_1)$: Words/Words, (C–B) − (A–B$_r$) = −0.26 ± 0.16;

Words/Nonsense, (C–B) − (A–B$_r$) = −0.63 ± 0.21;

Nonsense/Words, (C–B) − (A–B$_r$) = −0.20 ± 0.37;

Nonsense/Nonsense, (C–B) − (A–B$_r$) = −0.46 ± 0.55.

$E(Z_2)$: Words/Words, (C–B) − (A–B$_r$) = −0.76 ± 0.32;

Words/Nonsense, (C–B) − (A–B$_r$) = −1.27 ± 0.48;

Nonsense/Words, (C–B) − (A–B$_r$) = −2.14 ± 0.52;

Nonsense/Nonsense, (C–B) − (A–B$_r$) = −1.12 ± 0.75.

Differences between C–D and A–C in the first stage gave no consistent pattern, and apparently were nonsignificant.

$E(Z_1)$: Words/Words, (C–D) − (A–C) = 0.03 ± 0.18;

Nonsense/Words, (C–D) − (A–C) = −0.29 ± 0.52;

Words/Nonsense, (C–D) − (A–C) = −0.23 ± 0.50;

Nonsense/Nonsense, (C–D) − (A–C) = 0.44 ± 0.80.

In the second stage, A–C appears to have been consistently harder than C–D, although one condition did not give a significant difference, and another was borderline.

$E(Z_2)$: Words/Words, (C–D) − (A–C) = −0.28 ± 0.28;

Nonsense/Words, (C–D) − (A–C) = −0.82 ± 0.43;

Words/Nonsense, (C–D) − (A–C) = −0.52 ± 0.42;

Nonsense/Nonsense, (C–D) − (A–C) = −0.51 ± 0.65.

For reasons discussed earlier in this chapter, we expect that in Stage 2, the difference between A–B$_r$ and C–B should be greater than the difference between A–C and C–D. This second-order difference was in the predicted direction for all four conditions (as it was also in James' data—recall Figure 7-1), and it was significant in two of the four cases.

$E(Z_2)$: Words/Words, (C–B)−(A–B$_r$)−(C–D)+(A–C) = −0.48±0.42;

Nonsense/Words, (C–B)−(A–B$_r$)−(C–D)+(A–C) = −0.45±0.65;

Words/Nonsense, (C–B)−(A–B$_r$)−(C–D)+(A–C) = −1.63±0.67;

Nonsense/Nonsense, (C–B)−(A–B$_r$)−(C–D)+(A–C) = −0.60±1.00.

One final comparison of interest involves Stage 1. In the conditions with nonsense responses, there were strong differences between groups with new responses and groups who had the first-list responses during transfer.

$E(Z_1)$: Words/Nonsense, $\frac{1}{2}[(C-D) + (A-C)] - \frac{1}{2}[(C-B) + (A-B_r)]$
$$= 1.03 \pm 0.31;$$

Nonsense/Nonsense, $\frac{1}{2}[(C-D) + (A-C)] - \frac{1}{2}[(C-B) + (A-B_r)]$
$$= 2.82 \pm 0.49.$$

Clearly, it was an advantage for C–B and A–B$_r$ to be able to use the responses they had used in the first list.

However, current associationist theory attributes the advantage of response familiarity to a definite process of response learning that is assumed to occur as a component of all associative learning. This would produce an advantage of having the first-list responses in the conditions with word responses, although of course the amount of that advantage would be considerably smaller than in nonsense responses and could be counteracted by interference from backward associations. The data gave no evidence of any advantage.

$E(Z_1)$: Words/Words, $\frac{1}{2}[(C-D) + (A-C)] - \frac{1}{2}[(C-B) + (A-B_r)]$
$$= -0.01 \pm 0.12;$$

Nonsense/Words, $\frac{1}{2}[(C-D) + (A-C)] - \frac{1}{2}[(C-B) + (A-B_r)]$
$$= 0.03 \pm 0.28.$$

Discussion and Revision of Earlier Proposals

We have proposed mechanisms that could produce negative transfer in either the first or second stage of learning during transfer. There is further evidence here of negative transfer in the second stage, which we attribute to interference caused by the retrieval system that we assume is acquired during the learning of List 1. Furthermore, the amount of negative transfer observed in Stage 2 is greater for A–B$_r$ than for A–C, consistent with the idea that more extensive changes in the retrieval systems are required for A–B$_r$ to be mastered.

The other potential source of negative transfer that we hypothesized was interference from first-list encodings of stimuli. Some evidence for this was obtained; James found significant negative transfer in the first stage of A–C, and Greeno found significant first-stage negative transfer in two A–B$_r$ conditions. However, the amount of negative transfer in the first stage was considerably less than in the second stage in both the A–C and A–B$_r$ conditions in all of Greeno's observations, and only in the case of James' A–C condition was there greater negative transfer in the first stage than in the second. We think this represents a further failure of a prediction implied by associationist theory: that negative transfer should be greater earlier, rather than later, in learning. The reason, as we have said before, is that negative transfer caused by stronger associations should be greater than negative transfer caused by weaker associations, and the first-list associations should be expected to grow weaker, if they change in strength at all, during the course of second-list learning.

The results in this section also contradict our earlier expectation (Greeno, James, & DaPolito, 1971) that in the first stage negative transfer caused by interfering encodings of stimuli and responses would be symmetrical. Our earlier conclusion clearly overlooked the importance of response familiarity in the case of nonsense responses, and allowance for that must be made. We find that the major facilitating effect of familiarity with responses was in the first stage, as would be expected if familiarity with responses facilitates encoding. This agrees with conclusions obtained in the study of acquisition, particularly in Humphreys' experiment and in its replication, discussed in Chapter 4. There is some uncertainty now regarding what should be said about the case of meaningful responses. The lack of difference between conditions with old and new responses could be due to a lack of importance of response familiarity in encoding when responses are meaningful, or it could be due to a fortuitous cancelling of the advantage of familiarity with a disadvantage of first-list encodings of the kind hypothesized earlier. We are inclined to prefer the hypothesis of no effect, since it seems simpler and therefore more susceptible to future empirical test.

In addition, the general pattern of findings now available, including Greeno's experiment reported here and Pagel's (1973) study described in a previous section of this chapter, indicates that differences in the first stage between C–B and A–B$_r$, and apparently also between C–D and A–C, are probably common. The differences seem to be small in most cases, so that significant effects are often not obtained. However, all the significant effects that have been obtained have been in the direction of negative transfer in conditions having the same stimuli in transfer as in initial training. Thus, we are led to the conclusion stated at the beginning of this chapter, that persistence in encoding produces negative transfer primarily on the stimulus side.

TRANSFER WITH SYNONYMOUS RESPONSES: GOGGIN'S EXPERIMENT

We are grateful to Judith Goggin, who provided the last data we will discuss in this chapter. Her experiment used lists of eight CVC-adjective pairs; the first (A–B) list was presented to a criterion of one perfect trial, and all subjects received 20 trials on the appropriate second list. The conditions

Table 6-16 Analysis of First Stage in Goggin's Data

Condition	$1-s$	a	$E(Z_1)$
C–D	.404	.551	2.08
A–C	.358	.267	3.40
A–B$_r$	.211	.298	3.65
A–B$'$	.704	.265	2.12
A–B$'_r$	.549	.261	2.73

to be discussed here were C–D, A–C, A–B$_r$, A–B$'$, and A–B$'_r$. In group A–B$'$, each response was a synonym of the response in List 1 that was paired with the same stimulus. In group A–B$'_r$, the synonymous responses were paired with different stimuli from their counterparts in List 1.

The version of the two-stage model that was acceptable for all groups used the restriction $e = q$, $b = d$, the same restriction used for Greeno's transfer experiment. In Table 6-16 we give the estimated values of parameters that are involved in the first stage of learning, along with the calculated values of $E(Z_1)$, the expected number of trials in the initial state. Tests of significance were carried out for the differences in the values of a. It was found that C–D differed significantly from all the other groups, $p < .01$ in all cases, but that none of the other four groups differed from each other. Note that this does not indicate equality in the total amount of negative transfer in Stage 1. It is evident that A–B$'$ had little or no negative transfer relative to C–D in the mean number of trials needed to accomplish the first stage of learning. However, this equality resulted from two compensating effects: first, A–B$'$ had more items that were through the first stage after the first trial; second, those items that remained in the initial state after the first trial had a rate of learning approximately equal to those of the other transfer conditions.

Table 6-17 shows the parameter values estimated for the second stage of learning, using the identifying restriction $c = 0$. The parameter $t/(1 - s)$ is shown, since this is the conditional probability of completing the second stage on the first trial, given that the first stage is completed. Tests of significance were carried out, testing the hypothesis that the three second-stage learning parameters $t/(1 - s)$ c, and d were identical across pairs of groups. On this test, significant differences were obtained between C–D and three of the four

Table 6-17 Analysis of Second Stage in Goggin's Data

Condition	$t/(1-s)$	d	$1-r$	p	$E(Z_2)$
C–D	.849	.536	.576	.510	1.29
A–C	.372	.394	.174	.474	2.84
A–B$_r$	.296	.330	.792	.432	3.70
A–B$'$	.533	.392	.547	.428	2.33
A–B$'_r$	.198	.280	.178	.299	3.82

transfer groups: A–B$'(p < .05)$, A–B$_r(p < .01)$, and A–B$'_r(p < .01)$; also, A–B$'$ differed significantly from A–B$_r(p < .05)$.

Goggin's data for C–D, A–C, and A–B$_r$ are consistent with the general trends that we have found throughout our analyses. The strongest negative transfer was obtained for A–B$_r$ in the second stage. Negative transfer was also obtained, though apparently to a lesser degree, for A–C in the second stage, and for both A–C and A–B$_r$ in the first stage.

In addition to confirming earlier results, Goggin's data provide new information about the effects of having responses synonymous with those of an earlier list. The most interesting suggestions come from the A–B$'$ condition. Tables 6-16 and 6-17, combined with the results of the significance tests mentioned above, indicate that there was negative transfer in A–B$'$ during the second stage, and that there was negative transfer for some items in the first stage—that is, those items that did not escape the initial state immediately. Statistical tests comparing A–B$'$ and A–C on the learning parameters other than s(that is, a, c, d, and $t/(1 - s)$) showed no significant difference. However, when s was added to the set, a clear rejection of parameter invariance between A–B$'$ and A–C was obtained, $\chi^2(3) = 42.1$, $p < .01$.

The possibility comes to mind that in A–B$'$, some items benefit from a form of positive transfer, at least in the encoding stage, that has the same form as the positive transfer discussed in Chapter 5. If the subject recognized the synonymy of a List-2 response and the corresponding List-1 response, that relation could be used as a basis for encoding the pair in List 2. On the other hand, consider items whose relations with List-1 items were not recognized. These would not be comparable with C–D control items, since C–D items have new stimuli, and A–B$'$ items have stimuli that were used in List 1. These items, for which positive transfer fails, should suffer negative transfer of the A–B, A–C variety.

The pattern of results obtained for Goggin's A–B$'$ group fits with this story, since the probability of storing a representation on the first trial $(1 - s)$ was high for A–B$'$, but in all other respects A–B$'$ was apparently indistinguishable from the A–C condition. Note that the facilitation in storage seems not to have been followed by very substantial facilitation in learning to retrieve. This would be expected if only a fraction of the A–B$'$ items transferred positively, on the hypothesis that learning to retrieve involves developing a system of relationships among various items in the list.

The results regarding A–B$'_r$ are less interesting, but seem sensible. None of the three strong negative transfer groups—A–B$_r$, A–B$'_r$ and, A–C—differed significantly from either of the others in any of the learning parameters. One might imagine that A–B$'_r$ would include components of processes involved in A–C and A–B$_r$ transfer, with recognized items like A–B$_r$ and unrecognized items like A–C. Were this the case, then if A–B$_r$ differed substantially from A–C, the results for A–B$'_r$ might be found to share features of the other two or to show intermediate values of parameters. In Goggin's data, A–C and A–B$_r$ did not differ significantly in either stage of learning, and it is therefore reasonable that A–B$'_r$ did not differ significantly from either of them.

SUMMARY AND DISCUSSION

We have reported five empirical findings about negative transfer:

1. The quantitative effect of negative transfer found in the second stage of learning, as defined by a two-stage Markov model, was uniformly greater than that found in the first stage. This is firmly established for A–B$_r$, relative to C–B, but also seems to hold for A–C relative to C–D.

2. The amount of negative transfer in the second stage found in A–B$_r$ (relative to C–B) was greater than that found in A–C (relative to C–D).

3. When nonsense responses were used, there was positive transfer in the first stage for conditions in which responses were the same in both initial training and transfer; there appears to have been no positive or negative transfer due to responses when the responses were meaningful.

4. When negative transfer did occur in the first stage, its rather small effect consistently retarded A–C compared to C–D, and A–B$_r$ compared to C–B— that is, it seems to have been due to the presence of first-list stimuli in the transfer list that were paired with new responses.

5. When numerals were used as stimuli or responses, overtraining on A–B caused no measureable increase in negative transfer in an A–B$_r$ list. Using pairs of adjectives, overtrained subjects showed more negative transfer in the first stage than did subjects trained only to criterion. With six-item lists, there was a compensating decrease in negative transfer in the second stage. With a longer list of 10-adjective pairs, overtraining increased negative transfer in both stages of learning.

In addition to these five findings, we have noted Pagel's (1973) finding that there was less negative transfer in A–B$_r$ with similar nonsense stimuli than with dissimilar nonsense stimuli or with similar word stimuli. This was primarily an effect involving the second stage, where most of the negative transfer occurred in the other conditions.

Finally, we have presented an interesting but highly tentative finding arising from analysis of Goggin's data collected with an A–B′ condition. A–B′ differed from A–C only in one parameter—the probability of completing the first stage of learning on the first study trial. This suggests that A–B′ is partly a positive transfer and partly a negative transfer paradigm, with the difference occurring in an all-or-none manner, similar to the positive transfer reported in Chapter 5. Because it is based on a single observation, this suggestion must be taken as tentative for now.

Relation to Associationist Theory

We believe that two of these findings differentiate between the cognitive theory of association and the associationist theory of interference. These are, first, that more negative transfer occurs in the second stage of learning than the first stage and, second, that overtraining on the A–B list does not generally increase negative transfer in A–B$_r$. Both findings seem to contradict the implication of interference theory, that associations will cause more negative transfer if they are stronger than if they are weaker.

The other results seem compatible with associative interference theory as we understand it. The greater negative transfer found in A–B$_r$ than in A–C is explained by the response selector mechanism, and we consider it possible that a mechanism similar in function to response-set selection might operate in some situations, although we think the mechanism probably would involve an organized representation of relations among pairs rather than simply among responses, and we call it a retrieval plan. We think it more likely that the difficulty in A–B$_r$ is caused by a need for more extensive modification of the first-list retrieval network, but the fact is explained by either theory.

The positive transfer found for C–B and A–B$_r$ with nonsense responses agrees nicely with the associationist assumption of a response-learning phase in associative learning. The lack of an effect of response familiarity when responses are meaningful could be interpreted as evidence against the hypothesis of response learning. However, the possibility exists that the advantage of response learning is compensated by a disadvantage in C–B and A–B$_r$ of interference due to backward associations.

Relation to Encoding Variability Theory

Martin's position (1972) and ours seem entirely consistent at the level of concepts and principles. The conceptual similarity may have been obscured by Martin's labeling his view as a theory of encoding variability, and our use of the phrase "principle of persistent encoding"; these are simply two sides of the same hypothesis. Negative transfer occurs (at least in part) because subjects do not vary encodings with complete flexibility. This persistence retards learning in some transfer tasks. However, in conditions favoring changes in encoding, the resulting variability would decrease the amount of negative transfer to be expected.

Martin (1968) has argued that if two sets of stimuli differ in their ease of recoding, there should be less negative transfer found in lists composed of pairs with the stimuli that admit easier recoding. That seems a reasonable deduction to us. Martin then assumed that nonsense stimuli are easier to recode than meaningful words, he derived the prediction that A–B, A–C transfer should be greater for lists with word stimuli than with nonsense stimuli, and he gave evidence supporting that prediction. The empirical results presented in this chapter are inconsistent on whether more or less negative transfer is obtained with word stimuli than with nonsense stimuli. We question whether it is possible to compare amounts of negative transfer meaningfully in conditions involving different kinds of material, considering the present state of nonquantitative theory about parameters of learning. However, it is customary to compute percentage of transfer relative to the difficulty of learning the initial list, and that probably provides a reasonable index that is comparable among conditions. The usual procedure uses each subject's first-list performance as a base for that subject's percentage of transfer. We cannot obtain estimates of difficulty in the two stages separately for individual subjects simply because each individual gives too few observations. However, we have computed percentages of transfer for groups of subjects, using the formula

$$\% \, T_i = \frac{Z_{i1} - Z_{i2}}{Z_{i1}} \times 100,$$

where Z_{i1} is the value of $E(Z_i)$ for the initial A–B list, and Z_{i2} is the value of $E(Z_i)$ for the transfer list. The values obtained for the 16 conditions in Greeno's transfer experiment are in Table 6-18.

If we take the amount of negative transfer in A–C as the difference between $\%T$ for A–C and C–D, then with word responses in both stages of learning there was less negative transfer with word stimuli ($+2.1\%$ and -12.6%) than there was with nonsense stimuli (-9.6% and -33.4%). The direction of the difference accords with Martin's assumptions. However, with nonsense

Table 6-18 Percentage of Transfer for Greeno's Experiment

Stimuli	Responses	Paradigm	$\%T_1$ (First Stage)	$\%T_2$ (Second Stage)
Words	Words	A–C	5.0	49.4
Words	Words	C–D	2.9	62.0
Words	Words	A–B$_r$	−5.8	36.5
Words	Words	C–B	12.3	70.6
Nonsense	Words	A–C	35.6	12.6
Nonsense	Words	C–D	45.2	46.0
Nonsense	Words	A–B$_r$	30.9	−11.8
Nonsense	Words	C–B	51.8	39.8
Words	Nonsense	A–C	33.1	21.4
Words	Nonsense	C–D	38.1	40.0
Words	Nonsense	A–B$_r$	56.2	−18.7
Words	Nonsense	C–B	60.7	59.3
Nonsense	Nonsense	A–C	28.0	31.4
Nonsense	Nonsense	C–D	22.0	40.8
Nonsense	Nonsense	A–B$_r$	60.4	21.8
Nonsense	Nonsense	C–B	66.7	42.2

responses, the amount of negative transfer appears to have been greater in both stages with word stimuli (-5.0% and -18.6%) than with nonsense stimuli ($+6.0\%$ and -9.3%), which seems inconsistent with Martin's conclusion. The situation with A–B$_r$ transfer is similar in some respects. If we take the amount of negative transfer as the difference in $\%T$ between A–B$_r$ and C–B, then the amount of negative transfer in Stage 1 was about equal for both words and nonsense stimuli, both where responses were words (-18.2% and -20.9%) and where they were nonsense (-4.5% and -6.4%). In the second stage, the pattern was similar to that found for A–C transfer. When the responses were words, there was less negative transfer for word stimuli (-34.1%) than nonsense (-51.6%), but when responses were nonsense, there was more negative transfer for word stimuli (-78.0%) than nonsense (-20.4%).

It is not clear to us that this failure to corroborate Martin's finding should be taken as critical evidence against the hypothesis that ease of recoding should produce decreased negative transfer, as both Martin's theory and ours would predict. The problem is in the assumption that it is harder to find new encodings when words are used as stimuli. We wonder whether it may sometimes be easier to find new encodings for word stimuli, especially when the possibilities for mediational and imaginal encodings are included. In any case, we are dubious about comparisons based on such arbitrary indices as percentage transfer in cases where different bases have to be introduced for measurement.

On Inference from Parameter Estimates

Greeno, James, and DaPolito (1971) remarked that the duration of the first stage of learning, estimated by $E(Z_1)$, is "highly correlated" with the number of errors occurring before the first response. This was intended as a didactic remark, to provide intuition regarding the meaning of the statistic. Postman and Underwood (1973) have taken the correlation rather more seriously than we suspect it should be taken, and have presented observed mean trials of first correct responses from some previously published experiments that show substantial differences between C–B and A–B$_r$ in the number of errors before a correct response occurs. The statistics are accompanied by the following remarks (among others):

> Since the measures considered by Greeno et al. were fragmentary and based on parameter estimates of unknown validity, we present in Table 2 more direct measures of the index said to be highly correlated with the duration of the first stage, viz., the number of errors before the first correct response to an item. (Postman & Underwood, 1973, p. 35) In accounting for whatever discrepancies there appear to be between the findings of Greeno et al. and ours, we must for the present limit ourselves to the comment that our measures were determined from the actual experimental observations, whereas theirs were parameter estimates. (Postman & Underwood, 1973, p. 36)

Postman and Underwood's remarks raise several issues. The one we can deal with most easily is the question of what we meant by saying that the duration of Stage 1 is correlated with the trial of the first correct response. Both are random variables according to the model we use to measure learning, and they are positively correlated. We think the correlation is usually quite large. The correlation depends on parameter values, and its formula is quite complicated for the general model. It becomes manageable for simplified versions of the model, and if $r = e$, $s = 1 - a$, $t = ab$, $b = c = d$, and $e = q$, the square of the correlation is

$$\rho^2 = \frac{(1 - a)(p + qc)^2}{(1 - a)(p + qc)^2 + a^2 q(1 - c)}.$$

One set of experimental observations that we have utilized here satisfied the simplifying restrictions that justify this relatively simple expression for the correlation. They are the data obtained by James (1968), presented in this chapter. Using the parameter values given in Table 6-10, the correlations between number of trials in Stage 1 and the number of errors before the first correct response were .82, .88, .69, and .84 for conditions A–C, C–D, A–B$_r$, and C–B, respectively.

The theorem that gives a formula for the correlation between trial of first correct response and trial of transition from the initial state of the Markov chain refers to a single set of parameter values, operating in some experimental condition. If values of statistics are compared, as we have compared values of $E(Z_1)$ and Postman and Underwood have compared the trial of first correct response, and if it is claimed that these measure the same thing, a different meaning of the term "correlation" is involved. Use of one statistic to indicate changes produced in another statistic may be justified, but that requires an argument that the factors influencing the two statistics have effects of similar magnitudes on both of them. Consider an extraneous example: Height and body weight are correlated. Suppose we want to test the hypothesis that carbohydrate intake influences body weight. We divide subjects into two groups, and feed one a high carbohydrate diet, the other a low carbohydrate diet. Then we assess the effect of this manipulation by measuring the heights of the subjects in the two groups.

Of course, the example only shows the possibility that use of a correlated index can give misleading results. We do not know the extent to which $E(Z_1)$ and the number of errors before a correct response are influenced by the same variables, and it certainly would be convenient if it turned out that we could use the mean trial of the first correct response instead of spending the effort and computer time needed to obtain parameter estimates. In this regard, we present the empirical results obtained in Greeno's transfer experiment in Table 6-19. Asterisks in the table refer to cases in which we judge there are

Table 6-19 Comparison of Statistics for Estimating Effects of Transfer (Greeno's Experiment)

Stimuli	Responses	Para-digm	Trials before First Correct	$E(Z_1)$	Trials between First Correct & Criterion	$E(Z_2)$
Words	Words	A–C	1.94	1.35*	.45	1.13*
Words	Words	C–D	1.80	1.38	.34	.85
Words	Words	A–B$_r$	1.94	1.50*	.76	1.42
Words	Words	C–B	1.48	1.24	.24	.66
Nonsense	Words	A–C	3.00	1.94**	.96	2.15**
Nonsense	Words	C–D	2.13	1.65	.54	1.33
Nonsense	Words	A–B$_r$	2.81	2.08	1.50	2.75
Nonsense	Words	C–B	2.32	1.45	.63	1.48
Words	Nonsense	A–C	3.64	3.01	.98	2.16
Words	Nonsense	C–D	3.41	2.78	.60	1.65
Words	Nonsense	A–B$_r$	2.88	1.97**	2.03	3.26
Words	Nonsense	C–B	2.01	1.77	.43	1.12
Nonsense	Nonsense	A–C	5.87	5.26	1.99	3.76
Nonsense	Nonsense	C–D	6.32	5.69	1.60	3.25
Nonsense	Nonsense	A–B$_r$	3.95	2.89	2.66	4.29
Nonsense	Nonsense	C–B	3.45	2.43	1.72	3.18

discrepancies between the conclusions that would be reached using the two statistics.

Our conclusions involve the relative amounts of transfer observed in the two stages. It is comforting that in the majority of cases, approximately the same conclusion would be reached using either measure. However, there are a few substantial exceptions. The most striking is the comparison between A–C and C–D with nonsense stimuli and word responses. Using the estimates of mean trials before first correct response and mean trials between first correct and criterion, A–C is .87 trials worse in the first stage and only .42 trials worse in the second stage. However, using the estimates of $E(Z_1)$ and $E(Z_2)$, A–C is only .29 trials worse in the first stage and is .78 trials worse in the second stage. In general, the estimates obtained from the model give smaller estimates of effects in the first stage and larger estimates of effects in the second stage than do the means of directly countable statistics.

The difference that seems to characterize the two measurements relates to theoretical issues in an important way. We have argued that the greater amounts of negative transfer measured in the second stage are evidence against associative interference theory, and if the alternative measures shown in Table 6-19 were used, our evidence would be considerably attenuated. This forces the issue of comparative validity of the two statistics.

It seems to us that Postman and Underwood have neglected some elementary concepts in statistics when they remarked that their measures "were determined from the actual experimental observations," in contrast to $E(Z_1)$

and $E(Z_2)$, which are "parameter estimates." The contrast is nonexistent; all parameter estimates are determined from actual experimental observations. Furthermore, a statistic such as the difference between mean trials before first correct response in two experimental conditions is a parameter estimate; it estimates the magnitude of an experimental effect on that aspect of performance, and statistical methods for evaluating the reliability of such effects are derived from exactly the same principles as those that justify the tests of hypotheses we have presented in our discussion.

It seems to us that there are two important methodological differences between using an index like trials before the first correct response and an index like $E(Z_1)$. One is that trials before first correct response is much easier to compute. (Perhaps this is what Postman and Underwood referred to when they said their measures "were determined from the actual experimental observations.") The more significant difference is that $E(Z_1)$ is derived from explicit assumptions about the nature of the learning process, while no such assumptions are provided to justify the use of mean trials before first correct response. We believe that the question of the validity of our parameter estimates is well defined; the estimates are valid if the assumptions of the model are correct. There is no way to prove that they are; however, since the assumptions are explicit and sufficiently detailed to specify a probability distribution over the experimental outcome space, it is possible to bring actual experimental observations to bear on the question of whether the assumptions are correct. The question of validity seems more serious for a measure like mean trials before the first correct response, since no theory is provided to connect that parameter estimate with a psychological process.

chapter 7

Forgetting: Proactive Interference

In this chapter and the next we have two main purposes. We will present specific information about procedures and results of experiments on forgetting by DaPolito (1966) and James (1968) that have not been published previously, although their main findings have been summarized (Greeno, James, & DaPolito, 1971). We also show how the Gestalt and information-processing ideas of association we have been using can be applied to the interpretation of some main facts about forgetting. In this chapter we discuss DaPolito's studies and the theory of proactive forgetting, because the theoretical issues seem simpler, and because the findings and hypotheses we present here will be used in our discussion of retroaction in Chapter 8.

Suppose a subject learns an association A–C, after having learned A–B earlier. The subject's retention of A–C may be less successful because of the earlier A–B learning. Thus, the interfering effect of learning A–B operates on the association learned later in time, and for this reason it is called proactive interference.

There is a difficult problem in distinguishing proactive interference with retention, from negative transfer; indeed, we will assert that the two processes are not identifiably different. The difficulty arises because tests of retention must by definition involve material learned earlier. If retention is poor, it may indicate that the material was not learned well—if it had been learned well enough, why should it not be remembered?

At the theoretical level, the needed distinctions can be clearly made. We propose the following: Let Condition C denote a control condition and

Condition I denote a condition where some interference is known to occur. We will say that the two conditions are equal in learning if the same information is stored at the end of training in both conditions. (Note that this allows for negative transfer in that it may take longer for learning to occur in Condition I than in Condition C. The point of the definition is to specify what is meant by an equal state of knowledge when learning is complete.) We will say that the two conditions are equal in retention over a specified interval if equal amounts and kinds of information are lost during the interval. If unequal amounts and kinds of information are present at the beginning of the retention interval, equal retention has to be defined in relation to a theoretical function, and equal retention would occur if the two conditions involved equal displacements along the same function, differing only in their starting positions. Finally, we will say that Condition I and Condition C are equal in retrieval if there are no differences produced at the time of testing. If equal amounts and kinds of information are in memory when the test occurs, equal retrieval implies that performance will be the same. If the conditions are unequal in information available when the test occurs, then equal retrieval must be defined in relation to a theoretical function that specifies test performance as a function of information in memory, and equal retention would mean performance according to the same function, with conditions differing only in the input to the function.

Because theories differ in the loci of interference that they specify, it is important to be clear about different possibilities. McGeoch (1942) explained forgetting using a concept of response competition. This explanation assumes equal storage and retention of information in memory for A–C associations, whether or not they were preceded by A–B, but assumes a difficulty in retrieval for A–C in the interference condition where A–B had been learned previously.

A version of Gestalt theory that has had some credence (Wulf, 1938) assumes that losses in retention are due to assimilation of memory traces. If A–B has already been learned, studying A–C creates similar traces in memory, and the trace of A–C may lose its identity by becoming assimilated with A–B. This theory explains forgetting as poorer retention of information in Condition I than in a comparable condition where the A–C trace would be retained more completely.

The hypothesis that we think most plausible is that A–C items (or other materials that suffer proactive interference) are not encoded as well at the time of learning as are their comparable controls; therefore, the occurrence of greater forgetting in Condition I is due to a difference in the amount and kind of information stored in memory when the items are studied. Of course, any theory that assumed less learning of A–C would predict less retention; thus, associationist assumptions that A–B interferes with learning of A–C could also explain greater forgetting of A–C.

It would be helpful if it could be determined which of the three possible loci was responsible for the detriment in performance that we identify as proactive interference. Unfortunately, we probably cannot. We can observe only the output of all three processes: learning, retention, and retrieval. A difference in performance on a test between two conditions could be produced at any of the three stages. It might be thought that if a list of A–C items was trained to the same criterion of learning in a Condition I (with previous A–B training, for example) and in a Condition C, then equal storage of information had been achieved. However, that equality clearly need not always be achieved. One obvious possibility is that when criterion is reached, more items in one condition than the other stay in short-term memory; large differences in the amount of information stored in long-term memory about the items in the two conditions could occur. More significantly, representations stored in long-term memory may have varying degrees of resistance to forgetting due to interference from later events.

While it seems unlikely that we can discriminate between theories by finding at what point interference occurs, other empirical questions do seem to permit differentiation. The one we will focus on is statistical dependence in recall performance between pairs of items that would be expected to interfere with each other. In the case to be studied in detail here, two items, A–B and A–C, have the same stimulus and different responses. After the two items have been studied along with a number of other items the items are tested. In each test the stimulus A is presented and the subject tries to give both of the responses. The resulting observations permit estimation of the probabilities of recalling both responses, $P(B)$ and $P(C)$, and of conditional probabilities $P(C|B)$ and $P(C|\bar{B})$.[1]

According to most theories, interference between A–B and A–C occurs in a way that should produce a negative dependency between recall of B and C. Thus, we should expect $P(B|C)$ to be less than $P(B|\bar{C})$, at least at first thought. In DaPolito's experiments, the surprising result $P(B|C) = P(B|\bar{C})$ was obtained; that is, recall of the two responses was stochastically independent. There has been a good deal of discussion of the implications of independence of performance on pairs of items since DaPolito's results were obtained, including questions about artifacts in the statistical tests (Hintzman, 1972; Martin & Greeno, 1972) and questions about whether statistical independence should be taken as evidence contradicting various theoretical assumptions (Martin, 1971; Postman & Underwood, 1973). Because the issues are relatively complex, we will postpone detailed discussion of theoretical implications until we have presented the experimental findings. However, it may be useful to give a rough sketch of the general view that leads to the expectation of negative dependency. This rough sketch in fact characterizes the state of mind

---

[1] $P(C|B)$ is the probability that response C is given correctly, given that response B is given correctly. $P(C|\bar{B})$ is the probability that response C is given correctly, given that response B is not given correctly.

that was shared by DaPolito and Greeno when DaPolito's experiments were begun.

The argument uses five assumptions. First, there is some mechanism that produces interference between A–B and A–C when both have been studied. Whatever that mechanism is, it can cause A–C to be forgotten more rapidly if A–B has been learned previously than if A–C has been studied as the first association involving stimulus A. The second assumption is that A–B associations vary in strength. The third assumption is that on the average, stronger A–B associations are more likely to cause interference with retention of A–C than weaker associations. (In some theories, this is the same as the assumption that stronger associations cause more negative transfer—the assumption that Chapter 6 says follows from associationist theory and that we argue is contradicted by some of the results we report regarding negative transfer. In other theories, however, the processes causing negative transfer and those causing proactive interference are separate.) The fourth assumption is that stronger A–B associations will have higher probabilities of recalling B when the test is given. The fifth assumption is that if more interference occurs for an A–C pair, the probability of recalling C will be lower. A straightforward derivation gives the conclusion that $P(C|B)$ should be less than $P(C|\bar{B})$.

DAPOLITO'S EXPERIMENT 1

To examine effects of single presentations of interfering paired associates, DaPolito used a procedure that has been termed a "miniature experiment" (Estes, Hopkins, & Crothers, 1960). For example, a design consisting of two reinforced trials followed by two test trials with no knowledge of results may be represented by $R_1 R_2 T_1 T_2$, where R_1 denotes a single exposure of a stimulus-response pair, R_2 denotes a second study presentation, and T_1 and T_2 denote tests where the stimulus is presented and the subject is asked to give the response. The sequence of R's and T's refers to the sequence of events for a single item. The experiment includes several items which may have different sequences, with interspersed study and test presentations of the different items.

Normally, if an item has a sequence of study trials, the same pair is presented on all trials, then on a test, the subject is asked to give the single response paired with the stimulus being presented. DaPolito's experiments involved a modification. Some of the pairs had successive study trials corresponding to the A–B, A–C transfer paradigm. On tests, subjects were asked to give two responses to each stimulus. (This involves a variant of a testing procedure called modified modified free recall (MMFR), Melton, 1961.) Although some items in the list were paired with only one response, subjects were asked to give two responses to all items in order to avoid influencing their performance by decisions about whether items had one or two responses. The need to give bogus responses to some items did not seem to disturb subjects, especially since the set of possible responses used was a well-defined set of numerals specified to the subject in advance.

Materials and Procedure

The learning materials were two lists, each consisting of 14 symbol-number pairs. There were three different pairings of stimulus and response terms, each being used for 12 of the 36 subjects who participated in the experiment. The relationship between eight items in List 1 and eight in List 2 corresponded to the A–B, A–C paradigm; four items were given A–B presentations in both of the successive lists; the relationship between two items in each list was analogous to the A–B, C–D paradigm. A summary of the list structure is presented in Table 7-1.

The total set of responses used for any two lists consisted of the numerals 1–24. The 16 stimuli were commonly experienced symbols. They consisted of typewriter signs: ampersand, question mark, dollar sign; geometric figures: triangle, square; playing card forms: heart, club, diamond; Greek letters: sigma, phi, chi; and frequently observed forms: flag, half-moon, arrow, bell, cross. Some of the forms were used by Polson, Restle, and Polson (1965) and are shown in Figure 3-2 in Chapter 3. Photographs of each symbol were centered in the left half of a 5- by 8-inch white card; the numbers were centered at the right half of each card. These locations corresponded with the display windows of the exposure apparatus.

A given list of 14 pairs was used as List 1 for six subjects and List 2 for six subjects. Six random orders were used, each being used for six subjects. For each subject the presentation order was randomized with the restriction that one-half the items representing each paradigm occurred in the first half of the series of study presentations while the remaining items occurred in the last half.

Presentation of the two lists was separated by the experimenter rereading a portion of the instructions. On each study trial the stimulus-response pair was shown for 4 seconds and there was a 4-second interpair interval.

Table 7-1 Relationships Among Items Presented on Successive Reinforced Trials in DaPolito's Experiment 1

Experimental Condition	Training Paradigm		Number of Instances in Lists
	R_1	R_2	
Two-Reinforcement Control	A–B	A–B	4
Interference	A–B	A–C	8
RI Control	A–B	—	2
PI Control	—	C–D	2

Upon completion of the second list, the subject was instructed that (1) tests would be given where only the stimulus terms would be presented; (2) some of the stimuli had two correct responses while some had only one correct response; (3) for those stimuli having two correct responses the subject was to recall both in any order; (4) for those stimuli having only one correct response the subject was to recall that response and then select any other number from 1–24 as a second response.

Approximately 1.5 minutes intervened between the end of training and the beginning of the test procedure. For each stimulus the subject was given as much time as required to give two numbers. No knowledge of results was given on test trials. Six orders of presentation of test stimuli were used, each order being used for six subjects. These test sequences were randomized with the restrictions (1) that at least four other learning presentations and/or tests (i.e., 32 seconds) intervened between the last study trial and the test for any item and (2) that one-half of the items representing each paradigm was tested in the first half of the test block with the remaining items being tested in the last half of the test block. Items tested in the first half of Test 1 were not necessarily in the first half of Test 2 since each test sequence was independently randomized with the above restriction. Test 2 followed Test 1 after a 1.5-minute pause.

Results

Proportions of correct responses are shown in Table 7-2. Apparently no retroactive forgetting was caused by the presentation of A–C, as shown by the fact that the first-list B responses were given correctly as often in the A–B, A–C condition as in the RI controls. However, a substantial proactive effect caused the proportion of correct C responses to be significantly less than the proportion of correct responses for the C–D controls, for Test 1, $t(35) = 3.34$, $p < .01$; for Test 2, $t(35) = 4.24$, $p < .01$.

The data in Table 7-2 suggest that the A–C items may have been retained

Table 7-2 Proportions of Correct First-List (R_1) and Second-List (R_2) Responses in DaPolito's Experiment 1

Condition	Paradigm R_1	R_2	MMFR Test 1		MMFR Test 2	
			Correct First-List Response	*Correct Second-List Response*	*Correct First-List Response*	*Correct Second-List Response*
Two-reinforcement Control	A–B	A–B	.757	—	.736	—
Interference	A–B	A–C	.534	.340	.552	.288
RI Control	A–B	—	.542	—	.556	—
PI Control	—	C–D	—	.583	—	.569

Table 7-3 Proportions of Correct Response on Test 2 Conditional on Test-1 Performance

Condition	Item	$P(C_2 \mid C_1)$	$P(C_2 \mid I_1)$
Interference (A–B, A–C)	First List (B)	.961	.082
Interference (A–B, A–C)	Second List (C)	.776	.037
Control (A–B, —)	First List (B)	.974	.061
Control (—, C–D)	Second List (D)	.905	.100

less well between Test 1 and Test 2 than the items in other conditions. A more precise indicator of retention is the conditional proportion of correct responses on Test 2 given a correct response on Test 1. These values are denoted $P(C_2 \mid C_1)$ in Table 7-3. Proportions of correct response on Test 2 given incorrect on Test 1 are denoted $P(C_2 \mid I_1)$. The main result shown in the table is the lower value of $P(C_2 \mid C_1)$ for A–C items compared to all the other groups. This indicates that retention was considerably less good for the A–C items than for the A–B items or for the controls.

The most important result of the experiment, shown in Table 7-4, gives the proportions of joint events for the tests of A–B, A–C items. The outcome labelled BC refers to the subject giving both the B and C responses on a test. $B\bar{C}$ means that B was given correctly but C was missed. $\bar{B}C$ means that B was missed and C was given correctly, and $\overline{BC}$ means that neither B nor C was given correctly on the test. The expected proportions were obtained in the usual manner for testing independence of two variables. The probabilities $P(B)$ and $P(C)$ were estimated from the marginal proportions of correct responses for the two items. Then, if the responses are statistically independent, the expected proportions of joint outcomes should be

$$P(BC) = P(B)P(C), P(B\bar{C}) = P(B)(1 - P(C)),$$
$$P(\bar{B}C) = (1 - P(B))P(C), P(\overline{BC}) = (1 - P(B))(1 - P(C)).$$

For example, for Test 1 in Table 7-4, the marginal proportion of B is .534,

Table 7-4 Proportions of Joint Outcomes on Tests of A–B, A–C Items and Proportions Expected from Assumption of Response Independence

	$P(BC)$	$P(B\bar{C})$	$P(\bar{B}C)$	$P(\overline{BC})$
Test 1, Observed	.201	.333	.139	.326
Test 1, Expected	.182	.352	.158	.308
Test 2, Observed	.163	.389	.125	.323
Test 2, Expected	.159	.393	.129	.319

and the marginal proportion of C is .340. This gives the expected proportion of BC as .534 × .340 = .182; the expected proportion of B$\bar{\text{C}}$ is .534 × .660 = .352, and so on. As is clear from looking at the table, the hypothesis of independence cannot be rejected in these data. The statistics obtained for the chi-square tests of independence were $\chi^2(1) = 1.69$ for the first test, and $\chi^2(1) = .09$ for the second test.

The chi-square test assumes independent observations. In the experiment, there were eight items in the A–B, A–C condition for each subject. Lack of independence can influence the obtained value of chi-square, but we would expect a smaller effect of averaging if we divided the subjects into subgroups based on overall performance. Subjects were divided into three subgroups based on their performance on items from all conditions in Test 1. Call these the Best, Medium, and Worst subjects, respectively. Table 7-5 shows the observed proportions of joint outcomes in Test 1 for these three groups of subjects, along with expected proportions based on assuming independent responses. In none of the three cases was there any evidence of dependence between the responses: the largest value of chi square was obtained for the Best subjects ($\chi^2(1) = 1.07$, $p = .30$). There appears to be no evidence here that the independence obtained for the whole group was produced by averaging across subjects whose various dependencies cancelled each other.

Discussion

DaPolito failed to obtain evidence of retroactive interference. This lack of evidence seemed surprising when the result was obtained, and it still is not well understood. However, recent experiments by Tulving and Watkins (1974) have shown that relative amounts of retention of A–B and A–C items are greatly influenced by the presence or absence of immediate tests of the A–B items prior to study of A–C. Since the strong expectation of retroactive interference is based mainly on evidence obtained when A–B is tested prior to study of A–C, and since DaPolito did not test A–B prior to presenting A–C, the absence of retroactive interference may not be as anomalous as it seemed at the time.

Table 7-5 Proportions of Joint Outcomes on Test 1 for Three Subgroups of Subjects, and Proportions Expected from Response Independence

	$P(BC)$	$P(B\bar{C})$	$P(\bar{B}C)$	$P(\overline{BC})$
12 Best Subjects, Observed	.344	.354	.115	.187
12 Best Subjects, Expected	.320	.378	.139	.163
12 Medium Subjects, Observed	.146	.458	.094	.302
12 Medium Subjects, Expected	.145	.459	.095	.301
12 Worst Subjects, Observed	.115	.188	.208	.489
12 Worst Subjects, Expected	.098	.205	.225	.472

On the other hand, the absence of retroactive interference makes a cleaner situation regarding inferences for theory. DaPolito's experiments apparently involved proactive interference without concomitant retroaction. Thus, the empirical properties of forgetting can be used here to make inferences about the effect of A–B on retention of A–C, without uncertainty about effects operating in the opposite direction.

The difference in performance between the A–C items and the C–D controls probably was due in part to A–C items being learned less well. We know from many experiments, including those described in Chapter 6, that A–B learning produces negative transfer for A–C. In addition to weaker learning (or because of it, depending on assumptions) there apparently was poorer retention of A–C items than of A–B and control items. We are thus inclined to infer that the proactive interference produced by A–B includes a steeper forgetting function for A–C items; the information stored about A–C is retained less well in memory because of the previous study of A–B.

The surprising finding of response independence in MMFR has important implications for theory that we have already noted in a general way, and will comment on in more detail later. Although DaPolito failed to find evidence of artifacts when he divided subjects into groups of more nearly homogeneous ability, the potential importance of the finding of independence seemed to require a direct experimental test. This requirement was met in the next experiment.

DAPOLITO'S EXPERIMENT 2

The results of Experiment 1 seem to support the inference that the interfering effect of an A–B association is independent of the strength of that association—that is, the results contradict the idea that stronger associations should have greater interfering effects. A strong test of that idea is provided if A–B associations are caused to vary in strength by receiving varying numbers of presentations. If there is equal retention of A–C in conditions where A–B varied in the number of study presentations, the empirical support for the hypothesis of independence would be strengthened considerably.

Method

As in Experiment 1, a mixed-list design was used. The training sequences used for experimental and control conditions are shown in Table 7-6. The letters R_1, R_2, R_3, and R_4 represent cycles of study trials in which subjects received paired presentations of stimulus and response terms. The two successive tests (T_1 and T_2) that followed the completion of R_4 were unpaced MMFR-type recall tests as employed in Experiment 1.

Each row of Table 7-6 describes the sequence of paired-associate items presented over the four reinforced trials for each experimental and control

Table 7-6 Sequences of Stimulus and Response Changes over Reinforced Trials for Items in Each Condition of DaPolito's Experiment 2

Condition	Spacing	Training Paradigm				Number of Instances in List
		R_1	R_2	R_3	R_4	
3–OL Interference		A–B	A–B	A–B	A–C	3
3–OL Control		A–B	A–B	A–B	C–D	3
2–OL Interference	I	e–B	A–B	A–B	A–C	1
2–OL Control	I	e–B	A–B	A–B	C–D	1
2–OL Interference	II	A–B	e–B	A–B	A–C	1
2–OL Control	II	A–B	e–B	A–B	C–D	1
2–OL Interference	III	A–B	A–B	e–B	A–C	1
2–OL Control	III	A–B	A–B	e–B	C–D	1
1–OL Interference	I	e–B	e–B	A–B	A–C	1
1–OL Interference	II	e–B	A–B	e–B	A–C	1
1–OL Interference	III	A–B	e–B	e–B	A–C	1

condition. It may be helpful to refer to the training cycles R_1, R_2 and R_3 as original learning (OL) since the last reinforced cycle (R_4) is analogous to the interpolated learning in the more conventional homogeneous-list designs. Thus the first three training cycles permitted one, two, or three presentations of first-list (A–B) pairs, whereas a single paired presentation of "second-list" (A–C or C–D) pairs occurred on the last training cycle (R_4). For experimental and control conditions receiving one or two paired presentations during OL, the filler items represented by e–B (i.e., new stimulus with the same first-list response) were included to control for frequency of occurrence of first-list response terms. As shown in Table 7-6, there were three possible spacings for critical first-list (A–B) pairs receiving one or two paired presentations during OL. It should be noted that the control condition 2–OL (spacing I) was also an appropriate control for condition 1–OL (spacing III) when recall of the control pair e–B is compared with the recall of A–B in the 1–OL interference condition. Similarly, the 2–OL control condition (spacing II) also provided a RI control for the interference condition 1–OL (spacing II) when the control item e–B is compared against the A–B pair in condition 1–OL (spacing II). Also, the 2–OL control (spacing III) provided an RI control comparison for the A–B pair in 1–OL (spacing I). Thus the 2–OL control conditions served two functions and were not duplicated for conditions receiving one paired presentation during original learning.

Items were presented in the same way as in Experiment 1. The materials for learning were word-number pairs (e.g., Gem-12). The stimulus terms were English three-letter monosyllables taken from Appendix D of Underwood and Schulz (1960). The numerals 1–30 were used as the set of possible responses. There were three arrangements of stimulus-response terms and each arrangement was used for 20 of the 60 subjects who participated. For a given arrangement, the second-list (A–C and C–D) pairs were used as first-list pairs for 10 subjects. In this case the response terms for e–B items changed appropriately, but the stimulus terms remained the same.

Procedures for test items were also the same as in Experiment 1. There were six orders for presentation of test stimuli and each was randomized with the same restrictions as used in Experiment 1 except that items representing each condition were tested equally often in each half of the test blocks over every 20 subjects.

Results

The main new result involves comparison of A–C performance in the various conditions with different numbers of A–B presentations. The data are shown in Table 7-7. The results obtained with different spacing of presentations have been pooled; statistical analysis showed differences in performance of A–B items that were differently spaced, but not on the corresponding A–C items that are the main focus of the analysis. Each proportion in Table 7-7 is based on 180 observations.

Analyses of variance were carried out, and showed that the large effect of number of presentations on A–B performance was strongly significant, $F(2,108) = 57.4$, $p = $ nil. As in Experiment 1, there was no evidence that retroactive forgetting occurred; the small difference between A–B interference items and their controls was not significant, $F(1,54) = 0.13, p > .75$, nor was the interaction between interference vs. control and number of presentations, $F(2,108) = 1.51, p > .10$. The apparent proactive detriment on performance of A–C was reliable: A–C items were significantly different from the C–D controls, $F(1,54) = 33.9$, $p = $ nil, and there was a significant interaction between interference vs. control and the test, apparently due to a retention loss of the C–D items that was numerically greater than the loss of A–C items between the tests, $F(1,54) = 4.67, p < .05$.

Table 7-7 Proportion of Correct First-List (R_1) and Second-list (R_2) Responses on Each Test in DaPolito's Experiment 2

Condition	Paradigm (Spacings Pooled)	MMFR Test 1 $P(R_1)$	MMFR Test 1 $P(R_2)$	MMFR Test 2 $P(R_1)$	MMFR Test 2 $P(R_2)$
1–OL Interference	. . . A–B . . . . A–C	.494	.300	.461	.300
1–OL RI Controls	. . . A–B . . . . ——	.528	——	.505	——
2–OL Interference	. . A–B . . A–B . A–C	.728	.289	.694	.256
2–OL RI Controls	. A–B . . A–B . ——	.733	——	.700	——
2–OL PI Controls	—— —— C–D	——	.483	——	.439
3–OL Interference	A–B A–B A–B A–C	.822	.317	.828	.328
3–OL RI Controls	A–B A–B A–B ——	.767	——	.744	——
3–OL PI Controls	—— —— —— C–D	——	.488	——	.428

Table 7-8 Proportions of Joint Outcomes and Expected Proportions from Independence

Number of A–B Presentations	Test		$P(BC)$	$P(B\bar{C})$	$P(\bar{B}C)$	$P(\bar{B}\bar{C})$	χ^2
1	1	Observed	.133	.361	.167	.339	.51
1	1	Expected	.148	.346	.152	.354	
2	1	Observed	.222	.506	.067	.205	.37
2	1	Expected	.210	.518	.079	.194	
3	1	Observed	.278	.544	.039	.139	1.22
3	1	Expected	.261	.561	.056	.122	
1	2	Observed	.139	.322	.161	.378	.02
1	2	Expected	.138	.323	.162	.377	
2	2	Observed	.156	.539	.100	.205	1.63
2	2	Expected	.178	.517	.078	.227	
3	2	Observed	.289	.539	.039	.133	1.25
3	2	Expected	.272	.556	.056	.116	

The major result was that A–C performance appears to have been totally unaffected by the number of presentations given to A–B. The small differences shown in Table 7-7 were comfortably nonsignificant, $F(2,108) = 1.12$, $p >$ .25, as were all the interactions of number of A–B presentations with other experimental variables.

Items within the various experimental conditions were analyzed to test the statistical independence of responses. The results are in Table 7-8, which gives the proportions of joint outcomes observed and expected on the hypothesis of independence, and the values of the chi-square test statistic for independence. All the conditions gave data in agreement with the independence hypothesis.

Table 7-9 shows the conditional probabilities of correct response on Test 2, depending on Test-1 performance. Retention of A–C items as measured by $P(C_2 | C_1)$ again appears poorer than retention of A–B items and controls, although in this experiment the differences were not as large as they were in Experiment 1.

Table 7-9 Proportions of Correct Response on Test 2 Conditional on Test-1 Performance

Condition	Item	$P(C_2 | C_1)$	$P(C_2 | I_1)$
Interference (A–B, A–C)	First List (B)	.908	.134
Interference (A–B, A–C)	Second List (C)	.767	.082
Control (A–B, —)	First List (B)	.888	.154
Control (—, C–D)	Second List (D)	.811	.076

Discussion

The results of this experiment provide very strong support for the conclusion that the proactive effect of A–B associations is independent of their strengths. There must have been a considerable difference in the strength of A–B associations in the different conditions; the probability of correct response was increased from .49 to .82 by increasing the number of presentations from one to three. Yet the amount of interference with A–C performance was equally great in all three of the conditions.

Given the lack of difference between conditions, it is not surprising that the analysis of items within conditions showed that responses were independent. Strength of A–B associations surely varied among items in a single experimental condition, but the amount of variation probably was not as great as that produced between conditions. In any case, the results of the statistical analysis and the result of the experimental manipulation were consistent.

The measures of retention obtained by estimating $P(C_2 | C_1)$ are consistent with the conclusion in Experiment 1 that at least part of the detrimental effect on A–C performance is proactive interference with retention of A–C, in addition to whatever effect there is of direct negative transfer.

PROACTIVE INTERFERENCE IN RECOGNITION

There are several reasons for supposing that the proactive interference occurring in DaPolito's experiments should be associated with the first stage of learning rather than the second. First, the effect was obtained when items were given a single presentation. Although second-stage effects could be observed in a single presentation because for some items both stages can be accomplished on a single trial, with a single presentation of A–C, first-stage effects should predominate.

A second reason is theoretical. According to the conceptualization we developed in Chapter 4, the first stage involves storing a representation of a pair in memory, and the second stage involves learning to retrieve the representation reliably. The retrieval learning that occurs in the second stage involves important components of stimulus discrimination and learning of relations among pairs in the list. It seems unlikely that processes affecting retrieval learning would have very much effect in DaPolito's experiments, since the sequence of study trials had the character of a series of individual items. Subjects probably did not develop very much of a retrieval system for any of the items; therefore the difficulty with A–C items should not be due to a less efficient retrieval system for those items.

A third reason for supposing that DaPolito's proactive interference operates on storage, rather than on retrieval, is connected with the theory of retroactive interference that we will discuss in Chapter 8. We will argue that retroactive forgetting may be due primarily to interference that occurs between retrieval systems in which different organizations are required for retrieval of the A–B and the A–C items. On this hypothesis, the absence of any measurable retroactive interference would be a further indication that retrieval learning played little or no role in the effects observed in DaPolito's experimental situation.

If these arguments and hypotheses are correct, we should expect to find proactive effects in recognition memory of the same order of magnitude as those observed in recall. A recognition test requires retrieval of less information than a recall test; it therefore provides a more direct assessment of stored information. If it were found that proactive effects of the kind observed in DaPolito's other experiments were greatly reduced when testing was done by a recognition method, we would have reasons for doubting several aspects of the analysis developed thus far.

Method

Materials for learning were the picture-numeral pairs used in DaPolito's Experiment 1. There were 2 cycles of study presentations with 12 items in each cycle. In both cycles, 6 stimuli appeared with different responses in the A–B, A–C paradigm. In addition, there were 6 A–B items in the first cycle whose stimuli did not appear in the second cycle; and similarly, 6 C–D items in the second cycle had new stimuli. These additional 12 items served as retroactive interference and proactive interference controls, respectively. There were 3 arrangements of stimulus and response terms, each arrangement used for 15 of the 45 subjects who participated in the experiment. Instructions and presentation procedure were the same as in Experiments 1 and 2.

After the study presentations were completed, a two-alternative forced-choice recognition test was given for each pair. In each test, a stimulus was presented with two numerals (both from the set 1–24), of which one was correct. An advantage of testing for recognition is that order of testing the A–B and A–C pairs can be controlled. (In recall, the subject controls the order of output of B and C when A is presented, and it is possible that the first response output could interfere with retrieval of the other response.) For items in the A–B, A–C interference condition, one-half of the A–C pairs were tested in the first half of the test block with their corresponding A–B pairs tested in the last half; the remaining A–C pairs were tested in the last half of the test block with their corresponding A–B pairs in the first half. Items in each control condition were similarly divided between the two halves of the sequence of test trials.

Prior to the test, subjects were instructed as follows: (1) On every test a symbol would appear with two numbers–one correct number and one wrong number. (2) In every case, only one number was correct. (3) The subject was to pronounce the correct number previously associated with the symbol. No explicit mention was made of the fact that some symbols had two correct numbers and would appear twice in the list. If the subject asked whether some symbols would appear more than once he was told that this might happen. Each test item was presented for 4 seconds with a 4-second interitem interval.

Results

Performance on the recognition tests is reported in Table 7-10. Performance was evidently worse in the second half of the test block for all conditions. There was significant proactive interference for items tested in both halves, evidenced by reliable differences between A–C items and C–D controls, first half: $t(44) = 5.14$, $p < .001$; second half: $t(44) = 2.67$, $p < .02$. The difference between A–B interference items and RI controls in the second half of the test block was not significant, $t(44) = 1.42$, $.10 < p < .20$.

The analysis of the hypothesis of independence is given in Table 7-11. The result with recognition corresponds to all the previous tests; the data were consistent with the independence hypothesis.

Discussion

The experiment showed sizable proactive interference in recognition, consistent with expectations based on the earlier results. Performance on

Table 7-10. Proportions of Correct Choices in DaPolito's Recognition Experiment

Condition	Paradigm R_1	R_2	Half of Test Block	Proportion Correct R_1 Recognitions	Proportion Correct R_2 Recognitions
Interference	A–B	A–C	First	.882	.718
Interference	A–B	A–C	Second	.785	.645
Interference	A–B	A–C	Pooled	.833	.681
RI Control	A–B	—	First	.874	
RI Control	A–B	—	Second	.852	
RI Control	A–B	—	Pooled	.863	
PI Control	—	C–D	First		.911
PI Control	—	C–D	Second		.807
PI Control	—	C–D	Pooled		.859

Table 7-11 Proportions of Joint Outcomes and Expected Proportions assuming Independence for DaPolito's Recognition Experiment

Pair Tested in First Half	Pair Tested in Second Half		$P(BC)$	$P(B\bar{C})$	$P(\bar{B}C)$	$P(\overline{BC})$	χ^2
A–B	A–C	Observed	.578	.304	.067	.051	.52
A–B	A–C	Expected	.569	.313	.076	.042	
A–C	A–B	Observed	.570	.215	.148	.067	.23
A–C	A–B	Expected	.564	.221	.154	.061	

A–B and A–C was independent, also making the recognition performance consistent with earlier findings obtained with recall tests.

IMPLICATIONS FOR THEORY

The empirical fact of independence of A–B and A–C performance in the mixed-list situation used by DaPolito seems thoroughly established. Consequently, we need to discuss what conclusions are required regarding theory of proactive interference.

In our view, the implications of the result are very strong. We think that independence of A–B and A–C performance found where there was substantial proactive interference requires the rejection of nearly all the plausible hypotheses that were available for explaining proactive forgetting. These include hypotheses of response competition, assimilation of memory traces, and interference between associations at the time of encoding the A–C item. We will start by giving a detailed argument against response competition, and then argue that the same considerations apply to the other hypotheses we have mentioned.

The theoretical problem for hypotheses such as response competition does not arise from the finding of independence alone; that fact could be accommodated if it were not for the concomitant finding of proactive interference acting on the A–C pairs. Any hypothesis must postulate a mechanism that is strong enough to produce the detriment in retention of A–C that was observed and allow for independence of A–B and A–C at the same time. DaPolito's evidence is especially incisive, partly because there was no retroactive interference in his experiments. This allows theoretical leverage to be applied precisely on mechanisms that produce influence of previously learned material on new associations. Another important factor is the lack of any clear list structure in the materials presented by DaPolito. This makes hypotheses that depend on listwide organization extremely implausible, forcing the result to be applied to mechanisms involving individual items.

Response competition is assumed to produce proactive forgetting because, when two responses are connected to the same stimulus, they interfere with each other's performance. In DaPolito's experiments, such interference would have to have been strongly asymmetric—the B response apparently interfered with the C response, but not vice versa. And a B response should not have an interfering effect just because it was presented; the interference occurs because the interfering response is connected with the stimulus in the subject's memory. Thus, some learning of the A–B association has to be postulated for there to be an effect due to response competition.

A reasonable expectation might be that if an A–B association had not been learned well enough for the B response to occur on the MMFR test (or to be chosen in a recognition test), then it would not be strong enough for the B response to produce interference. We have worked out the implications of this idea for DaPolito's first experiment. For Test 1, the data give the estimate $P(B) = .534$. Suppose that without interference, the C responses would be just as likely as the B's, that is, $P(C|\bar{B}) = P(B)$. (It would be just as reasonable to equate $P(C|\bar{B})$ with the proactive interference control items, which would give nearly the same result for these data.) A second item of data is that $P(C)$ was .340. By the rule of total probability,

$$P(C) = P(C|\bar{B})P(\bar{B}) + P(C|B)P(B).$$

Substituting the empirical values for $P(B)$, $P(\bar{B})$ and $P(C)$, and using the assumption that $P(C|\bar{B}) = P(B)$, we can solve for $P(C|B)$.

$$.340 = (.534)(.466) + P(C|B)(.534); \quad P(C|B) = .170.$$

With values of $P(B)$ and $P(C|B)$ we can calculate theoretical values for the joint outcomes; for example,

$$P(BC) = P(B)P(C|B) = (.534)(.170) = .091.$$

The theoretical values obtained in this way are shown in Table 7-12, along with the empirical values repeated from Table 7-4, and goodness-of-fit chi-square statistics. This hypothesis clearly is well outside the acceptable range.

The assumption that $P(C|\bar{B}) = P(B)$ was used in a way that made a correct prediction about the amount of negative transfer. It made a very inaccurate prediction about the dependence between B and C. Is it possible for a different hypothesis that still assumes response competition to predict independence and still allow the amount of proactive interference that was obtained? There seem to be three possibilities; unfortunately, one of them seems very implausible and the other two very improbable.

The implausible solution is to assume that all the items studied receive sufficient associative strength to produce equal amounts of response competition. The difficulty is in assigning equal effect in interference to responses that are clearly unequal in other ways—namely, retrievability in a recall test and recognizability in a forced-choice test. On the other hand, it could be

Table 7-12 Proportions of Joint Outcomes and Proportions Expected from Assumption that $P(C|\bar{B}) = P(B)$

	$P(BC)$	$P(B\bar{C})$	$P(\bar{B}C)$	$P(\bar{B}\bar{C})$	χ^2
Test 1, Observed	.201	.303	.139	.326	75.3
Test 1, Expected	.091	.443	.249	.217	
Test 2, Observed	.163	.389	.125	.323	128.3
Test 2, Expected	.040	.512	.248	.200	

assumed that a study trial always produces at least a small increase in associative strength, and that the maximum interfering effect of A–B on A–C is achieved with whatever amount is taken to be the minimum increment.

The improbable solutions assume that the amount of proactive interference does depend on the associative strength of the A–B item, but that some other factor causes the quantitative relationships found in the data. These solutions are necessarily quantitative in form. To explain apparent independence in spite of a hypothesis such as response competition that implies negative dependence, it must be assumed that there is some compensating factor that operates in just the right quantity to cancel the expected dependence.

One candidate for a mechanism that would tend to obscure negative dependence between A–B and A–C is stimulus differentiation. It is quite likely that items acquiring relatively strong A–B associations also have relatively differentiated stimuli, and good differentiation should facilitate learning and retention of A–C. We assume that when two associations with the same stimulus have been learned, they can be stored in the same retrieval network, but they will be found at different terminal nodes of the network. The simplest case is diagramed in Fig. 7-1, which shows a feature test that presumably is preceded by a number of other tests, but is the last test before identification of two associations, A–B and A–C. Suppose that p is the probability of reaching the feature just above these two associations when the subject tries to retrieve either of the items. Then let q be the probability of retrieving the A–B item, given that the search reached the final feature, and let r be the probability of retrieving A–C, given that the final feature was reached.

If separate tests were given for the two items we would have

$$P(B) = pq, \ P(C) = pr,$$

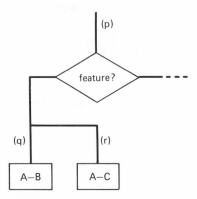

Figure 7-1   Portion of a retrieval network showing hypothetical links needed to retrieve A-B and A-C items.

and if independence of the *tests* could be assumed,

$$P(B \cap C) = p^2 qr.$$

However, for a MMFR test, it is more reasonable to assume that an attempt is made to search the network and retrieve both of the items. On a single test of both items, we would have

$$P(B \cap C) = pqr, \, P(B \cap \bar{C}) = pq(1-r), \, P(\bar{B} \cap C) = p(1-q)r,$$
$$P(\bar{B} \cap \bar{C}) = 1 - p + p(1-q)(1-r).$$

From this it follows that

$$P(B) = pq, \, P(C) = pr,$$

as before, but $P(BC)$ is *pqr* in the MMFR situation.

The finding of independence between retention of A–B and of A–C is that $P(C)$ remains constant in spite of variations in $P(B)$. The finding was strongest in DaPolito's Experiment 2, where variation in $P(B)$ was produced experimentally. If something like Figure 7-1 represents the situation, independence of A–B and A–C means that *pr* was constant, even though *pq* was considerably larger for items with more presentations. According to the hypothesis of response competition, r should become smaller if q is increased. But both p and q should increase with the number of presentations of A–B. Therefore, r could decrease because of response competition, but an increase in p could compensate for that, leaving *pr* approximately constant. The only difficulty with this explanation is the coincidence that must be assumed regarding the compensating changes in p and r. The conclusion that r was simply unaffected by changes in q is more parsimonious, and more falsifiable in future research, and thus seems a potentially more productive conclusion.

The other factor that can be considered in trying to explain independence of A–B and A–C retention is variation of parameter values. The values of p, q, and r almost certainly are not constant, despite efforts to construct relatively homogeneous sets of items and sample subjects from a relatively homogeneous population. Furthermore, the parameter values for subjects and items probably do not vary independently. Skillful subjects probably have relatively high values of all the parameters for most of the items, and some items with stimuli easy to relate to responses might have relatively high values of all the parameters.

To analyze effects of possible intersubject and interitem differences, we must consider parameters as random variables. If the parameters of the process are p, q, and r, then in an MMFR test,

$$EP(B) = E(pq), \, EP(C) = E(pr), \, EP(B \cap C) = E(pqr).$$

The possible relationships among three varying parameters are very complicated, but our main theoretical interest here has to do with dependencies
between q and r, so for simplicity, assume that p is a constant. Then

$$E(pq) = pE(q), \ E(pr) = pE(r), \ E(pqr) = pE(qr).$$

By the definition of covariance,

$$E(qr) = \text{Cov}(q, r) + E(q)E(r) = \text{Cov}(q, r) + \frac{1}{p_2}[EP(B) \cdot EP(C)].$$

We are interested in conditions where retention of B and C are independent;
that is,

$$EP(B) \cdot EP(C) = EP(B \cap C) = E(pqr) = p \cdot \text{Cov}(q, r) + \frac{1}{p}[EP(B) \cdot EP(C)].$$

A few algebraic transformations show that the retention of B and C are
independent if and only if

$$EP(B) \cdot EP(C) = -\frac{p^2}{1 - p} \text{Cov}(q, r).$$

The hypothesis of response competition implies that $\text{Cov}(q, r)$ should be
negative, and this agrees with the results, since $p^2/(1 - p)$ will be positive.
However, it seems very improbable that the values of p and $\text{Cov}(q, r)$ so
that $-(p^2/1 - p) \text{Cov}(q, r)$ should just equal the value of $EP(B) \cdot EP(C)$
would be obtained in so many cases.

It seems to us that the arguments against response competition can be
applied with the same cogency against two other hypotheses. One is that the
A–B association leaves a memory trace, and the trace of A–C is subject to
assimilation to the trace of A–B. The other theory is that because A–B has
been stored with some relational encoding, the set of relational mediators
available for encoding A–C is reduced; therefore, it is more likely that the
subject will fail to find an encoding, or if one is found, it is likely to be less
stable or distinctive. Both of these theories suffer from the same difficulties
as the response competition hypothesis. If they are made to depend on the
strength of A–B learning, they cannot accomodate independence. To predict
independence, they must assume that minimal learning produces maximum
interference, which is implausible. And if they are combined with another
compensating process, the compensation must be so precise that the assumptions become extremely improbable.

In our own search for an explanation of DaPolito's findings, we have been
led to the hypothesis of interference based on stimulus encoding that we
presented at the beginning of Chapter 6. We believe that the representation
of the stimulus in memory will generally be influenced by the subject's effort

to represent the stimulus-response pair. And if we assume that the encoding of the stimulus tends to persist, it will generally be a poorer representation for relating the stimulus to another response in A–C than would be likely if the stimulus had not been in the A–B pair.

Our hypothesis of persistent encoding falls into the same class as the implausible versions of response competition, trace assimilation, and associative interference. That is, it explains independence by assuming that mere study of the A–B items produces whatever interfering effect there will be, whether or not the study leads to successful learning of the A–B pair. We think this assumption is more plausible regarding stimulus encoding than it is regarding the other mechanisms considered because, under conditions generally used in paired-associate experiments, recognition of stimuli should be easy after a single trial. To study relations between stimulus recognition and recall of association, it is necessary to use longer lists and more confusable items than are necessary to make a reasonable task for learning associations (see Martin, 1967, for an example). Recognition of a stimulus depends on keeping an encoded representation of the stimulus in memory. We therefore think it is reasonable to suppose that, at least with relatively distinctive stimuli, the encodings given stimuli by subjects are likely to persisit and influence later attempts to learn.

It may be that the empirical finding of independence depends on having a situation where A–B items are not organized to different degrees for retrieval. Underwood (1949) presented an A–B list for different numbers of trials, then presented an A–C list to a criterion of one perfect trial. Retention of the A–C list was less in conditions where the A–B list had been studied longer. We would suppose that the A–B retrieval system produced interference with A–C retention, causing more interference in cases where subjects became better organized for A–B retrieval. Runquist's (1957) results are consistent with this interpretation. He ranked the A–B items by their inferred strength, using the number of times they were given correctly during original learning. There was no dependence of recall of A–C items on the inferred strength of the A–B interfering items. This fits with DaPolito's results, and shares with DaPolito's situation the feature that stronger and weaker items were all presented together, not allowing the "strong" items to become integrated into a more coherent retrieval system.

chapter 8

Forgetting: Retroactive Interference

When a list of A–B associations has been learned and the subject is then asked to learn a second list, a later test of retention for A–B generally shows that the interpolated learning has interfered with recall of A–B. A–B retention is lower after interpolated learning in the A–C or the A–B$_r$ paradigm than in the C–D or C–B paradigm, but these less interfering situations also have been shown to produce forgetting relative to control conditions.

COGNITIVE THEORY OF RETROACTION

Difficulty in recall may be caused by loss of stored information about the items themselves, or by interference with procedures that are needed to retrieve stored information. In the theory of retrieval that we presented in Chapter 2, recall of associations depends on an active process of testing features of stimuli. After learning an A–B list, interpolated learning requires the development of a new retrieval network involving the features of the second list of associations. We believe the most likely hypothesis to explain forgetting is that development and use of a new retrieval system interferes with use of the first network by making part or all of that network inaccessible.

Previous analyses of forgetting based on retrieval networks have considered two processes (Feigenbaum, 1963; Hintzman, 1968). One is a change in the network by adding features to be tested or a change in the connective structure involving different consequences linked to the outcome of a test. EPAM or SAL would naturally make such changes in the network when new stimuli sharing features with the A–B list were presented. The other mechanism, considered by Hintzman, is the creation of a pushdown stack of responses at a terminal node of the retrieval network. This provides a means for the system to retain information about previous responses but still perform an interpolated task correctly.

The mechanism we propose involves the process of adding features and modifying connections that is indigenous to the idea of a retrieval network, but also applies the notion of pushdown stacks to retain previous connective structure throughout the network (cf. Anderson & Bower, 1973, Chap. 12). Suppose the A–B network contains a test for feature *g*. The upper panel of Figure 8-1 shows a test for *g*, and tests for features *h* and *j* that might be consequent on the outcome of testing for *g*. Now suppose that in interpolated learning, a test for *g* is still useful but, if *g* is absent, the system needs to test for feature *k* instead of *j*. Our hypothesis is that a test for *k* will be located at the top of a pushdown stack stored at the "no" branch from the test for *g*.

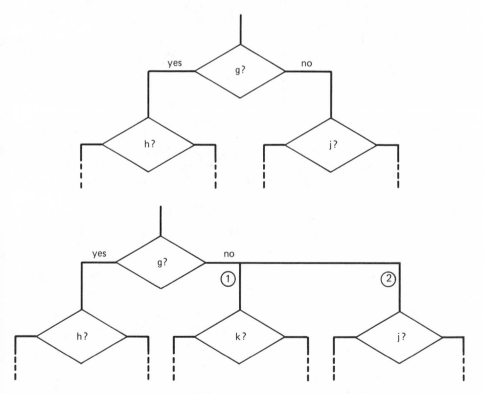

Figure 8-1 Portion of a retrieval network—initially (above) and after modification where test for feature *j* is pushed down in memory.

The node previously located at that branch is pushed down to the second location in the stack, where it is held in storage.

A retrieval network with pushdown storage at each branch is an extremely flexible system. It is possible for such a system to learn not to respond in the old way before a new element is added, by pushing down the stack and entering a null symbol in the top cell of the slot. Various mechanisms are available for the system to err—one of the easiest to implement would be a probability of mistakenly retrieving the second item in the stack. Another straightforward system would involve a nonzero probability of losing the item from the top of the stack between the addition of the new branch and the next test of the item for which it was developed. This would cause the more recently built branch to be lost from memory and the previous branch to occupy the first position.[1]

Figure 8-2 illustrates a network with some pushed-down branches. The list shown has the same stimuli as the one diagrammed in Figure 2-7, but the responses have been changed, and the network has been modified mainly by adding branches just above the terminal nodes. This is the simplest kind of modification and is the kind of change we think is probably typical in the A–B, A–C paradigm.

A modified network like Figure 8-2 will support correct performance of the interpolated list of items, assuming that the subject reliably retrieves the contents of the top position of each pushdown stack. The structure as shown in Figure 8-2 does not contain information needed to retrieve items from the first list when a retention test is given. An assumption made by some theorists (Anderson & Bower, 1973; Norman & Rumelhart, 1970; Shiffrin, 1970) is that contextual information in the form of list-membership tags are associated with information about items stored in memory, and this contextual information is used when a test requires differentiation between items on the basis of their list membership.

In an EPAM-type net there are two ways to incorporate information about context. One is to include nodes that test for features that are distinctive between contexts. An example for Figure 8-2 would be to have another test node on the "yes" branch from "INITIAL G?" that would test "SECOND LIST?"; if the response is yes, then it would recognize *GAC-JOHN*, if no,

---

[1] It may be important to emphasize that the model of pushdown storage does not presuppose a physical system in which information is literally stacked in positions above or below other items of information. The assumption of pushdown memory storage merely requires that information be stored in a way that implies a precedence ordering on retrieval. In a pushdown store automaton, information stored lower in the stack cannot be retrieved without first retrieving the information stored higher in the stack. In human memory, we suppose that the precedence is imposed by the retrieval process; retrieval probably occurs on the basis of links that provide access to the current items. Rearrangement of the stack would then be accomplished if a different set of memory links were active at the time of a later test, and this sort of change could occur because of a change in context or in a number of other factors.

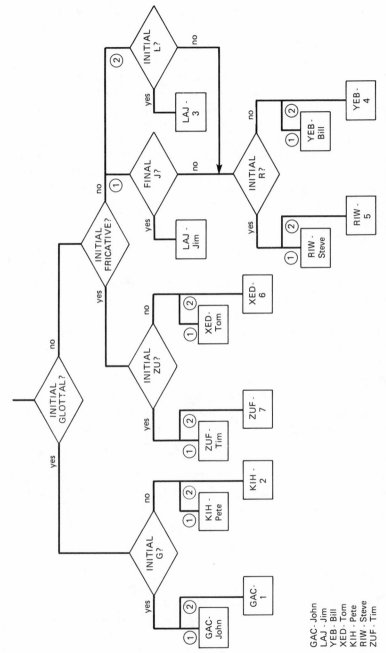

Figure 8-2 Possible retrieval network acquired during A-C interpolated learning. Compare Figure 2.7.

GAC - John
LAJ - Jim
YEB - Bill
XED - Tom
KIH - Pete
RIW - Steve
ZUF - Tim

then recognize *GAC*-1. In effect, this technique makes a single retrieval network for both lists, using features that discriminate between the lists in exactly the way that features of items are used.

Although we can conceive of situations where list-context information would be stored as features to be tested in the retrieval network, that technique seems unlikely as a general procedure. For one reason, in the interpolated list, tests for list membership are not needed and their addition to the network would add unnecessary complexity to the retrieval structure.

The second way to incorporate contextual information is to store it when the memory stack is pushed down along with the information that specifies a feature to be tested or a pattern that is described in the terminal node. If this were done, the subject would have the information needed to retrieve items from the first list, but the information would have to be found by searching through memory in a fairly complicated way. Specifically, information would have to be taken out of memory stacks and tested for the contextual information found as part of the information. This idea is similar to the two-stage mechanism that Kintsch (1970) hypothesized for recall, in that it involves retrieval of items from memory and an editing to select the items that belong in the set being searched for.

According to this group of ideas, subjects always have the information needed for correct performance on a retention test; the problem is whether they can find it. On this point we agree with a majority of recent theorists (e.g., Anderson & Bower, 1973; Shiffrin, 1970) who have argued that the probability of recalling an item depends mainly on the complexity of the search process required to retrieve the item from memory.

In most theories, difficulty of search depends on the number of memory locations that must be examined. Although that factor also contributes to difficulty of search in this system, there is still another important factor. If the subject searches through the retrieval network from the top down, there will be opportunities to pass by the entries to sections of memory containing some items. For example, in Figure 8-2, if the search process neglects to test the initial *L* on the "no" branch from "INITIAL FRICATIVE?" the item *LAJ*–3 will not be retrieved unless the search returns to the highest level a second time.

There could be situations in which the conditions of a test would lead to a thorough search for pushed-down branches at high-level nodes. However, one factor probably works against retrieval at high-level nodes compared to retrieval of pushed-down branches that are located lower in the network: the connections leading to high-level nodes in the interpolated retrieval network have to be used for many of the interpolated items. In Figure 8-2, the connection to "FINAL J?" would be used each time *LAJ-JIM*, *RIW-STEVE*, or *YEB-BILL* was retrieved in the interpolated list. By contrast, lower-level retrievals are used on fewer occasions—the connection to *RIW-STEVE* is used only when that individual item is tested. It might be expected, then, that subjects would build up stronger tendencies to ignore first-list information stored at higher levels in the network, making retrieval of *LAJ*-3 less likely than retrieval of items like *RIW*-5 in many test conditions.

What do these ideas imply about forgetting in the various experimental paradigms? In the control condition C–D, the usual case probably involves developing a new retrieval network for the items in the second list. It is known that retention of A–B items is not perfect after C–D interpolated learning. The most likely explanation is that some stimulus features shared by the A–B and C–D items are used in the retrieval network for C–D after being used for A–B. Development of the C–D network would then cause some nodes in the A–B network to be pushed down into memory, and retrieval of these nodes could be impaired. An interesting implication is that if stimuli in A–C and C–D share more features, learning of C–D should cause more forgetting of A–B; this agrees with the findings (Gibson, 1940).

At times, forgetting of A–B is greater after C–B interpolated learning than after C–D learning, although the difference is generally very small. Recall our assumption that subjects encode a representation of each stimulus-response pair, using relational properties of the two elements when they can. This assumption implies that when the same responses are used in the two lists, stimulus properties shared between the lists are more likely to be included in the encodings. The situation is potentially quite complicated. There can be instances where a feature used in identifying an A–B pair will also be useful in identifying the C–B pair with the same response. This can lead to facilitation—both of second-list learning and, we would suppose, of retention. On the other hand, it need not. We think facilitation would be produced if the shared feature were used to form a grouping of items in the way discussed in Chapter 5. Otherwise, the feature would be embedded in a network of feature tests, and when the feature has been tested, different consequences would generally follow in the C–D network than did in the A–B network. This situation would produce pushdown storage of the nodes of the A–B network and consequent difficulty of retrieving the A–B item or items involved. It must be remembered that difference between retention in the C–B and C–D conditions is generally small and often negligible. Retrieval networks consist of tests on stimulus features, and when new stimuli are used, the presence of old responses apparently has only small effects in increasing the probability of using the same features for C–D that were used for A–B.

The amount of forgetting after A–C or A–B$_r$ learning should be considerably greater than in the C–D and C–B conditions, because the same stimuli are used in the two tasks and there will naturally be greater overlap between the features used in the interpolated and the A–B retrieval networks. The diagram shown in Figure 8-2 illustrates what we propose as a typical result of interpolated learning in the A–C network. Most of the retrieval network from the A–B list remains intact and most of the pushdown storage is created at low-level nodes. Unlike the situation for C–D and C–B, the A–B network has been modified to permit retrieval of new items, and the standard empirical findings regarding forgetting in A–C indicate that subjects do not find it easy to retrieve the first-list items after the interpolated items have been incorporated into the network.

Note that the network used for A–C in Figure 8-2 uses nearly all the same stimulus features as were used for A–B items. This is a consequence of the assumption made in Chapter 6 concerning negative transfer—that is, that subjects will tend to persist in their encodings of stimuli from List 1. As a further consequence, the encodings of items in the A–C list will often make learning and retention more difficult. Figure 8-3 shows a network for the list of A–C items that might be developed by a subject who had no prior experience with the stimuli. Several relations among responses based on phonemic similarity correspond to the stimulus features built into the network of Figure 8-3, and if these were noticed, a subject might be able to learn and retain the list more easily. The network shown in Figure 8-2 represents our idea that encodings are carried over from the first list and influence the encodings of items in A–C; comparison with Figure 8-3 indicates why this may produce negative transfer and proactive forgetting.

We think that a general difference between A–C and A–B$_r$ is in the frequency with which higher-level, as opposed to lower-level, nodes are modified in developing the retrieval network for the interpolated list. In the A–C condition, new responses are used and persistence of stimulus encoding dominates the organization of the retrieval network. However, in A–B$_r$, the first-list responses are present. Relations among the response terms that were noticed and used in A–B learning will still influence the subject's organization of retrieval. This will lead to a tendency for higher-level nodes to be modified in order to produce at least some groupings that correspond to response relations carried in from List 1. An example of A–B$_r$ encoding is given in Figure 8-4. The effect of response-based grouping is illustrated by the use of middle letters such as the initial test for "MIDDLE A ?". This particular feature happens to discriminate the two items with responses 1 and 2 which are grouped together. Recall (or note in Figure 8-4) that the two items with responses 1 and 2 were also assumed to be grouped for the A–B list, but in that case their common feature was an initial glottal consonant.

This hypothesis implies that performance in retention tests could be quite different, depending on the kind of test given. It is known that, if subjects are required to recall responses, retention of associations is often poor following A–C interpolated learning but if multiple-choice tests are given, performance of A–B following A–C is much better and exceeds retention performance in the A–B$_r$ paradigm. Our interpretation is that following A–C, subjects retain more of the initial retrieval system. When a stimulus is presented, subjects

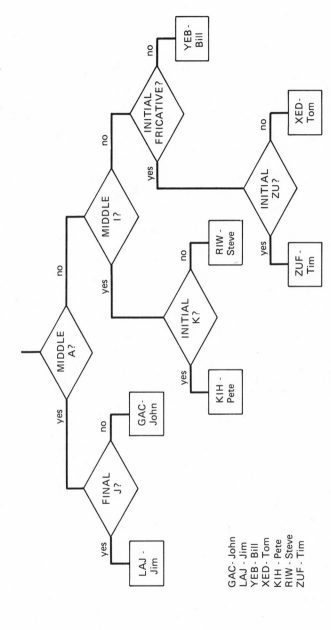

Figure 8-3 Possible retrieval network acquired without prior A-B learning of these A-C items. Compare Figure 8.2.

GAC - John
LAJ - Jim
YEB - Bill
XED - Tom
KIH - Pete
RIW - Steve
ZUF - Tim

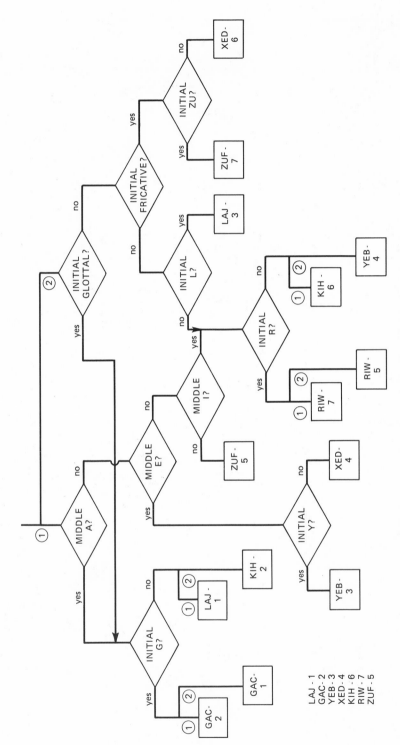

Figure 8-4 Possible retrieval network acquired during A-B$_r$ interpolated learning. Compare Figures 2.7 and 8.2.

can sort through the retrieval network and get quite close to the terminal nodes where the associations are stored. If the first-list responses are presented in the test, they can easily reinstate the last link or so needed to determine which response went with which stimulus. However, after the higher-level modifications that we suppose occur in A–B$_r$ learning, the features used in retrieving associations prevent the subject from getting near some of the associations, and the presentation of the first-list responses (which of course are also the second-list responses) is not a sufficient cue for retrieval of the A–B associations.

Martin (1972), identified another possible reason for the good retention of A–B items on multiple-choice tests. Martin's idea relates to the hypothesis that stimulus features used to represent associations are those that fit into a relational unit involving the response. We think that subjects generally persist in the initial encoding, but a change in the response paired with the stimulus can bring about a change in the features used in the pair's encoding (Weaver, 1969). To the extent that different features of stimuli are used in the retrieval of second-list associations, presentation of the first-list responses should serve as reminders of the stimulus features needed to retrieve the first-list items. This would be more effective in A–C than in A–B$_r$, because during A–B$_r$ learning, subjects continue to see the responses previously paired with all the stimuli and must repress features used for first-list retrieval to permit successful performance on the transfer list.

ASSOCIATIONIST THEORY OF RETROACTION

In the years preceding World War II, associationist theory was strongly developed by American functionalist psychologists. These scientists were unwilling merely to analyze and appreciate association as a solution for intellectual problems such as the genesis of abstract ideas. They wanted to understand what use associations have for persons, and their theoretical questions had a distinctly practical aspect. Much attention was given to the question of why associations are forgotten, and the main outlines of interference theory were developed. McGeoch (1942) developed the idea of response competition, which stated that failure to respond correctly on a test of material learned earlier is attributed to the existence of associations other than the one needed, and results in interference among alternative responses. Results obtained by Melton and Irwin (1940) convinced them that competition among responses was not a sufficient factor to explain important aspects of forgetting, and they introduced the concept that associations learned earlier would become unlearned if later material of an interfering kind had to be memorized. Associationist theory was thus extended to the analysis of forgetting; unlearning and response competition were the main operative concepts in explaining failures to retain learned associations.

Recent analyses have considered detailed aspects of associative unlearning. Major components of the current associationist theory of retroaction were presented by McGovern (1964); thorough reviews and discussions of the theory have been given by Keppel (1968) and Postman and Underwood (1973). McGovern's analysis used the concept of unlearning and dealt with forward, backward, and contextual associations. The main idea is that if there is a first-list association from x to y, then if x appears in the second-list situation without y, there will be some unlearning of the first-list association. The most likely mechanism for producing unlearning is thought to be elicitation of the first-list response during learning of the second list, a condition in which the response is not reinforced.

The theory implies that forward associations from A to B will tend to be unlearned during interpolated learning of A–C or A–B$_r$. Backward associations will tend to be unlearned when the interpolated list is C–B or A–B$_r$. And contextual associations will tend to be unlearned during interpolated learning of A–C or C–D. Assuming that the most important factor in retention is the strength of forward association, this theory explains why forgetting is greater after A–C or A–B$_r$ interpolated learning than after C–D or C–B. Whether A–C or A–B$_r$ produces more forgetting depends on the relative importance of contextual associations (unlearned in A–C) and backward associations (unlearned in A–B$_r$), and the same is true regarding C–D and C–B interpolated learning.

Another important concept in the associationist theory of forgetting is the hypothesis of a response selector mechanism (Underwood & Schulz, 1960)—the idea that once a response pool has been formed, the set of responses can be suppressed or recovered more or less as a unit. Postman (1963a) considered implications of the response selector mechanism regarding retroactive interference, viewing it as a process that can strongly influence the availability of responses. An important use of the concept was by Postman and Stark (1965) who pointed out that a response-set selector might protect forward associations from unlearning during A–C interpolated learning, explaining experimental results in which performance after A–C interpolated learning is quite poor if the responses must be recalled but is much better (sometimes nearly perfect) if the responses are provided, as they are in a multiple-choice recognition test (Postman & Stark, 1969).

COMPARISON OF THEORIES

In preceding chapters, associationist and cognitive theories were shown to diverge at numerous points. This has led to discussion of data that we conclude favor the views we characterize as a cognitive theory of association. With regard to retroactive forgetting, our theory has much in common with the associationist theory as that has developed in recent years. Although things happen in different ways according to the two theories, many of the same things do happen.

According to associationist theory, first-list associations are unlearned during second-list learning. According to the cognitive theory we have presented, first-list associations are pushed down in memory storage and are therefore harder to retrieve. The outcome of these two mechanisms should produce similar effects. For example, the idea that unlearning occurs through a process analogous to extinction of a conditioned reflex has led association theorists to expect spontaneous recovery of unlearned associations. The experimental evidence has been uneven, but some studies report an apparent increase in strength of first-list items during a retention interval following interpolated learning (see Keppel, 1968; Postman & Underwood, 1973). Increase in performance on first-list items relative to second-list items, or even absolute increases in first-list performance, would not be surprising in the theoretical framework we have presented. The simplest hypothesis would suggest rearrangement of the pushdown stacks during retention intervals, with items lower in the stack moving up and taking the places of items that had occupied higher positions. Indeed, Hintzman (1968) assumed such a mechanism in his assumption that responses were stored in pushdown stacks at terminal nodes of SAL's discrimination net.

There is a feature of the cognitive theory that might lead to a differentiating prediction from associationist theory, if the associationist theory did not include the idea of response-set interference. Since the cognitive theory assumes that pushdown storage can occur anywhere in the retrieval network, on some occasions subsets of items should be retrieved or forgotten as a group. It should be possible, then, to construct paired-associate lists in which the relations among items would produce the kinds of clusters whereby subjects would tend to recall either all or none of the items in the cluster. Although such experiments would add to our knowledge about the organization of associative memory, they would not differentiate between cognitive and associative theories, because the foreseeable results could also be explained using the concept of response-set interference. If subjects do form cognitive structures analogous to the list of responses, then the formation of those structures probably involves learning subgroups of associations similar to the groupings of responses that occur during free recall learning (Mandler, 1967; Tulving, 1962), and these subgroups would show the kinds of clustering that are predictable from the theory of retrieval networks.

In case of competition between specific responses, as with unlearning of associations, it seems that the predictions of cognitive theory presented here do not differ from those of the associationist theory. The storage of two or more items in a pushdown stack makes possible the uncertainty in retrieval, and the effect of such uncertainty would probably be indistinguishable from the effect of competition between responses.

The main departure between the theories involves the concept of response-set interference, but even here the ideas have much in common. The hypothesis of competition between sets of responses provides associationist theory with a mechanism that affects subsets of items or the whole list, and such a mechanism clearly is required. The hypothesis of response-set formation is consistent with ideas of response learning, and it would be expected that a coherent response pool might be formed as a part of the process of response learning during learning of a list. However, evidence presented in Chapter 4 seems to us to argue agianst the process of response learning as this has been developed, and therefore also reduces the plausibility of the idea of response-set learning.

On the other hand, the idea of interference between retrieval plans follows directly from the hypothesis that a retrieval network is acquired by subjects in learning to retrieve items from the list. This hypothesis is supported by the evidence of strong effects of stimulus variables in later stages of learning, as well as by the finding that most negative transfer appears to operate in the second stage of learning, when the retrieval network is assumed to be acquired. Thus, it seems to us that the idea of a retrieval network is at least as plausible as the idea of a pool of responses. However, both conceptualizations assign major significance to processes operating at the level of the list—an important similarity between the two.

JAMES' EXPERIMENT

We turn now to empirical results obtained by James (1968), who studied retention after interpolated learning using a series of different kinds of tests. The tests were developed to provide a variety of measures that might show the impossibility of a theory using only the concept of strength of individual associations.

Estimates of negative transfer in James' experiment were presented in Chapter 6. Recall that James presented an A–B list of ten adjective pairs, learned to a criterion of one perfect trial by all subjects, followed by interpolated learning in four different paradigms: A–C, C–D, A–B$_r$, and C–B. In addition to the groups with interpolated training to a criterion of one perfect recitation (the data reported in Chapter 6), still another group in each paradigm was given just two study and two test cycles on the interpolated list, after learning the A–B list to criterion.

Following the interpolated learning, subjects were given a series of tests to measure their retention of the initial A–B items. The first test was a MMFR test in standard form. The subject was given a sheet of paper listing all the stimuli from both lists in random order and was asked to write the correct response or responses beside each stimulus term. The subject was allowed to work as long as she or he thought fruitful, then was asked to list any additional responses not yet written that she or he could remember. Finally, the subject was asked to indicate the list membership of each stimulus.

Following MMFR, the subject was given a response completion task. Each response from the first list was tested by presenting a frame formed by deleting all letters except the first and one other letter. Two different sets of frames were constructed, and one-half of the subjects in each paradigm were tested on each set. For example, the response MANLY was tested using the frames M – – – Y and M A – – –.

In a third test, recall of List-1 responses was measured. The subject was given a sheet of paper containing the stimuli from the first list and was asked to write the correct response from List 1 beside each stimulus.

The final test in the series was a matching test for the List-1 items. The subject received a sheet of paper with the stimuli and responses from the first list and was asked to match each stimulus with its correct response, matching all the stimuli and using no response more than once.

On all four tests, subjects were encouraged to get as many correct as possible. There was no time limit on any of the tests. Intervals between successive tests were approximately 1 minute.

Results

A summary of James' main results is given in Table 8-1. These data are from conditions where interpolated learning was taken to criterion. We will discuss the results of each test in some detail; however, note the main finding that on the MMFR test given immediately after interpolated learning, A–C produced considerable forgetting—substantially more than A–B_r produced. However, on a test given after some of the responses were recalled by special prompting, the A–C group did as well as the A–B_r group. Finally, in a matching test the A–C group's performance exceeded that of the group with A–B_r interpolated learning.

It is important to note performance on the first list, since all subjects learned the same items in interpolated learning and different items in the initial A–B list. The mean trials to criterion in the four conditions were as follows: A–B_r, 4.8; A–C, 5.3; C–B, 5.3; C–D, 6.2. The differences in trials to criterion were not reliable, $F(3, 119) = 1.72, p > .10$. In analysis of the mean

Table 8-1 Proportions of Items Remembered from First List

Interpolated Learning	MMFR Test	Response Completion	List-1 Recall	List-2 Matching
A–B_r	.81	.98	.69	.72
A–C	.57	.72	.70	.94
C–B	.88	.94	.89	.93
C–D	.88	.89	.93	.97

number of errors in List 1, the *F*-ratio was larger, but also not significant, $F(3, 119) = 2.63, p > .05$.

Differences in difficulty of interpolated learning have already been discussed in Chapter 6. We note here the differences in mean trials to criterion among the four paradigms in the groups where interpolated learning was taken to criterion. These constituted differences in the delays between initial learning and the tests of recall. The mean trials to criterion on List 2 were as follows: A–B$_r$, 6.7; A–C, 6.1; C–B, 3.1; C–D, 3.7.

MMFR Results

Table 8-2 presents the full results of the MMFR test. In "strict" scoring, an item was counted correct only if the response was given with its stimulus and identified correctly as to list membership. In lenient scoring, an item was scored as correct if its response occurred anywhere. Substantially higher scores for C–B and A–B$_r$, and small increases ranging from .01 to .04 for C–D and A–C were shown in lenient scoring. Analysis of variance for List-1 recall showed significant effects of paradigms, $F(3,119) = 8.95, p < .01$, of the amount of interpolated learning, $F(1,119) = 7.13, p < .01$, and in the interaction between paradigms and amount of interpolated learning, $F(3,119) = 5.00, p < .01$. Pairwise comparison carried out using the Newman-Keuls test showed that the group receiving A–C training to criterion was poorer than any other group, $p < .01$; all other differences were nonsignificant. Regarding List-2 recall, only the effect of amount of interpolated training was significant, $F(1,119) = 76.7, p < .01$.

Two trials of interpolated learning produced only a modest amount of retroactive forgetting in each of the paradigms. When training was continued to criterion, A–C produced a substantial decrement on MMFR performance, but other conditions produced little additional forgetting. We note especially the failure to find significant retroactive forgetting in the A–B$_r$ paradigm; this conflicts with other findings (e.g., Postman, 1964; Postman &

Table 8-2 Proportion Correct on MMFR Test

Amount of Interpolated Training	Paradigm	List 1 Strict	List 1 Lenient	List 2 Strict
Criterion	A–B$_r$	.811	.994	.994
Criterion	A–C	.572	.606	.961
Criterion	C–B	.878	.978	.978
Criterion	C–D	.883	.889	.989
Two Trials	A–B$_r$	.839	.928	.678
Two Trials	A–C	.839	.872	.667
Two Trials	C–B	.911	.989	.778
Two Trials	C–D	.867	.878	.756

Stark, 1969) and the discrepancy is probably due to a difference in the manner of testing. When A–B$_r$ training has produced significant first-list forgetting, tests have been given by presenting one item at a time and requiring the subject to give the two responses for that item. With all items presented simultaneously, subjects could write in the responses they knew, then use a process of elimination to help sort out responses to other items, changing responses to some items if later responses helped them remember items they missed earlier, and so on. James' results appear to agree with Keppel's (1968) conjecture that A–B retention after A–B$_r$ interpolation will vary substantially between single-item and whole-list testing procedures.

Response Completion

Table 8-3 gives full results of the response completion test. Statistical analysis of the unconditional performance showed that the main effect of the paradigm differences and the interaction between paradigms and amount of interpolated training were both significant, $F(3,119) = 14.53$, $p < .01$; $F(3,119) = 6.35$, $p < .01$. Newman-Keuls tests showed that the A–C group with criterion training was reliably poorer than all other groups, and no other pairs of groups differed reliably.

The two columns to the right in Table 8-3 show performance on the response completion test conditionalized on whether the first-list response was given correctly (by strict scoring) in the MMFR test. It is interesting that the decrement in first-list recall after A–C learning was present for items that were correct in MMFR as well as for items that had been missed. It seems unlikely that .175 of the B responses that were recalled in MMFR were forgotten before the response completion test. A more likely hypothesis is that some responses that could be retrieved with the stimulus (and possibly the second-list response) presented as a cue could not be retrieved in the absence of that cue. Finally, we note that the response fragments given failed to serve as reliable retrieval cues for all responses. The A–C criterion group failed to

Table 8-3 Performance on Response Completion Test (Test 2)

Amount of Interpolated Training	Paradigm	$P(C_2)$	$P(C_2 \mid C_1)$	$P(C_2 \mid I_1)$
Criterion	A–B$_r$	.978	.981	.941
Criterion	A–C	.717	.825	.571
Criterion	C–B	.944	.937	1.000
Criterion	C–D	.894	.931	.619
Two Trials	A–B$_r$	.956	.974	.862
Two Trials	A–C	.883	.921	.690
Two Trials	C–B	.917	.933	.750
Two Trials	C–D	.894	.949	.542

give 33 of the B responses correctly (nearly two per subject) of the 77 that were missed on MMFR. Although the values of $P(C_2 | I_1)$ are similar for the two C–D groups and the A–C criterion group, it should be noted that in the C–D groups only a few items were missed in MMFR—21 in C–D criterion and 24 in C–D with two trials. Thus, there were probably selection factors operating rather strongly to make the values of $P(C_2 | I_1)$ as low as they were in the C–D conditions.

Recall after Response Completion

Table 8-4 gives results of the test for List-1 recall following the response completion test. Analysis of variance for the unconditional performance gave significant effects of the paradigms, $F(3,119) = 8.18$, $p < .01$; of the amount of interpolated learning, $F(1,119) = 15.15$, $p < .01$; and of their interaction, $F(3,119) = 3.86$, $p < .05$. Newman-Keuls tests showed that the A–B$_r$ and A–C criterion groups were not different from each other, but both were reliably poorer than all the other groups, $p < .01$.

Significance tests were applied to determine reliability of change in performance between the MMFR test and the test of recall following response completion. These comparisons were made by simple t-tests on the differences in performance between Test 1 and Test 3 for individual subjects in each group. Improvement in performance would be expected in conditions A–C and C–D if recall of responses in Test 2 aided recall of associations. Indeed, significant improvement was found for both of the A–C groups, $p < .01$, and for the C–D criterion group, $p < .05$. Surprisingly, there was also significant improvement for the C–B group with two trials of interpolated learning, $p < .05$. The A–B$_r$ criterion group showed a significant decrement in performance between Test 1 and Test 3, $p < .01$. This was almost surely not caused by the response completion test; rather, we think it must have occurred because of the change in test conditions. In Test 3, subjects were asked only

Table 8-4 Performance on First-List Recall (Test 3) Following Response Completion (Test 2)

Amount of Interpolated Learning	Paradigm	$P(C_3)$	$P(C_3 \| C_1)$	$P(C_3 \| I_1)$	$N(I_1 \cap C_2)$	$P(C_3 \| I_1 \cap C_2)$
Criterion	A–B$_r$	.694	.788	.294	32	.219
Criterion	A–C	.700	.981	.325	44	.409
Criterion	C–B	.889	.975	.273	22	.273
Criterion	C–D	.933	.994	.476	13	.692
Two Trials	A–B$_r$	.872	.947	.483	25	.560
Two Trials	A–C	.889	.967	.486	20	.650
Two Trials	C–B	.956	.994	.562	12	.583
Two Trials	C–D	.906	.968	.500	13	.692

to fill in the responses from the first list. We infer from their poorer performance that the requirement of giving second-list responses in the MMFR test must have had a facilitating effect on recall of first-list responses.

The second and third columns of data in Table 8-4 show performance on Test 3 conditional on whether the correct response was given in Test 1. From $P(C_3|C_1)$, we can conclude that retention was uniformly high—virtually no items were forgotten during the interval between the tests. The value of $P(C_3|C_1)$ was low only in the A–B$_r$ criterion condition and we believe this was probably due to facilitation of performance on Test 1, as we noted above.

The values of $P(C_3|I_1)$ all seem too high to be attributed to guessing, and it therefore seems likely that there was recovery of associations between Test 1 and Test 3 in all conditions. This could have occurred because of the response completion test, in which recall of responses may have caused associations to be reactivated, improving prospects for recall in the forward direction in Test 3. This idea is consistent with the high values of $P(C_3|I_1 \cap C_2)$ given in the last column. (The number of cases in individual conditions tends to be small; however, with values above .50 in all the conditions with two trials of interpolated learning, it seems likely that the high values were not due to chance.)

Finally, we note that while response recall in Test 2 must have facilitated recall of some items in Test 3, especially for the A–C groups, response recall did not ensure recall of all items in the recall test. Indeed, in the A–C criterion group, more than one-half of the items that were missed in MMFR and then recalled in Test 2 were missed again in the List-1 recall test given as Test 3.

Matching Test

The results obtained in the matching test are shown in Table 8-5. In analysis of variance, reliable effects were obtained due to paradigms, $F(3,119)$

Table 8-5 Performance on Matching (Test 4) and Conditional Performance on List-1 Recall (Test 3)

Amount of Interpolated Learning	Paradigm	$P(C_4)$	$P(C_4|C_3)$	$P(C_4|I_3)$
Criterion	A–B$_r$	.722	.888	.345
Criterion	A–C	.939	.992	.815
Criterion	C–B	.933	.988	.500
Criterion	C–D	.967	.992	.583
Two Trials	A–B$_r$	.906	.968	.478
Two Trials	A–C	1.000	1.000	1.000
Two Trials	C–B	.978	1.000	.500
Two Trials	C–D	.972	.982	.882

$= 58.56, p < .01$; degree of interpolated learning, $F(1,119) = 59.56, p < .01$; and their interaction, $F(3,119) = 16.7, p < .01$. Newman-Keuls tests showed that A–B$_r$ with criterion was reliably worse than every other group, $p < .01$, and A–B$_r$ with two trials was reliably worse than all the other two-trial groups as well as the criterion C–D group, $p < .05$.

When a matching test is given, some improvement would occur if no information were added other than the set of alternative answers. James tested the hypothesis that the improvement in performance from Test 3 to Test 4 was entirely due to guessing. Suppose that only the items known by the subject were given correctly on Test 3. Then, when Test 4 occurred, the subject would have to guess the remaining items. Given n unknown items, the probability of matching j of them by guessing is

$$P(j, n) = \frac{1}{j!}\left(1 - 1 + \frac{1}{2!} - \frac{1}{3!} + \cdots \pm \frac{1}{(n-j)!}\right)$$

(Feller, 1950, p. 97). Let X be the number of items matched by guessing from n unknown items. It turns out that regardless of n,

$$E(X) = 1, \quad V(X) = 1.$$

Thus, according to the hypothesis, the expected number of correct responses on Test 4 should be one greater than the number of correct responses on Test 3 (we consider only subjects who missed one or more items in Test 3). The standard error of the difference (Test 4 minus Test 3) should equal the square root of the number of subjects having one or more errors on Test 3.

A statistical test was formed by computing the expected increase from Test 3 to Test 4, and subtracting that from the observed increase, dividing the difference by the theoretical standard deviation. Call this ratio z. Under the null hypothesis that the matching test presented no new effective information, z should be asymptotically distributed as a standard normal deviate.

In three groups, James found that improvement from Test 3 to Test 4 was significantly greater than could be expected by guessing. These included both A–C conditions: for A–C criterion, $z = 7.22$, $p < .001$; for A–C with two trials, $z = 4.02$, $p < .01$. The C–D group with two trials also showed a significant increment, $z = 2.23$, $p < .05$. Apparently, the matching test provides information helpful especially in A–C to retrieval of associations beyond that provided by the reinstatement of responses achieved in the response completion test.

The two columns to the right in Table 8-5 show performance in matching conditional on the List-1 recall observed in Test 3. The most notable fact is the low performance in A–B$_r$, especially on items missed on Test 3. (The results for C–B are also low, although we hesitate to draw conclusions from these, due to the small number of items missed on Test 3 in these conditions.)

Apparently in A–B$_r$, if a response could not be recalled when the stimulus was presented, there was relatively little chance of its being remembered when the response was also presented, as it is in a matching test.

Discussion

Several features of James' results are consistent with both the cognitive interpretation and concepts of associative interference theory. First, the relatively small amount of forgetting after C–B or C–D interpolated learning is a standard finding. The result agrees with the idea that forward associations are most important in recalling A–B items, and these associations are lost primarily when stimuli from the first list are present during interpolated learning. The result also agrees with the cognitive hypothesis that forgetting occurs because the retrieval network for the A–B items is modified during interpolated learning. The network consists of tests for stimulus features, and because the A stimuli are not used in C–B or C–D, it is expected that the network for retrieving A–B should be disturbed much less than in A–C and A–B$_r$.

Another finding that agrees with both theories is that in A–C and A–B$_r$, where substantial forgetting occurred, there was more forgetting when interpolated learning was continued to criterion than when only two trials of interpolated learning were given. This also is a standard finding (e.g., Barnes & Underwood, 1959) and is explained in associative interference theory by the greater number of opportunities during criterion learning for unreinforced elicitations of A–B responses; hence, for a greater amount of unlearning. The explanation in the theory of retrieval networks is similar. With only two trials of interpolated learning, subjects will not have developed sufficient retrieval networks for the interpolated lists. The further training given the criterion groups led to further modifications of the A–B retrieval network; hence, it led to greater amounts of forgetting.

Some performance features in the A–C condition are difficult to explain using the theory of associative and response-set interference. First, in that theory most of the poor performance in MMFR would be attributed to suppression of the first-list responses. Performance on the matching test was very good for the A–C subjects. If many of the first-list associations had been unlearned, matching would not have been successful. It is possible that some of the improvement from A–C's MMFR performance on the matching test was due to recovery of unlearned associations. However, since other investigators (Postman & Stark, 1969) have observed good performance on matching tests for A–B given immediately after A–C learning, we conclude that performance on James' matching test probably indicates that individual A–B associations were not unlearned to a great extent in the A–C condition.

A question arises of why there would be so much response-set suppression in A–C when in C–D there was only a small amount. (Both conditions require use of a new set of responses in interpolated learning.) In this connection, Postman and Underwood (1973, p. 24) said, "The usual difference in retention loss between the A–C and C–D paradigms does not in itself bear on the question of the relative weight of response-set interference and item-specific unlearning in determining RI (retroactive inhibition). The degree of suppression of the first-list repertoire and consequent dominance of second-list responses are expected to be related to the amount of negative transfer." This seems a rather vague hypothesis, but we suppose it means that in A–C the use of first-list stimuli keeps the B responses active longer during interpolated learning; therefore, a greater amount of inhibition must be built up to permit the interpolated learning to occur.

It seems to us that this hypothesis conflicts with the results we reported in Chapter 6 regarding negative transfer in A–C. Most of the negative transfer (relative to C–D) occurs in the second stage of learning, after the probability of the correct response has increased to a nonzero value. If it were assumed that the first stage of learning mainly involves acquisition of responses, then the explanation of forgetting given above would seem to imply that more negative transfer should appear during the first stage of interpolated learning, an explanation contrary to the empirical results. Furthermore, it seems unnecessarily awkward to assume that forgetting results from suppression of responses but that the amount of suppression is largely determined by whether first-list stimuli are used in the interpolated task. It seems more parsimonious to assume that since stimuli make such a great difference in the amount of forgetting, the process of forgetting probably involves something that the subject does regarding the stimuli as well as the responses.

Other aspects of A–C performance also argue against an idea of interference that involves just responses rather than the whole associative system. On the response-completion test, subjects were able to give .57 of the A–B responses they missed in MMFR. The fragments shown to the subjects thus provided some assistance in retrieving responses. However, a substantial number of responses given correctly in MMFR were missed in the completion test, $P(C_2 | C_1)$ was .825. The usual concept of response availability is that it operates as a precondition for correct recall of an association–that is, if the response is available and if the stimulus-response connection is retained, then the response will be given on the test. But this being so, responses that were available in MMFR surely should have been available during response completion where extra cues were provided. Thus, it is surprising that as many as one-sixth of the responses given correctly in MMFR should have been missed in response completion.

Another fact about A–C performance that embarrasses the simple idea of response availability involves first-list recall after response completion. One would think that if response unavailability in its simple form was the cause of most retroaction in A–C, then A–B associations should be recalled in nearly all cases where the B response was reinstated by the fragment shown in response completion. The fact was that first-list recall was successful in fewer than one-half of the cases where an item was missed in MMFR but the response was correct in the response completion test, $P(C_3 | I_1 \cap C_2)$ was .409.

We consider it more in accord with these findings to conclude that forgetting in A–C involves loss of information about the stimulus-response connections rather than just the responses. On the other hand, this lost information must be recoverable, since presentation of the first-list responses provides an occasion where most of the information needed for correct performance is recovered. We think the most reasonable hypothesis is that when both the stimuli and responses are present on a matching test, subjects can enter the retrieval network using both the stimulus features and the response terms and conduct a search for pairings that were associated in the first list. (Anderson and Bower's, 1973, MATCH system provides a mechanism for doing this.) The good performance on matching tests after A–C interpolated learning is consistent with the expectation that search starting from both ends should lead to success more often than search emanating from a single entry point.

Finally, we consider performance of subjects in the A–B$_r$ condition. If we take the performance on MMFR as a measure, we must conclude that there was practically no unlearning of individual associations. However, in the tests of first-list recall and matching, there were many errors. Some forgetting may have occurred from Test 1 to Test 4, but forgetting should have been relatively slight for first-list associations for which there was already a long delay and much interference by the time Test 1 occurred.

The main criterion for an explanation of the A–B$_r$ performance is that A–B associations must still have been in memory, but retrieval of many of them required mediation by the pairings used in interpolated learning. This could be a property of retrieval using an EPAM net that had been modified considerably with pushdown storage creating multiple branches at many nodes. Suppose the subject initially wrote out the second-list responses (as most of them did). Now assume that a retrieval process begins for one of the stimuli. Because the network has been modified for A–B$_r$ learning, one or more choice points are encountered. However, because the second-list response term has already been written down, the subject can look ahead in the search, see which path leads to the response already written, and take the alternative path. Of course, terms such as "look ahead" and "take the alternative path" must be interpreted metaphorically here—we do not believe that the tests and choices correspond to conscious activity. However, the hypothesis that second-list responses were used to sort out the first-list associations corresponds to our intuitions and informal observations of subjects in the MMFR test.

Why would A–B$_r$ performance be inferior to A–C performance in the matching test? Our best hypothesis is that because each B term corresponded to just one terminal node in the retrieval network, presentation of the response terms from A–B gave A–C subjects more useful information. In A–B$_r$, each response term from List 1 also was a response term from List 2, and therefore would have to be represented at two terminal nodes of the final network. It would not be possible, then, to simply initiate a network search both from a stimulus and response term, looking for an intersection path. The response-anchored search would have to start from two places, and this would make the system less efficient.

We have been unable to think of any plausible explanation for performance in the A–B$_r$ condition based on associative interference theory. The problem is that for second-list responses to mediate retention of A–B, connections must have been formed between the two responses for a stimulus during interpolated learning. It is known that subjects can be induced to learn an interpolated list through mediation, with the first-list responses as intermediate terms. However, such learning generally requires rather explicit instructions and is facilitated by similarity between each second-list response and its mate from the first list (for example, the use of synonyms). In the standard A–B$_r$ situation, continued use of the first-list response would increase intralist interference for the interpolated learning, and it would seem unlikely that subjects would adopt it as a strategy. Consequently, it seems unlikely that subjects would form the response-response associations that apparently are needed for facilitating first-list retention through mediation.

INDEPENDENCE OF RESPONSE RECALL

In Chapter 7 we presented data obtained by DaPolito indicating that, in a MMFR test, recall of the A–B and A–C associations are stochastically independent. An important feature of DaPolito's results was the absence of retroactive forgetting. Because of this, we are able to draw relatively strong conclusions from the independence of responses regarding the mechanism of learning that causes negative transfer and proactive forgetting.

For reasons we will discuss later, the theoretical strength of a finding of independence is not as great when retroaction occurs. However, independence has been tested in several experiments where retroactive forgetting took place, and the results have nearly always been consistent with the null hypothesis of independent recall.

Koppenaal's Data

Results obtained by Koppenaal (1963) were analyzed by DaPolito (1966) regarding the hypothesis of independence. Koppenaal's experiment included

Table 8-6 Analysis of Independence of Responses in MMFR from Koppenaal's (1963) Experiment

Retention Interval	P(correct) in Control	P(B)	P(C)	P(C|B)	P(C|B̄)	χ²
One Minute	.990	.663	.944	.934	.963	.15
20 Minutes	.950	.669	.888	.888	.887	.00
90 Minutes	.850	.664	.894	.922	.842	1.71
Six Hours	.900	.744	.850	.815	.951	3.43
24 Hours	.860	.644	.738	.738	.737	.00
Three Days	.780	.613	.631	.643	.613	.05
Seven Days	.570	.500	.419	.475	.363	1.64

an A–B, A–C transfer condition as well as a single-list control condition. All lists were learned to a criterion of one perfect trial. Recall was tested with a MMFR test in the transfer condition and a standard recall test in the control condition. There were seven different retention intervals for subjects in different groups.

Table 8-6 shows the results of DaPolito's analysis. Note the substantial amount of retroactive forgetting in all seven tests. The performance on A–C items was apparently as good as on the control items during tests given the same day as learning, although this probably indicates only that the requirement of learning to criterion forced learning to occur to a level that compensated for the negative transfer that undoubtedly occurred. Both proactive and retroactive forgetting is seen in the tests given one or more days after the lists were learned. The results in all the tests were consistent with the hypothesis of independent recall of responses.

Postman's Data

Table 8-7 shows DaPolito's analysis of Postman's (1964) data from MMFR tests given after A–B, A–C and A–B, A–B$_r$ training. The sets refer to different lists given to different groups of subjects. These data also show strong agreement with the hypothesis of independent recall of responses.

Table 8-7 Analysis of Response Independence in Postman's (1964) Experiment

Paradigm	Set	P(B)	P(C)	P(C|B)	P(C|B̄)	χ²
A–B, A–C	1	.458	.368	.287	.435	2.76
A–B, A–C	2	.590	.645	.635	.661	.02
A–B, A–C	3	.618	.777	.831	.690	3.11
A–B, A–B$_r$	1	.465	.368	.343	.428	.77
A–B, A–B$_r$	2	.645	.562	.516	.647	1.79
A–B, A–B$_r$	3	.645	.673	.698	.627	.47

Table 8-8   Analysis of Independence in MMFR in James' Experiment

Amount of Interpolated Learning	Paradigm	$P(B \cap C)$	$P(B \cap \bar{C})$	$P(\bar{B} \cap C)$	$P(\bar{B} \cap \bar{C})$	χ^2
Criterion	AB, AC, Observed	.54	.03	.42	.01	2.33
Criterion	AB, AC, Expected	.56	.02	.41	.02	
Two Trials	AB, AC, Observed	.54	.29	.12	.04	1.32
Two Trials	AB, AC, Expected	.56	.28	.11	.05	

James' Data

The data obtained in the A–C conditions of James' (1968) experiment were also analyzed regarding the hypothesis of independence in MMFR. The results are in Table 8-8. The data agreed with the hypothesis of independence, but the tests were not very stringent, due to the high level of A–B recall in the group with two interpolated trials, and of A–C recall in the criterion group. The two-trial group showed no retroactive forgetting, so its performance provides further evidence for independence when only proactive forgetting and negative transfer occur.

Wichawut and Martin's Data

A stronger test of response independence involving retroaction was given in Wichawut and Martin's (1971) experiment. They presented a 16-item A–B list until the subject had given at least one correct response to every item. A second list was presented for 12 trials, in which A–C and C–D items were intermixed. In it, 4 A–B items had no A–C items, 4 had A–C items that appeared 4 times, 4 had A–C items that appeared 8 times, and 4 had A–C items that appeared 12 times. A MMFR test was given after the interpolated learning.

The varying number of A–C presentations produced different amounts of A–C recall, as would be expected. The values of $P(C)$ observed were .64, .79, and .85, respectively, with 4, 8, and 12 presentations. In each condition, data were consistent with the hypothesis that B and C responses were independent. But the most important finding was that $P(B)$ was not affected by the number of interpolated A–C trials. The values of $P(B)$ obtained were .73, .62, and .72 with 4, 8, and 12 A–C presentations, respectively, and the difference was not reliable, $F(2, 70) = 2.07$, $p > .10$. As with the experiment of DaPolito (1966) in which number of A–B presentations did not affect A–C recall, Wichawut and Martin's results provide a case where the independence of responses cannot have been a statistical artifact, since the varying strength of A–C was produced by an experimental manipulation.

Discussion

We argued in Chapter 7 that independence of responses in DaPolito's experiments had a strong theoretical implication—it contradicts any hypothesis in which the proactive interfering effect of an association depends directly on the strength of that association. The situation is more complicated when retroactive forgetting is involved. Here we have to consider possible reciprocal effects—effects of the strength of A–B on the retrievability of its interpolated counterpart, and also effects of the strength of an interpolated item on the retrievability of its mate from the A–B list.

We have argued previously (Greeno, James, & DaPolito, 1971; Martin & Greeno, 1972) that the concepts of associationist theory should lead to the expectation of a negative dependency between recall of B and C responses to the same stimulus: that is,

$$P(B \cap C) < P(B) \cdot P(C).$$

We have thus interpreted the consistent finding of independence as a contradiction of the associationist ideas of unlearning and response competition as explanations of forgetting. The argument leading to this prediction has some elements in common with the position taken in Chapter 7. It might be thought that stronger A–B associations would interfere more with the learning of their corresponding A–C associations than would weaker A–B associations. Conversely, if some individual A–C association were learned rapidly, the effect would be to weaken its corresponding first-list association more than the average.

Postman and Underwood (1973) have argued that there is no reason to expect negative dependency between responses on the basis of associationist theory. They seem to assume that the existence of an A–B association produces no interference with learning an A–C association with the same stimulus. Unlearning occurs because the B response from A–B is elicited during interpolated learning, rather than through any interaction between the associative connections. Indeed, they derive the prediction that there should be a positive dependency between the B and C responses for corresponding associations. The reasoning is that if A–C is learned relatively early in interpolated learning, the effect will be to block the elicitation of A–B, and therefore prevent unlearning.

We find Postman and Underwood's analysis puzzling for two reasons. First, if the assumption is made that two associations to a stimulus can be made as easily as one, then we do not understand why negative transfer should occur. Second, the mechanism of blocking elicitation of first-list responses through strengthening of second-list associations seems to suggest that stronger second-list associations indeed interfere more with first-list associations than with weaker ones. On the other hand, since a positive dependency between individual responses has not been reported, perhaps we should conclude that their suggestion of such a mechanism should be considered only as a possibility rather than a definite hypothesis implied by the basic assumptions of associative interference theory.

Nevertheless, we think there is a version of associative interference theory that is compatible with the finding of independent responses when retroactive forgetting occurs. The idea is that stronger first-list associations interfere for a longer time with second-list learning; consequently, they lose more of their initial strength. The result could be that all first-list associations eventually finish at the same strength—or more realistically, finish with a distribution of strengths that is independent of the intial strengths. We conclude, then, that independence of responses in MMFR is not evidence against associative interference theory when retroactive forgetting has occurred. We note, however, that this version of the theory does imply that stronger first-list associations will cause more negative transfer and proactive interference than weaker ones, and so is still inconsistent with results reported earlier in Chapters 6 and 7.

CONCLUSIONS

The concept of a retrieval network provides the basis for a theory of retroactive forgetting in which it is assumed that the network is modified by interpolated learning through addition of pushdown storage with initial branches of the network pushed down in memory. This theory explains some facts that were previously explained by the hypothesis of response-set interference, and the theory of retrieval networks also appears to have some advantages regarding details of interrelationships between performance on different tests. The theory is consistent with findings of response independence in MMFR when retroaction occurs, and although we now can see a way to make associative interference theory similarly consistent with that finding, the associationist mechanism we see as a cogent explanation of independence is still not consistent with salient facts about negative transfer and proactive interference.

chapter 9

Conclusions

We have now completed our presentation of evidence against associationist theory. Although we have a high regard for this theory, considering it one of the strongest intellectual achievements thus far developed in scientific psychology, we also think it is wrong, and the main content of this book has given the empirical basis for our conclusion that the main assumptions of associationist theory are incorrect.

There are three main attacks against associationist theory. One is based on analyses of complex human information processing in the understanding of natural language, problem solving, and other complex task environments. Theoretical work in these areas has proceeded rapidly in recent years, but the concepts of associationist theory appear to be too weak to be of any great use in representing the processes that occur.

A second attack is based on analyses of verbal learning tasks such as recognition or free recall. The theories reviewed in Chapter 3 seem to provide good understanding of the process of storing information in memory, but they do not use the basic concepts of associationism in a strong way. The theories of recognition and recall that seem to be most useful and empirically valid are based on concepts of storing and retrieving information, with little or no involvement of processes of forming connections between mental elements.

On the basis of these two attacks alone, associationist theory could be set aside as being irrelevant to the analysis of processes that we now find we can understand better using other concepts. Such a judgment would undermine the strong claim of associationism—that formation of undifferentiated connections between mental elements is the basic process in acquiring knowledge. However, it would leave the psychological theory of learning in a rather untidy condition. A vast body of experimental work has been developed using the task of paired-associate memorizing. This experimental work has been interpreted using the concepts of associationist theory and has been seen by many as providing evidential support for the assumptions of that theory. The evidence we have presented argues against that interpretation and provides a third kind of attack against associationist theory. We believe the evidence shows that associationist assumptions are incorrect, even for the experimental task of memorizing paired associates.

The paired-associate memorizing experiment has provided the paradigm case of forming new mental connections, and results obtained in that situation have provided the main empirical guidance in developing many of associationist theory's concepts. We recognize the difficulties and uncertainties of attacking a theory in its own data base; in fact, that has been thought by some to be impossible in principle (Kuhn, 1962). Our view is that critical discussions of interpretation regarding common data are not only possible, but essential in the growth of scientific knowledge. And to set aside a set of concepts as important as those of associationist theory without careful consideration of the main data on which that theory rests would involve a serious intellectual disservice.

The theory we have proposed as an alternative to associationist theory combines a Gestalt interpretation of the nature of association and an assumption about the process of retrieval based on recent theories of human information processing. The Gestalt idea is that association is one form of cognitive organization and that learning a new association consists of forming a new mental unit with the associated elements as components. The general form of an association, then, is a relational structure that represents the associated elements in an interactive way. The information-processing analysis of retrieval assumes that to retrieve the learned associations, the subject develops a cognitive system that can be represented as a network of tests of stimulus features. Because of the relational nature of the basic associative learning, the features included in the network will be influenced by the response terms. Sufficient features must be included to allow discrimination among stimuli. Relationships among different items will be reflected in an organization of the retrieval network that permits retrieval to occur in an efficient way.

We now review the main conclusions regarding applications of this cognitive theory to various aspects of paired-associate memorizing:

First, consider response learning and stimulus encoding. Analyses of these hypothetical processes have been developed mainly during the 1960s as major amendments to the classical associationist assumptions. The major phenomena explained by these hypotheses can be as well accommodated to a cognitive theory.

When the response term of an association is complex and unfamiliar to the subject, the organized unit that must be stored to represent the association will be harder to achieve than when the response term is already unitary. Therefore, it is to be expected that associations with more meaningful responses will be easier to learn and that practice, especially on nonmeaningful responses, will facilitate later paired-associate memorizing. It is not necessary, however, to conclude that response learning occurs as a separate phase of paired-associate memorizing. It seems more appropriate to consider integration of the response as part of the process of representing the association as a relational structure.

Selective encoding of stimulus features is implied by the assumption of a retrieval network consisting of feature tests that are added as needed for stimulus discrimination. Thus, findings that subjects can give the correct response when shown some components of a stimulus but not when shown other components are a natural consequence of the assumptions of a cognitive theory; additional attentional mechanisms or encoding processes are not required as they are for associationist theory. Subjects' tendencies to use imaginal encodings and other elaborations of stimulus-response pairs seem easily understood when it is assumed that the main process in associative learning is formation of a relational structure that includes the associated elements as components. A pictorial image or a proposition can often permit a subject to use relational materials already stored in memory in forming the new associative unit.

In Chapter 4 we presented analyses of acquisition of paired associates based on a two-stage Markov model of learning. The results led us to conclude that the stages of learning can be identified with the two main processes specified in the cognitive theory. The first stage involves storage of a relational representation of the stimulus-response pair. The second stage involves inclusion of a pair's stimulus features in a retrieval system that permits the pair to be retrieved successfully on tests. The main expectation is that difficulty of the first stage should be determined jointly by variations in stimuli and responses, both of which affect the difficulty of achieving a memorable encoding, but that difficulty of the second stage should be determined primarily by variations in the stimuli, which affect the difficulty of forming a sufficient retrieval system.

The results were in general agreement with these expectations. Stimulus similarity and stimulus meaningfulness both had large effects on the mean number of trials needed to accomplish the first stage; so too did response meaningfulness, response word frequency, and response pronounceability. In the second stage, the effect of stimulus similarity was always at least as large as it was in the first stage, and in most cases stimulus similarity had a considerably larger effect on second-stage difficulty than on first-stage difficulty. Stimulus concreteness had a very large effect on the second stage, making learning essentially all-or-none when concrete stimuli were used. Stimulus meaningfulness also had marked effects on second-stage difficulty, especially when stimuli were difficult to distinguish or when nonsense responses were used. Response variables, in contrast, generally had either no effect or relatively weak effects in the second stage. Response pronounceability and response word frequency did not affect the second stage significantly, and response concreteness had a smaller effect on Stage 2 than stimulus concreteness had. Response meaningfulness affected the second stage substantially when stimuli were not meaningful. To explain this effect we suggest that there may be a kind of induced meaningfulness for nonsense stimuli when responses are words involving greater use of meaningful encodings for the nonsense items, and that with these encodings it is easier to develop a satisfactory retrieval system.

An interpretation of the associationist concepts of response learning, stimulus encoding, and forming a connection can be made that fits the main trends in our results. According to this interpretation, the first stage of the Markov model corresponds to learning the response and forming the stimulus-response connection; the second Markov stage corresponds to acquiring a distinctive and stable encoding of the stimulus. This view would be quite similar to ours, especially if it were assumed that response learning and connection formation could go on simultaneously, forming a single process of storing information about the pair. However, we would still maintain that the information stored about each pair should be conceptualized as a relational structure with stimulus and response terms as components, and that the encodings of the stimuli acquired in the second stage should be conceptualized as a retrieval system, incorporating features that allow discrimination and efficiency of recall on tests.

In Chapter 5 we presented analyses of positive transfer. Results were consistent with the hypothesis that transfer to an individual item occurs in an all-or-none fashion, and that acquisition of a relationship between items that can be used for transfer is also an all-or-none process. Our interpretation of positive transfer is that subjects form relational groupings based on common features among items. The idea that these relations are found in an all-or-none fashion fits with a strong tradition in Gestalt psychology, in that apprehending such relations constitutes a form of insight. Further, the all-or-none character of recognition of a new item's membership in an acquired category agrees with the cognitive view of generalization based on attention to discrete features and seems inconsistent with the associationist analysis of transfer based on generalization of associative strength. As Restle (1965) has shown, theories that assume a continuum of associative strength can be made compatible with all-or-none results by making appropriate assumptions about individual differences. However, it seems likely that the assumptions needed to accomodate all-or-none learning of categories and all-or-none transfer might become quite complex, while the assumptions needed to explain these phenomena in cognitive theory are simple and straightforward.

In Chapter 6 we used the two-stage Markov model to analyze acquisition of paired associates under conditions of negative transfer. Our cognitive interpretation of negative transfer is that interference with storage of a pair occurs because of previous encoding of the stimulus in relation to the response it was previously paired with, and that interference with development of a retrieval system occurs because features and relationships useful to group items for one list of pairs for efficient retrieval will generally not be as useful for organizing a second list of pairs. In comparisons between A–B$_r$ and C–B, which use responses from the first list, the amount of negative transfer occurring in the second stage of learning was much greater than the amount of negative transfer in the first stage. In comparisons between A–C and C–D, results were not completely consistent, but most cases studied showed more negative transfer in the second stage than in the first. The greater amount of negative transfer in the second stage is consistent with the cognitive theory, and indicates that the major source of difficulty is developing a modified or new retrieval system based on old stimuli. The findings seem incompatible with the idea that negative transfer is caused by interference between associations, since that hypothesis seems to require that greater interference be produced by associations that have greater strength, and therefore implies that negative transfer should be greatest early in the process of learning the transfer list.

Further evidence against the idea that the amount of negative transfer varies directly with associative strength was obtained in comparisons in which overtraining was given for some subjects on the A–B list. In many conditions there was no measurable effect of overtraining on the amount of negative transfer in A–B$_r$. When effects of overtraining were obtained, they were usually small and were located in the first stage. We attribute these rather small effects to interference produced by interpair groupings that subjects probably acquire during overtraining.

When responses were nonsense syllables, A–B$_r$ and C–B conditions showed positive transfer relative to C–D, showing the advantage of previous familiarity with responses. However, A–B$_r$ always suffered greater negative transfer relative to C–B than was observed for A–C relative to C–D. This indicates that there is greater interference with the acquisition of a new retrieval system when the responses from the first list are present. We take this as support for the idea that A–B$_r$ requires extensive modification of the retrieval network, but in A–C more of the initial retrieval system can be maintained.

In Chapter 7 we discussed proactive interference. We presented results obtained by DaPolito in which recall and recognition of the two responses

2. modification; for example, a plant is a structure of a particular kind, namely, a living structure.
3. disjunction; the relation between members of a set of alternatives.
4. conjunction; the relation between members of a set of requirements.
5. connections between relations and their arguments; for example, the information that people use machines has the relation "use" connected to "people" and "machine" through this relation. The system must distinguish different forms of this kind of connection, since many relations are not symmetric.

In addition to the connections, Quillian's system uses quantitative modifiers to represent information such as plants frequently have leaves, or plants are not animals.

An example of a knowledge structure that can be constructed in Quillian's model is given in Figure 2-1. The diagram represents the information for the first dictionary definition for "plant": Living structure that is not an animal, frequently with leaves, getting its food from air, water, or earth. The diagram shows plants as members of the category "structure," modified by a conjunction of four concepts: they are living; they are not animal; they frequently

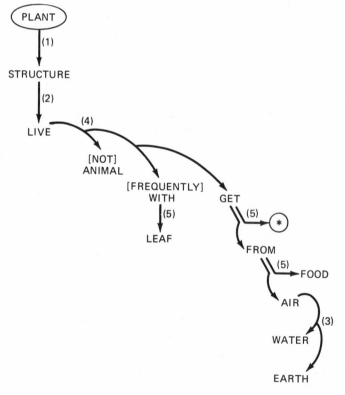

Figure 2-1 Knowledge structure for one meaning of "plant," in Quillian's (1968) model.

taken from experiments where the task was memorizing paired associates. Given the assumptions of associationist theory, paired-associate memorizing is as close as one can come to an ideal experimental task for studying basic learning mechanisms. Those who agree with our conclusion that memorizing paired associates involves storing relational representations of pairs and acquiring retrieval networks rather than forming undifferentiated connections may also conclude with us that the hypothesis of associationism must be fundamentally in error.

Associationism has been a pervasive and dominant theoretical framework, and its rejection has far-reaching consequences. For one, there is a considerable implication regarding the probable usefulness of such research as that reported in this book. If one believes that the basic mechanism by which humans acquire knowledge is formation of undifferentiated connections between ideas, then rote verbal learning, and especially paired-associate memorizing, provides the most appropriate task environment in which to observe acquisition of knowledge. But if we conclude that the basic mechanism of acquiring knowledge is formation of relational structure, then there is considerable question whether the information we obtain by observing rote verbal learning is as useful in furthering our understanding of basic learning processes as are observations that can be made in other task environments. The difficulty is not that performance in rote learning is irrelevant to theory. We have argued throughout this book that the fundamental process of learning, namely cognitive organization, is exactly what subjects do when they memorize paired associates. Moreover, other theorists (notably Mandler, 1967) have presented similar arguments concerning other rote learning tasks. The difficulty lies in the relatively weak structure of the materials that subjects learn in these tasks. Motivated by the belief that organization is a derivative of basic associative processes, investigators have tried to minimize the possibility that subjects will find organizing principles in the materials used in experiments. Nevertheless, subjects do find organizing principles, but the organizations found are relatively weak and extremely varied. If learning is organization, then we can study it better by presenting material in which the organization is relatively unambiguous, and by studying the subjects' processes of achieving a representation of that organized material.

This conclusion about research in rote verbal learning has been voiced many times, by scientists and other individuals who considered the study of meaningful learning more important than the study of basic mechanisms. Many persons have thought that experimental psychologists were perversely stubborn in continuing research that seemed unrelated to real problems of classroom instruction and of other practical settings where learning occurs. We emphatically reject that view. The most important contribution of scientists is to make possible an understanding of basic principles, not only because of the human importance of increased understanding in itself, but because genuine progress in basic understanding almost always brings with it enormous practical consequences. We believe the protracted study of rote verbal learning was not the product of a perverse insulation of science, but rather was the product of an incorrect theory. Given a different understanding of the nature of human knowledge and its acquisition, different settings will be chosen in which to study processes of learning. Only because of the assumptions of associationist theory has rote verbal learning been judged the most likely task environment in which to obtain information about learning, and we consider the work done using that task environment to have been the soundest work that could have been done, given the available knowledge and understanding.

Another implication involves fundamental beliefs about educational practice. If one believes that learning involves formation of undifferentiated connections, then instructional technology requires identifying the component connections involved in a skill or set of ideas, then presenting the ideas that need to be connected in appropriate combinations so that the connections will be formed. Important qualifications have been recognized, especially in Gagné's (1965) writing, consisting of the need to ensure the presence of prerequisites such as discriminative skills and ability to perform needed component responses. But if we conclude that learning is basically a process of modifying complex relational systems of cognitive structure, it follows that successful teaching requires a much deeper and more thorough understanding of a student's initial cognitive structure than we can obtain with present concepts and techniques. If we theorize that learning is formation of connections, then presentation of the materials to be connected should be a sufficient procedure for learning to occur. But if learning is a process of generating structure within an existing relational system, much more attention should be paid to the characteristics of that system, and there must be appropriate recognition of each student's active role in the learning process.

Finally, there are strong implications regarding our understanding of the nature of human knowledge. Associationism is required by the form of empiricism that asserts that knowledge is derived from experience. We have concluded that associationism is incorrect—that is, it does not correctly describe the basic process by which human beings acquire knowledge. It must follow that human knowledge is not derived from experience, but rather derives from some important general cognitive capabilities interacting with and growing in response to experience. The nature of those cognitive capabilities is still very much in doubt. Piaget has provided important proposals about their characteristics, and he has undoubtedly raised the right kinds of questions, but it will be many years before we can hope to achieve a satisfactory understanding of the complex processes and structures that support intellectual development. But whatever the base requirements for intellectual growth may turn out to be, there are some, and the implication is that innate ideas in some form are a factor in the knowledge we possess.

On the other hand, innate ideas do not determine the nature of our knowledge. We are able to modify our ideas, and when our experience conflicts with expectations that are implied by the ideas we have at the time, we do modify them. Experience is not sufficient to produce all we know, but it can be sufficient to produce changes in what we know by showing that what we thought we knew was false. While we reject empiricism of the extreme form, we maintain a very strong form of empiricism in which empirical evidence provides the only legitimate basis for resolving differences of opinion about the way things are. Indeed, we maintain that it is on the basis of empirical evidence that we have shown that the associationist theory of paired-associate memorizing is factually incorrect.

References

ADAMS, J. A. *Human memory*. New York: McGraw-Hill, 1967.

ANDERSON, J. R. Computer simulation of a language acquisition system: A first report. In R. L. Solso (Ed.), *Information processing and cognition: The Loyola symposium*. Hillsdale, N.J.: Erlbaum, 1975.

ANDERSON, J. R., & BOWER, G. H. *Human associative memory*. Washington, D.C.: Winston, 1973.

ASCH, S. E. The doctrinal tyranny of associationism. In T. R. Dixon & D. L. Horton (Eds.), *Verbal behavior and general behavior theory*. Englewood Cliffs, N.J.: Prentice-Hall, 1968.

ASCH, S. E. A reformulation of the problem of association. *American Psychologist*, 1969, *24*, 92–102.

ATKINSON, R. C. Optimizing learning a second vocabulary. *Journal of Experimental Psychology*, 1972, *96*, 124–129.

ATKINSON, R. C., BOWER, G. H., & CROTHERS, E. J. *An introduction to mathematical learning theory*. New York: Wiley, 1965.

ATKINSON, R. C., & CROTHERS, E. J. A comparison of paired-associate learning models having different acquisition and retention axioms. *Journal of Mathematical Psychology*, 1964, *1*, 285–315.

ATKINSON, R. C., & ESTES, W. K. Stimulus sampling theory. In R. D. Luce, R. R. Bush, & E. Galanter (Eds.), *Handbook of mathematical psychology* (Vol. 2). New York: Wiley, 1963.

ATKINSON, R. C., & SHIFFRIN, R. M. Human memory: A proposed system and its control processes. In G. H. Bower & J. T. Spence (Eds.), *The psychology of learning and motivation: Advances in research and theory* (Vol. 2). New York: Academic Press, 1968.

BARNES, J. M., & UNDERWOOD, B. J. "Fate" of first-list associations in transfer theory. *Journal of Experimental Psychology*, 1959, *58*, 97–105.

BARTLETT, F. C. *Remembering.* Cambridge, England: Cambridge University Press, 1932.

BATCHELDER, W. H. An all-or-none theory for learning on both the paired-associate and concept levels. *Journal of Mathematical Psychology*, 1970, *7*, 97–117.

BATCHELDER, W. H. A theoretical and empirical comparison of the all-or-none multilevel theory and the mixed model. *Journal of Mathematical Psychology*, 1971, *8*, 82–108.

BATTIG, W. F. Facilitation and interference. In E. A. Bilodeau (Ed.), *Acquisition of skill.* New York: Academic Press, 1966.

BATTIG, W. F. Paired-associate learning. In T. R. Dixon & D. L. Horton (Eds.), *Verbal behavior and general behavior theory.* Englewood Cliffs, N.J.: Prentice-Hall, 1968.

BERNBACH, H. A. A forgetting model for paired-associate learning. *Journal of Mathematical Psychology*, 1965, *2*, 128–144.

BERNBACH, H. A. Replication processes in human memory and learning. In G. H. Bower & J. T. Spence (Eds.), *The psychology of learning and motivation: Advances in research and theory* (Vol. 3). New York: Academic Press, 1969.

BJORK, R. A. *Learning and short-term retention of paired-associates in relation to specific sequences of interpresentation intervals* (Institute for Mathematical Studies in the Social Sciences Tech. Rep. No. 106). Stanford: Stanford University, 1966.

BORING, E. G. *A history of experimental psychology.* New York: Appleton-Century-Crofts, 1950.

BOUSFIELD, W. A. The occurrence of clustering in the recall of randomly arranged associates. *Journal of General Psychology*, 1953, *49*, 229–240.

BOWER, G. H. Application of a model to paired-associate learning. *Psychometrika*, 1961, *26*, 255–280.

BOWER, G. H. A descriptive theory of memory. In D. P. Kimble (Ed.), *Proceedings of the second conference on learning, remembering, and forgetting.* New York: New York Academy of Sciences, 1967. (a)

BOWER, G. H. A multicomponent theory of the memory trace. In K. W. Spence & J. T. Spence (Eds.), *The psychology of learning and motivation: Advances in research and theory* (Vol. 1). New York: Academic Press, 1967. (b)

BOWER, G. H. Imagery as a relational organizer in associative learning. *Journal of Verbal Learning and Verbal Behavior*, 1970, *9*, 529–535.

BOWER, G. H. A selective review of organizational factors in memory. In E. Tulving & W. Donaldson (Eds.), *Organization of memory.* New York: Academic Press, 1972. (a)

BOWER, G. H. Mental imagery and associative learning. In L. W. Gregg (Ed.), *Cognition in learning and memory.* New York: Wiley, 1972. (b)

BOWER, G. H. Stimulus-sampling theory of encoding variability. In A. W. Melton & E. Martin (Eds.), *Coding processes in human memory.* Washington, D.C.: Winston, 1972. (c)

BOWER, G. H., CLARK, M. C., LESGOLD, A. M., & WINZENZ, D. Hierarchical retrieval schemes in recall of categorized word lists. *Journal of Verbal Learning and Verbal Behavior*, 1969, *8*, 323–343.

BOWER, G. H., & THEIOS, J. A learning model for discrete performance levels. In R. C. Atkinson (Ed.), *Studies in mathematical psychology*. Stanford: Stanford University Press, 1964.

CALFEE, R. C., & ATKINSON, R. C. Paired-associate models and the effects of list length. *Journal of Mathematical Psychology*, 1965, *2*, 254–265.

CHANDLER, J. P. *Program STEPIT* (Program QCPE 66, Quantum Chemistry Program Exchange). Bloomington: Indiana University, 1965.

CHASE, W. G., & SIMON, H. A. Perception in chess. *Cognitive Psychology*, 1973, *4*, 55–81.

CHERNOFF, H., & LEHMANN, E. L. Use of maximum likelihood estimates in chi square tests of goodness of fit. *Annals of Mathematical Statistics*, 1954, *25*, 579–586.

CIEUTAT, V. J., STOCKWELL, F. W., & NOBLE, C. E. The interaction of ability and amount of practice with stimulus and response meaningfulness (m, m') in paired-associate learning. *Journal of Experimental Psychology*, 1958, *56*, 193–202.

COHEN, B. H., BOUSFIELD, W. A., & WHITMARSH, G. A. *Cultural norms for verbal items in 43 categories* (Tech. Rep. No. 22). Storrs: University of Connecticut, 1957.

COLLINS, A. M., & QUILLIAN, M. R. Retrieval time from semantic memory. *Journal of Verbal Learning and Verbal Behavior*, 1969, *8*, 240–247.

CROWDER, R. G. *Principles of learning and memory*. Hillsdale, N.J.: Erlbaum, 1976.

DALLETT, K. M. Implicit mediators in paired-associate learning. *Journal of Verbal Learning and Verbal Behavior*, 1964, *3*, 209–214.

DAPOLITO, F. J. *Proactive effects with independent retrieval of competing responses*. Unpublished doctoral dissertation, Indiana University, 1966.

DEGROOT, A. D. Perception and memory versus thought: Some old ideas and recent findings. In B. Kleinmuntz (Ed.), *Problem solving: Research, method, and theory*. New York: Wiley, 1966.

EBBINGHAUS, H. [*Memory: A contribution to experimental psychology*] (H. A. Ruger & C. E. Bussenius, trans.). New York: Columbia University, Teachers College, 1913.

EGAN, D. E., & GREENO, J. G. Theory of rule induction: Knowledge acquired in concept learning, serial pattern learning, and problem solving. In L. Gregg (Ed.), *Knowledge and cognition*. Hillsdale, N.J.: Erlbaum, 1974.

EKSTRAND, B. R. A note on measuring response learning during paired-associate learning. *Journal of Verbal Learning and Verbal Behavior*, 1966, *5*, 344–347.

ELLIS, H. C. Transfer and retention. In M. H. Marx (Ed.), *Learning: Processes*. New York: Macmillan, 1968.

ELLIS, H. C., & MULLER, D. G. Transfer in perceptual learning following stimulus predifferentiation. *Journal of Experimental Psychology*, 1964, *68*, 388–395.

ELLIS, H. C., & SHUMATE, E. C. Encoding effects of response belongingness and stimulus meaningfulness on recognition memory of trigram stimuli. *Journal of Experimental Psychology*, 1973, *98*, 70–78.

ESTES, W. K. Statistical theory of distributional phenomena in learning. *Psychological Review*, 1955, *62*, 369–377.

ESTES, W. K. Learning theory and the new "mental chemistry." *Psychological Review*, 1960, *67*, 207–223.

ESTES, W. K. Structural aspects of associative models for memory. In C. N. Cofer (Ed.), *The structure of human memory*. San Francisco: Freeman, 1976.

ESTES, W. K., & DAPOLITO, F. Independent variation of information storage and retrieval processes in paired-associate learning. *Journal of Experimental Psychology*, 1967, *75*, 18–26.

ESTES, W. K., HOPKINS, B. L., & CROTHERS, E. J. All-or-none and conservation effects in the learning and retention of paired associates. *Journal of Experimental Psychology*, 1960, *60*, 329–339.

FEIGENBAUM, E. A. The simulation of verbal learning behavior. In E. A. Feigenbaum & J. Feldman (Eds.), *Computers and thought*. New York: McGraw-Hill, 1963.

FELLER, W. *An introduction to probability theory and its applications* (Vol. 1) (2nd ed.). New York: Wiley, 1950.

FILLMORE, C. J. The case for case. In E. Bach & R. T. Harms (Eds.), *Universals in linguistic theory*. New York: Holt, Rinehart & Winston, 1968.

FRIJDA, N. Simulation of human long-term memory. *Psychological Bulletin*, 1972, *77*, 1–31.

GAGNÉ, R. M. *The conditions of learning*. New York: Holt, Rinehart & Winston, 1965.

GENTNER, D. Evidence for the psychological reality of semantic components: The verbs of possession. In D. A. Norman & D. E. Rumelhart, *Explorations in cognition*. San Francisco: Freeman, 1975.

GIBSON, E. J. A systematic application of the concepts of generalization and differentiation to verbal learning. *Psychological Review*, 1940, *47*, 196–229.

GIBSON, E. J., BISHOP, C. H., SCHIFF, W., & SMITH, J. Comparison of meaning-fulness and pronounceability as grouping principles in the perception and retention of verbal material. *Journal of Experimental Psychology*, 1964, *67*, 173–182.

GIBSON, J. J. *The senses considered as perceptual systems*. Boston: Houghton Mifflin, 1966.

GIBSON, J. J., & GIBSON, E. J. What is learned in perceptual learning? A reply to Professor Postman. *Psychological Review*, 1955, *62*, 447–450.

GOGGIN, J., & MARTIN, E. Forced stimulus encoding and retroactive interference. *Journal of Experimental Psychology*, 1970, *84*, 131–136.

GREENO, J. G. Paired-associate learning with short-term retention: Mathematical analysis and data regarding identification of parameters. *Journal of Mathematical Psychology*, 1967, *4*, 430–472.

GREENO, J. G. Identifiability and statistical properties of two-stage learning with no successes in the initial stage. *Psychometrika*, 1968, *33*, 173–216.

GREENO, J. G. How associations are memorized. In D. A. Norman (Ed.), *Models of human memory*. New York: Academic Press, 1970.

GREENO, J. G., JAMES, C. T., & DaPOLITO, F. J. A cognitive interpretation of negative transfer and forgetting of paired associates. *Journal of Verbal Learning and Verbal Behavior*, 1971, *10*, 331–345.

GREENO, J. G., & SCANDURA, J. M. All-or-none transfer based on verbally mediated concepts. *Journal of Mathematical Psychology*, 1966, *3*, 388–411.

GREENO, J. G., & SIMON, H. A. Processes for producing sequences. *Psychological Review*, 1974, *81*, 187–198.

HAMBURGER, H., & WEXLER, K. A mathematical theory of learning transformational grammar. *Journal of Mathematical Psychology*, 1975, *12*, 137–177.

HARRINGTON, A. L. Effects of component emphasis on stimulus selection in paired-associate learning. *Journal of Experimental Psychology*, 1969, *79*, 412–418.

HEINE, R. T. *Quantitative analysis of multitrial free recall learning* (Michigan Mathematical Psychology Program Report MMPP 70–12). Ann Arbor: The University of Michigan, 1970.

HILGARD, E. R., & BOWER, G. H. *Theories of learning* (3rd ed.). New York: Appleton-Century-Crofts, 1966.

HINTZMAN, D. L. Exploration with a discrimination net model for paired-associate learning. *Journal of Mathematical Psychology*, 1968, *5*, 123–162.

HINTZMAN, D. L. On testing the independence of associations. *Psychological Review*, 1972, *79*, 261–264.

HINTZMAN, D. L. Theoretical implications of the spacing effect. In R. L. Solso (Ed.), *Theories in cognitive psychology: The Loyola symposium*. Potomac, Md.: Erlbaum, 1974.

HOROWITZ, L. M., & PRYTULAK, L. S. Redintegrative memory. *Psychological Review*, 1969, *76*, 519–531.

HOVLAND, C. I., & KURTZ, K. H. Experimental studies in rote-learning theory: X, Pre-learning syllable familiarization and the length difficulty relationship. *Journal of Experimental Psychology*, 1952, *44*, 31–39.

HUESMANN, L. R., & CHENG, C. A theory for the induction of mathematical functions. *Psychological Review*, 1973, *80*, 126–138.

HULL, C. L. Quantitative aspects of the evolution of concepts. *Psychological Monographs*, 1920, *28* (Whole No. 123).

HULL, C. L. *A behavior system*. New Haven: Yale University Press, 1952.

HUMPHREYS, M. S., & GREENO, J. G. Interpretation of the two-stage analysis of paired-associate memorizing. *Journal of Mathematical Psychology*, 1970, *7*, 275–292.

HUMPHREYS, M. S., & YUILLE, J. C. *Errors as a function of noun concreteness*. Unpublished manuscript, 1971.

HUNT, E. B., MARIN, J., & STONE, P. I. *Experiments in induction*. New York: Academic Press, 1966.

IZAWA, C. The test trial potentiating model. *Journal of Mathematical Psychology*, 1971, *8*, 200–224.

JAMES, C. T. *A consideration and rejection of the associative theory of interference and forgetting*. Unpublished doctoral dissertation, Indiana University, 1968.

JAMES, C. T., & GREENO, J. G. Stimulus selection at different stages of paired-associate learning. *Journal of Experimental Psychology*, 1967, *74*, 75–83.

JAMES, C. T., & GREENO, J. G. Effect of A–B overtraining in A–B$_r$. *Journal of Experimental Psychology*, 1970, *83*, 107–111.

JENKINS, J. J., & RUSSELL, W. A. Associative clustering during recall. *Journal of Abnormal and Social Psychology*, 1952, *47*, 818–821.

JENSEN, A. R., & ROHWER, W. D., JR. Verbal mediation in paired-associate and serial learning. *Journal of Verbal Learning and Verbal Behavior*, 1963, *1*, 346–352.

JONES, M. R. Cognitive representations of serial patterns. In B. H. Kantowitz (Ed.), *Human information processing: Tutorials in performance and cognition*. Hillsdale, N.J.: Erlbaum, 1974.

JUDD, C. H. The relation of special training to general intelligence. *Educational Review*, 1908, *36*, 28–42.

KATONA, G. *Organizing and memorizing*. New York: Columbia University Press, 1940.

KEPPEL, G. Retroactive and proactive inhibition. In T. R. Dixon & D. L. Horton (Eds.), *Verbal behavior and general behavior theory*. Englewood Cliffs, N.J.: Prentice-Hall, 1968.

KINTSCH, W. All-or-none learning and the role of repetition in paired-associate learning. *Science*, 1963, *140*, 310–312.

KINTSCH, W. Recognition learning as a function of the length of the retention interval and changes in the retention interval. *Journal of Mathematical Psychology*, 1966, *2*, 412–433.

KINTSCH, W. Models for free recall and recognition. In D. A. Norman (Ed.), *Models of human memory*. New York: Academic Press, 1970.

KINTSCH, W. *The representation of meaning in memory*. Hillsdale, N. J.: Erlbaum, 1974.

KINTSCH, W., & KEENAN, J. Reading rate and retention as a function of the number of propositions in the base structure of sentences. *Cognitive Psychology*, 1973, *5*, 257–274.

KINTSCH, W., & MORRIS, C. J. Application of a Markov model to free recall and recognition. *Journal of Experimental Psychology*, 1965, *69*, 200–206.

KLAHR, D., & WALLACE, J. G. The role of quantification operators in the development of conservation of quantity. *Cognitive Psychology*, 1973, *4*, 301–327.

KOFFKA, K. *Principles of Gestalt psychology*. New York: Harcourt Brace, 1935.

KÖHLER, W. *The mentality of apes*. New York: Harcourt Brace, 1927.

KÖHLER, W. On the nature of associations. *Proceedings of the American Philosophical Society*, 1941, *84*, 489–502.

KÖHLER, W. *Gestalt psychology*. New York: Liverwright, 1947.

KOPPENAAL, R. J. Time changes in the strengths of A–B, A–C lists: Spontaneous recovery? *Journal of Verbal Learning and Verbal Behavior*, 1963, *2*, 310–319.

KUHN, T. S. *The structure of scientific revolutions*. Chicago: University of Chicago Press, 1962.

LAMING, D. *Mathematical psychology*. London: Academic Press, 1973.

LAUGHERY, K. R. Computer simulation of short-term memory: A component-decay model. In G. H. Bower & J. T. Spence (Eds.), *The psychology of learning and motivation: Advances in research and theory* (Vol. 3). New York: Academic Press, 1969.

LAWRENCE, D. H. The nature of a stimulus. In S. Koch (Ed.), *Psychology: A study of a science* (Vol. 5). New York: McGraw-Hill, 1963.

LINDLEY, R. H. Effects of controlled coding cues in short-term memory. *Journal of Experimental Psychology*, 1963, *66*, 580–587.

LOCKE, J. *An essay concerning human understanding* (A. C. Fraser, Ed.). Oxford, 1894.

MALTZMAN, I. Thinking: From a behavioristic point of view. *Psychological Review*, 1955, *62*, 275–286.

MANDLER, G. Organization and memory. In K. W. Spence & J. T. Spence (Eds.), *The psychology of learning and motivation: Advances in research and theory* (Vol. 1). New York: Academic Press, 1967.

MANDLER, G., & HEINEMANN, S. H. Effect of overlearning of a verbal response on transfer of training. *Journal of Experimental Psychology*, 1956, *52* 39–46.

MARTIN, E. Transfer of verbal paired associates. *Psychological Review*, 1965, *72*, 327–343.

MARTIN, E. Stimulus recognition in aural paired-associate learning. *Journal of Verbal Learning and Verbal Behavior*, 1967, *6*, 272–276.

MARTIN, E. Stimulus meaningfulness and paired-associate transfer: An encoding variability hypothesis. *Psychological Review*, 1968, *75*, 421–441.

MARTIN, E. Verbal learning theory and independent retrieval phenomena. *Psychological Review*, 1971, *78*, 314–332.

MARTIN, E. Stimulus encoding in learning and transfer. In A. W. Melton & E. Martin (Eds.), *Coding processes in human memory*. Washington, D.C.: Winston, 1972.

MARTIN, E., & GREENO, J. G. Independence of associations tested: A reply to D. L. Hintzman. *Psychological Review*, 1972, *79*, 265–267.

MARTIN, E., & NOREEN, D. L. Serial learning: Identification of subjective subsequences. *Cognitive Psychology*, 1974, *6*, 421–435.

MCGEOCH, J. A. *The psychology of human learning*. New York: Longmans, Green, 1942.

MCGOVERN, J. B. Extinction of associations in four transfer paradigms. *Psychological Monographs*, 1964, *78* (Whole No. 593).

MCGUIRE, W. J. A multiprocess model for paired-associate learning. *Journal of Experimental Psychology*, 1961, *62*, 335–347.

MELTON, A. W. Comments on Professor Postman's paper. In C. N. Cofer (Ed.), *Verbal learning and verbal behavior*. New York: McGraw-Hill, 1961.

MELTON, A. W., & IRWIN, J. McQ. The influence of degree of interpolated learning on retroactive inhibition and the overt transfer of specific responses. *American Journal of Psychology*, 1940, *53*, 173–203.

MILLWARD, R. An all-or-none model for noncorrection routines with elimination of incorrect responses. *Journal of Mathematical Psychology*, 1964, *1*, 392–404.

MINSKY, M., & PAPERT, S. *Perceptions*. Cambridge, Mass.: MIT Press, 1969.

MURDOCK, B. B., JR. The retention of individual items. *Journal of Experimental Psychology*, 1961, *62*, 618–625.

NAHINSKY, I. D. Statistics and moments-parameter estimates for a duo-process paired-associate learning model. *Journal of Mathematical Psychology*, 1967, *4*, 140–150.

NEISSER, U. *Cognitive psychology*. New York: Appleton-Century-Crofts, 1967.

NORMAN, D. A., & BOBROW, D. G. On the role of active memory processes in perception and cognition. In C. N. Cofer (Ed.), *The structure of human memory*. San Francisco: Freeman, 1976.

NORMAN, D. A., & RUMELHART, D. E. A system for perception and memory. In D. A. Norman (Ed.), *Models of human memory*. New York: Academic Press, 1970.

NORMAN, D. A., & RUMELHART, D. E. *Explorations in cognition*. San Francisco: Freeman, 1975.

PAGEL, J. C. A Markov analysis of transfer in paired-associate learning with high intralist similarity. *Journal of Verbal Learning and Verbal Behavior*, 1973, *12*, 456–470.

PAIVIO, A. *Imagery and verbal processes*. New York: Holt, Rinehart & Winston, 1971.

PAIVIO, A., YUILLE, J. C., & MADIGAN, S. Concreteness, imagery, and meaningfulness values for 925 nouns. *Journal of Experimental Psychology*, 1968, *76* (1, Pt. 2).

POLSON, M. C., RESTLE, F., & POLSON, P. G. Association and discrimination in paired-associates learning. *Journal of Experimental Psychology*, 1965, *69*, 47–55.

POLSON, P. G. *A quantitative study of the concept identification and paired-associates learning processes in the Hull paradigm*. Unpublished doctoral dissertation, Indiana University, 1967.

POLSON, P. G. A quantitative analysis of the conceptual processes in the Hull paradigm. *Journal of Mathematical Psychology*, 1972, *9*, 141–167.

POPPER, K. R. *Logik der Forschung*. Vienna: J. Springer, 1935.

POPPER, K. R. *Logic of scientific discovery*. New York: Basic Books, 1959.

POSNER, M. I., & KEELE, S. W. On the genesis of abstract ideas. *Journal of Experimental Psychology*, 1968, *77*, 353–363.

POSTMAN, L. Association theory and perceptual learning. *Psychological Review*, 1955, *62*, 438–446.

POSTMAN, L. Does interference theory predict too much forgetting? *Journal of Verbal Learning and Verbal Behavior*, 1963, *2*, 40–48. (a)

POSTMAN, L. One-trial learning. In C. N. Cofer & B. S. Musgrave (Eds.), *Verbal behavior and learning: Problems and processes*. New York: McGraw-Hill, 1963, (b)

POSTMAN, L. Studies of learning to learn II: Changes in transfer as a function of practice. *Journal of Verbal Learning and Verbal Behavior*, 1964, *3*, 437–447.

POSTMAN, L. A pragmatic view of organization theory. In E. Tulving & W. Donaldson (Eds.), *Organization of memory*. New York: Academic Press, 1972.

POSTMAN, L., & RILEY, D. A. A critique of Köhler's theory of association. *Psychological Review*, 1957, *64*, 61–72.

POSTMAN, L., & STARK, K. The role of response set in tests of unlearning. *Journal of Verbal Learning and Verbal Behavior*, 1965, *4*, 315–322.

POSTMAN, L., & STARK, K. Role of response availability in transfer and interference. *Journal of Experimental Psychology*, 1969, *79*, 168–177.

POSTMAN, L., & UNDERWOOD, B. J. Critical issues in interference theory. *Memory & Cognition*, 1973, *1*, 19–40.

QUILLIAN, M. R. Semantic memory, In M. Minsky (Ed.), *Semantic information processing*. Cambridge, Mass.: MIT Press, 1968.

REES, H. J., & ISRAEL, H. C. An investigation of the establishment and operation of mental sets. *Psychological Monographs*, 1935, *46* (Whole No. 210).

REITMAN, J. S. Computer simulation of an information-processing model of short-term memory. In D. A. Norman (Ed.), *Models of human memory*. New York: Academic Press, 1970.

RESTLE, F. Sources of difficulty in learning paired associates. In R. C. Atkinson (Ed.), *Studies in mathematical Psychology*. Stanford: Stanford University Press, 1964.

RESTLE, F. The significance of all-or-none learning. *Psychological Bulletin*, 1965, *62*, 313–324.

RESTLE, F., & BROWN, E. Organization of serial pattern learning. In G. H. Bower (Ed.), *The psychology of learning and motivation: Advances in research and theory* (Vol. 4). New York: Academic Press, 1970.

RESTLE, F., & GREENO, J. G. *Introduction to mathematical psychology*. Reading, Mass.: Addison-Wesley, 1970.

RIPS, L. J., SHOBEN, E. J., & SMITH, E. E. Semantic distance and the verification of semantic relations. *Journal of Verbal Learning and Verbal Behavior*, 1973, *12*, 1–20.

ROCK, I. The role of repetition in associative learning. *American Journal of Psychology*, 1957, *70*, 186–193.

ROSCH, E. On the internal structure of perceptual and semantic categories. In T. E. Moore (Ed.), *Cognitive development and acquisition of language*. New York: Academic Press, 1973.

RUMELHART, D. E. *The effects of interpresentation intervals on performance in a continuous paired-associate task* (Institute for Mathematical Studies in the Social Sciences Tech. Rep. No. 116). Stanford: Stanford University, 1967.

RUMELHART, D. E. A multicomponent theory of the perception of briefly exposed visual displays. *Journal of Mathematical Psychology*, 1970, *7*, 191–218.

RUNQUISIT, W. N. Retention of verbal associates as a function of strength. *Journal of Experimental Psychology*, 1957, *54*, 369–375.

SCHANK, R. C. Conceptual dependency: A theory of natural language understanding. *Cognitive Psychology*, 1972, *3*, 552–631.

SCHNEIDER, N. G., & HOUSTON, J. P. Retroactive inhibition, cue selection, and degree of learning. *American Journal of Psychology*, 1969, *82*, 276–279.

SELFRIDGE, O. G. Pandemonium: A paradigm for learning. In *The mechanization of thought processes*. London: Her Majesty's Stationery Office, 1959.

SELZ, O. *Über die Gesetze des geordneten Denkverlaufs*. Stuttgart: Spemann, 1913.

SELZ, O. [The revision of the fundamental conception of intellectual processes.] In J. M. Mandler & G. Mandler (trans.), *Thinking: From association to Gestalt*. New York: Wiley, 1964.

SHIFFRIN, R. M. Memory search. In D. A. Norman (Ed.), *Models of human memory*. New York: Academic Press, 1970.

SIMON, H. A., & GILMARTIN, K. A simulation of memory for chess position. *Cognitive Psychology*, 1973, *5*, 29–46.

SIMON, H. A., & KOTOVSKY, K. Human acquisition of concepts for sequential patterns. *Psychological Review*, 1963, *70*, 534–546.

SPENCE, K. W. The nature of discrimination learning in animals. *Psychological Review*, 1936, *43*, 427–449.

SUTHERLAND, N. S. Stimulus analyzing mechanisms. In *The mechanization of thought processes* (Vol. 2). London: Her Majesty's Stationery Office, 1959.

TRABASSO, T. R., ROLLINS, H., & SCHAUGHNESSY, E. Storage and verification stages in processing concepts. *Cognitive Psychology*, 1971, *2*, 239–289.

TULVING, E. Subjective organization in free recall of "unrelated" words. *Psychological Review*, 1962, *69*, 344–354.

TULVING, E., & WATKINS, M. J. On negative transfer: Effects of testing one list on the recall of another. *Journal of Verbal Learning and Verbal Behavior*, 1974. *13*, 181–193.

UNDERWOOD, B. J. Proactive inhibition as a function of time and degree of prior learning. *Journal of Experimental Psychology*, 1949, *39*, 24–34.

UNDERWOOD, B. J. An orientation for research on thinking. *Psychological Review*, 1952, *59*, 209–220.

UNDERWOOD, B. J. Studies of distributed practice: IX, Learning and retention of paired adjectives as a function of intralist similarity. *Journal of Experimental Psychology*, 1953, *45*, 143–149.

UNDERWOOD, B. J. Stimulus selection in verbal learning. In C. N. Cofer & B. S. Musgrave (Eds.), *Verbal behavior and learning: Problems and processes*. New York: McGraw-Hill, 1963.

UNDERWOOD, B. J. The representativeness of rote verbal learning. In A. W. Melton (Ed.), *Categories of human learning*. New York: Academic Press, 1964.

UNDERWOOD, B. J., REHULA, R., & KEPPEL, G. Item selection in paired-associate learning. *American Journal of Psychology*, 1962, *75*, 353–371.

UNDERWOOD, B. J., & RICHARDSON, J. Some verbal materials for the study of concept formation. *Psychological Bulletin*, 1956, *53*, 84–95.

UNDERWOOD, B. J., RUNQUIST, W. N., & SCHULZ, R. W. Response learning in paired-associate lists as a function of intralist similarity. *Journal of Experimental Psychology*, 1959, *58*, 70–78.

UNDERWOOD, B. J., & SCHULZ, R. W. *Meaningfulness and verbal learning*. Philadelphia: Lippincott, 1960.

VOSS, J. F. On the relationship of associative and organizational processes. In E. Tulving & W. Donaldson (Eds.), *Organization of memory*. New York: Academic Press, 1972.

WATSON, J. B. *Psychology from the standpoint of a behaviorist.* Philadelphia: Lippincott, 1919.

WEAVER, G. E. Stimulus encoding as a determinant of retroactive inhibition. *Journal of Verbal Learning and Verbal Behavior*, 1969, *8*, 807–814.

WERTHEIMER, M. *Productive thinking* (enlarged ed.). New York: Harper & Row, 1959.

WICHAWUT, C., & MARTIN, E. Independence of A–B and A–C associations in retroaction. *Journal of Verbal Learning and Verbal Behavior*, 1971, *10*, 316–321.

WILKS, S. S. *Mathematical statistics.* New York: Wiley, 1962.

WINOGRAD, T. Understanding natural language. *Cognitive Psychology*, 1972, *3*, 1–191.

WINSTON, P. Learning to identify toy block structures. In R. L. Solso (Ed.), *Contemporary issues in cognitive psychology: The Loyola symposium.* Washington, D.C.: Winston, 1973.

WOLLEN, K. A., & LOWRY, D. H. Effects of imagery on paired-associate learning. *Journal of Verbal Learning and Verbal Behavior*, 1971, *10*, 276–284.

WOOD, G. Organizational processes and free recall. In E. Tulving & W. Donaldson (Eds.), *Organization of memory.* New York: Academic Press, 1972.

WULF, F. Tendencies in figural variation. In W. D. Ellis (Ed.), *A source book of Gestalt psychology.* New York: Harcourt Brace & World, 1938.

YERKES, R. M. The mind of a gorilla: I. *Genetic Psychology Monographs*, 1927, *2*.

YOUNG, J. L. Reinforcement-test intervals in paired-associate learning. *Journal of Mathematical Psychology*, 1971, *8*, 58–81.

Author Index

Numbers in italics refer to the pages on which the complete references are listed.

233

Subject Index

Figure 2-4: From Kintsch, W., and Keenan, J., Reading rate and retention as a function of the number of propositions in the base structure of sentences. *Cognitive Psychology,* 1973, *4,* 259.

Figures 3-2, 3-3, 3-4, 3-5, 3-9: From Polson, M. C., Restle, F., and Polson, P. G., Association and discrimination in paired-associates learning. *Journal of Experimental Psychology,* 1965, *69,* 47-55. Copyright 1965 by the American Psychological Association. Reprinted by permission.

Tables 4-1, 4-2, 4-3, 4-4, 4-5, and Figures 4-1, 4-2, 4-3, 4-4, 4-5: From Humphreys, M. S., and Greeno, J. G., Interpretation of the two-stage analysis of paired-associate memorizing. *Journal of Mathematical Psychology,* 1970, *7,* 275-292.

Tables 4-6, 4-7, 6-4, 6-5: From Greeno, J. G., How associations are memorized. In D. A. Norman (Ed.), *Models of human memory.* New York: Academic Press, 1970.

Figures 5-1, 5-2, 5-3, and Tables 5-1, 5-2: From Greeno, J. G., and Scandura, J. M., All-or-none transfer based on verbally mediated concepts. *Journal of Mathematical Psychology,* 1966, *3,* 388-411.

Tables 5-3, 5-4: From Batchelder, W. H., A theoretical and empirical comparison of the all-or-none multilevel theory and the mixed model. *Journal of Mathematical Psychology,* 1971, *8,* 82-108.

Figures 5-4, 5-5, 5-6: From Polson, P. G., A quantitative analysis of the conceptual processes in the Hull paradigm. *Journal of Mathematical Psychology,* 1972, *9,* 141-167.